James Dean in Death

A Popular Encyclopedia of a Celebrity Phenomenon

WARREN BEATH

with PAULA WHEELDON

McFarland & Company, Inc., Publishers
Jefferson, North Carolina, and London

791.4302
Dean
B

LIBRARY OF CONGRESS CATALOGUING-IN-PUBLICATION DATA

Beath, Warren, 1951–
James Dean in death : a popular encyclopedia of a celebrity phenomenon / Warren Beath with Paula Wheeldon.
p.   cm.
Includes bibliographical references and index.

ISBN 0-7864-2000-6 (softcover : 50# alkaline paper)

1. Dean, James, 1931–1955 — Encyclopedias.   2. Dean, James, 1931–1955 — Death and burial — Encyclopedias.   I. Wheeldon, Paula.   II. Title.
PN2287.D33B44   2005
791.4302'8'092 — dc22   2005020840

British Library cataloguing data are available

Cover photograph ©2005 Image Source

Manufactured in the United States of America

McFarland & Company, Inc., Publishers
Box 611, Jefferson, North Carolina 28640
www.mcfarlandpub.com

Contents

Preface

The actor James Dean made only three films, all in the space of a year, before his death in an automobile collision at age 24. The films, especially *Rebel Without a Cause*, are still celebrated today, but it is Dean's death — the quintessential romantic tragedy of reckless youth cut short in its prime — that has had the larger impact on popular culture in America and even around the world. Dean's movies made him the subject of much fan devotion and many teen fantasies; his untimely death made him an immortal whose image would be revered, copied, and mercilessly hawked in myriad ways for decades— perhaps forever. Today, half a century after the fatal collision, the death of James Dean has spawned an industry and, for some, a way of life.

This book is an alphabetical compendium of information related to the death of James Dean and its impact on popular culture. It does not serve as a biography of Dean the man or the actor, though much information on both will be found herein. Instead, it constitutes a record of the Dean legend and its evolution — a process that brought it from the pages of 1950s fan magazines to the popular consciousness of today.

Among the book's entries, the reader will find names of persons associated with Dean's death (such as the officers at the crash site, or the coroner who attended to Dean's body) and those who have attached themselves to Dean's legacy since his death; titles of articles, books, movies, plays, record albums, and other popular entertainments related to Dean and his passing; places important to the story of Dean's last day and beyond (such as the restaurant where he ate his last meal, or sites now supposed to be haunted by his ghost); and descriptions of Dean memorabilia from death masks to salt and pepper shakers.

Information for the serious researcher is present in abundance. The book contains, for example, in its entirety and for the first time, the only

1

deposition about the automobile wreck given by the other driver, Donald Turnupseed. In another entry, a chronology follows, day by day, the lawsuit filed by Dean's passenger, Rolf Wuetherich, against both Dean's estate and Donald Turnupseed. Documents and photos, some never before published, are included.

At the same time, the book contains fascinating information for pop culture mavens, Dean fans, and anyone interested in the phenomenon of the celebrity death cult. Entries on memorabilia, fan clubs, and memorial events (e.g., DeanCon) show how, through dramatic circumstance, a entertainer whose career had barely begun became the subject of posthumous adulation — and how his death eventually became a legend more compelling than anything he accomplished in life.

The book is the result of thirty-five years of research — a quest that began when Warren Beath, at age 11, ran across a tabloid article titled "The Curse of James Dean's Death Car" and was instantly absorbed. Warren's father, a highway patrolman, was a friend to the officer who gave James Dean a speeding ticket just hours before his death, and that gave Warren a sense of personal connection to the actor and his legend. As Warren grew up, his interest in Dean continued, and he began to visit the crash site and then talk to people involved in the events—from a gas station attendant, to family members, to stars and Hollywood personalities who had been close to Dean. Much of the information in this book is drawn from years' worth of personal interviews.

Surprisingly, at the time Warren began his research, little was known or published about the exact circumstances of Dean's last day and the wreck that took his life. Warren began to collect records and photographs, and he intensified his search for people involved in Dean's Hollywood year and his fatal last day. Later the collection extended to include material related to the devoted following that developed in the wake of Dean's death. That collection gave rise to this book.

Our intention has been to include, as far as possible, everything that more than three decades years of research has uncovered in relation to Dean's death, the fascination it inspired, and how that fascination is expressed in popular culture. If the book is not exhaustive — and no book on this subject could be — we have at least attempted to include something from every category of expression of the posthumous Dean craze.

Warren Beath and Paula Wheeldon
Fall 2005

THE ENCYCLOPEDIA

A

accident

Actor James Dean died in a highway traffic accident on September 30, 1955, near 6:00 in the evening when his Porsche Spyder racing car collided with a 1950 Ford driven by college student Donald Turnupseed. Dean was heading west on Highway 466 (now 46) toward the "Y" junction with Highway 41 heading north when the eastbound Ford crossed into his lane with the intention of taking Highway 41. What was essentially an illegal left-hand turn resulted in a nearly head-on collision to the left fronts of both vehicles that left Dean dead in his car with a broken neck.

Turnupseed claimed throughout his life that he did not see Dean's car before his attempted turn, but he left two thirty-yard-long sets of skid marks with a thirty-yard interval in between that belies the statement. As pointed out by the California Highway Patrol at the inquest, the tire marks were in an arc that terminated at the collision point.

Though much was made at the ensuing inquest of the fact that Dean had previously been ticketed for speeding, had driven a local couple off the road, and perhaps was not wearing his prescription lenses that were a restriction of his driver's license, the actual accident was primarily the fault of the other driver. At the time of the collision Dean was in his own lane, and that was where the crash occurred. One investigating officer has said that had there not been a fatality, Turnupseed would have been cited for an illegal left-hand turn.

Also injured in the collision was Dean's mechanic, Rolf Wuetherich, who was in the Porsche with Dean.

See also crash sites; lawsuit; reenactment; simulation; velocity report.

Adams, Charles

Charles Adams was a resident of Bakersfield, California, who claimed that in 1954 he was newly out of the service and visiting relatives in the San Fernando Valley when James Dean approached him at a hamburger stand to admire his brand-new Mercury Montclair. They talked cars and became

Page 1 of the California Highway Patrol Vehicle Accident Report on the wreck that killed James Dean.

friends, and Adams claimed that Dean often called him late at night when Adams worked the graveyard shift as a dispatcher for the Bakersfield highway patrol office. After Dean was killed, Adams claimed that he went to see his father and stepmother, Winton and Ethel Dean, and that they seemed to find him sympathetic. He said they had unanswered questions about the crash that had claimed Jimmy's life. They began to call Adams at work, and he set about on his own private investigation of the accident.

He obtained a copy of the inquest transcript by typing it out himself

Page 2
Arrest or Citation Number

STATE OF CALIFORNIA
CALIFORNIA HIGHWAY PATROL
Vehicle Accident Report ★

CORONER'S COPY
00116

Veh. 1 .... Charge ....

Veh. 2 .... Charge ....

Local No. 0-66-55

City ....
County ....
Township ....
Division ....

State No. ....

LOCATION AND DATE

Accident Occurred on ....
At Intersection With ....
NAME OF STREET, ALLEY, HIGHWAY NO. (U. S., STATE, COUNTY) OR NAME
Not at Intersection .... Feet .... of ....
NAME OF STREET, ALLEY, HIGHWAY, ETC.
NORTH, E., S., W   NEAREST INTERSECTING STREET OR LANDMARK

Day of Week **Friday**
Date **30 Sept 55**
Time **1745** .... M

Motor Vehicle Involved with
1. Pedestrian X 2. Other Motor Vehicle ....3. Train ....4. Street Car ....5. Animal Drawn Vehicle ....6. Bicycle ....7. Animal (ridden, herded, unattended)
....8. Fixed Object ....9. Overturned in Roadway ....10. Ran Off Roadway ....11. Other Non-collision (fell from veh., fire, etc.) ....12. Other (explain in Remarks)

Vehicle No. 1

Driven by .... **Turnupseed** ....
NAME   STREET, CITY AND STATE ADDRESS   BEAT   PHONE
Nationality/Race ....
Company/Employer/Military Unit ....
NAME   ADDRESS
Age .... Sex .... Driv. Exp .... Driv. Lic .... Chauf's ...Oper's .... Occ ....
Veh. YEARS   STATE   NUMBER Veh. Lic. TYPE, AS REG., BEGIN., ETC. ICC
Make .... Yr .... Type .... Plate No. ....
(SEDAN, CAB, TRUCK, BUS, ETC.—DESC. TRAILER, IF ANY)   YEAR   NUMBER   STATE
Going .... On .... Parts of Vehicle Damaged .... Amount $ ....
NORTH, EAST, PARKED, ETC.)   STREET NAME, HIGHWAY NO., ALLEY, DRIVEWAY
Uses Road or Street Frequently .... Rarely .... Never Before .... Date Driver Last Used Road ....
Reg. Owner ....
NAME   STREET, CITY AND STATE ADDRESS
Distance Danger Was First Noticed .... Estimated Speed at That Time .... Estimated Speed at Moment of Accident .... Distance Vehicle Traveled After Impact .... Lawful Speed .... Max. Safe Speed Under Conditions Prevailing ....
FEET   M.P.H.   M.P.H.   FEET   M.P.H.   M.P.H.
Vehicle Removed to .... By ....

Vehicle No. 2

Driven by .... **Dean (FATAL)** ....
NAME   STREET, CITY AND STATE ADDRESS   BEAT   PHONE
Nationality/Race ....
Company/Employer/Military Unit ....
NAME   ADDRESS
Age .... Sex .... Driv. Exp .... Driv. Lic .... Chauf's ...Oper's .... Occ ....
YEARS   STATE   NUMBER Veh. Lic. TYPE, AS REG., BEGIN., ETC. ICC
Make .... Yr .... Type .... Plate No. ....
(SEDAN, CAB, TRUCK, BUS, ETC.—DESC. TRAILER, IF ANY)   YEAR   NUMBER   STATE
Going .... On .... Parts of Vehicle Damaged .... Amount $ ....
NORTH, EAST, PARKED, ETC.)   STREET NAME, HIGHWAY NO., ALLEY, DRIVEWAY
Uses Road or Street Frequently .... Rarely .... Never Before .... Date Driver Last Used Road ....
Reg. Owner ....
NAME   STREET, CITY AND STATE ADDRESS
Distance Danger Was First Noticed .... Estimated Speed at That Time .... Estimated Speed at Moment of Accident .... Distance Vehicle Traveled After Impact .... Lawful Speed .... Max. Safe Speed Under Conditions Prevailing ....
FEET   M.P.H.   M.P.H.   FEET   M.P.H.   M.P.H.
Vehicle Removed to .... By ....

Damage to Property Other Than Vehicles **none** .... $ ....
NAME OBJECT, SHOW OWNERSHIP, AND STATE NATURE AND AMOUNT OF DAMAGE

Total No. of Persons Injured **2**

INJURED

Name **Donald Gene Turnupseed** .... Address **1001 Academy Tulare** .... Phone ....
Age **23** Sex **M** Taken to... **not** .... By ....
Nature of Injuries: None X Minor ....Major ....Fatal Injured Was: ....Ped. X Driver ....Pass. ....Other Occupant in Veh. No. **1** in **frnt**
(RIGHT FRONT, LEFT REAR, ETC.)

Number Killed **1**

Name .... Address .... Phone ....
Age .... Sex .... Taken to .... By ....
Nature of Injuries: ....None ....Minor ....Major ....Fatal Injured Was: ....Ped. ....Driver ....Pass. ....Other Occupant in Veh. No .... in ....
(RIGHT FRONT, LEFT REAR, ETC.)

Witnesses

Name **Don Dooley** .... Address **Box 45 Shandon** Phone .... Where Was Witness **following #1**
(IN VEH. 1—FRS., 40 FT. R., ETC.)
Name .... Address .... Phone .... Where Was Witness ....
(IN VEH. 1—FRS., 40 FT. C., ETC.)

NOTE: Use another report form if 3 or more vehicles or additional injuries, fatalities and witnesses are involved.

Description of Accident and Circumstances Which Led to It

CALLED: 1750
10-07:   1820
10-08:   1055

Page 2 of the California Highway Patrol report.

on his typewriter, and he went out to the crash site, where he took numerous photos and even conducted skid-mark tests. He went to the garage at Cholame and obtained unpublished pictures of the wrecked car and the ambulance from ambulance driver Paul Moreno. He created two large diagrams that were detailed schemata of the crash to scale. He inked in the Ford's skid marks on the photos to show its path on the highway.

By 1957, he had completed a fourteen-month investigation. His motive, he said, was that he wanted to ease the minds of Jimmy's loved ones in California and Indiana by answering the questions that haunted them. Death was instantaneous, he deduced, and Jimmy had not suffered. He annotated the transcript and mounted it handsomely for presentation to Jimmy's father with the name "Winton Dean" embossed on the cover. He made three copies of text and diagrams, and sent one set to the James Dean Memorial Foundation in Fairmount, Indiana. Another went to Winton, and Adams kept the last. He received no money for his work, though he said he did ask Winton for one of Jimmy's little drawings; Winton told him it was still too early, maybe later.

It is unknown whether Adams ever actually met Winton Dean or even James Dean, but it is undeniable that he compiled the report, drew the diagrams, and took the photos. Into the eighties, Adams submitted to local radio interviews and would show the photos and diagrams, but he would not let anyone handle his actual report. He claimed to still be on affectionate terms with Dean's surviving relatives.

Adams, Christine

An artist and design student at California Polytechnic, Christine, like many fans, became interested in James Dean in high school after perusing a book on him. She has since immersed herself in Dean lore and let his legend and persona inspire her work.

Adams, Nick

Nick Adams, born Nicholas Adamschock the same year Jimmy Dean was born, was a real scene-stealer on the set of *Rebel Without a Cause.* He got into a fistfight with one girl, Beverly Long, and punched actress Steffi Sidney in the ribs during shooting so he could cop her sole line in the picture: "Watch out, Buzz, he's got a chain!" Director Nick Ray restored the line to her, but a lot of the cast found Adams impossible. Nevertheless, he seemed genuinely tight with Jimmy, as evidenced by their improvised banter in the wardrobe test for the film. The two did comedy skits for the amusement of the cast, and even talked about taking their act on the road to Las Vegas when they had some time after film commitments.

It was after Jimmy's death that Adams' actions began to annoy Jimmy's friends. Adams contributed to ghostwritten articles for fan magazines and the results were stories such as "The James Dean I Knew," "Jimmy's Happiest Moments" and "Jimmy Dean, Why We Loved Him." He was all over *Modern Screen, Screen Star,* and *Movie Life,* and well on his way to becoming *the* preeminent Dean pal in the teenage collective unconscious.

Not content with his determined public identification with Jimmy's ghost, he dated Natalie Wood, and showed up in Marion, Indiana, when the biopic *The James Dean Story* premiered in 1957.

Perhaps the real source of jealousy was that Nick got to fill in Jimmy's voice during the last bits of his appearance in *Giant*. The two actors had amused themselves with impressions of Hollywood celebrities, and Nick finally got to do Jimmy when he replaced Jett Rink's garbled speech at the end of the film. Nick Adams dubbed Jimmy's cinematic valedictory.

Things went badly for Nick. Though he had showed his own little streak of comedic genius in such films as *No Time for Sergeants* (1958), and even got a supporting actor Oscar nomination in 1963 for *Twilight of Honor,* the sixties found him in such humiliating pictures as *Monster of Terror* and the Japanese *Frankenstein Conquers the World.* In 1968 he was found dead in his El Roble Lane home in Beverly Hills, the victim of an apparent overdose of the paraldehyde he had been taking for drinking and depression. He had been involved in an ugly divorce and custody battle.

There is some controversy over whether Nick Adams actually dubbed Dean's voice in *Giant.* Another candidate is Daws Butler, who later became the cartoon voice of Fred Flintstone.

Albums *see* **Giant, the record;** *James Dean: Soundtrack Excerpts*

Alexander, Paul

The Most Ghoulish Interview Award has to go to Paul Alexander. Alexander's exclusive for his biography *Boulevard of Broken Dreams* was an audience with Jimmy's reclusive father, Winton Dean. Winton was in his eighties and suffering from advanced Alzheimer's disease when Alexander got to him in a convalescent home, slipping past attendants because he was accompanying Adeline Nall, Dean's high school drama teacher, who by many accounts was herself in her dotage. Otherwise, it's hard to imagine her being so oblivious as to breach the wishes of Dean's family by exposing the ailing Winton to an interview.

Almost Salinas

Originally called *Almost Cholame,* this 2002 independent production starring John Mahoney, Virginia Madsen, Ray Wise and Lindsay Crouse takes place at Cholame and the site of James Dean's death. Characters include grape farmer Zelder Hill, who gives tours of the crash site and talks obsessively about the day James Dean died forty years earlier. Allie's Diner in Cholame is soon visited by a film crew making a movie on Dean, and a beautiful Los Angeles writer whose life is in turnaround stumbles on a decades-old mystery.

Wrote Reel Movie Critic.com Lee Shoquist:

> Set in a small California town named Cholame, Allie's Diner is a longtime fixture on the quiet highway strip and run by one Max Harris (John Mahoney), a semi-cantankerous man still pining away for wife Allie (Lindsay Crouse), who walked out years ago.
>
> With the help of cook and right-hand-man Manny (Ian Gomez), Max decides to renovate the broken-down gas station next door. Head waitress Clare (Virginia Madsen) and retired grape farmer Zelder Hill (Nathan Davis, as quirky as they come) are also on hand, the former pretty much just standing around looking for love and the latter prattling on all day about James Dean and giving tours of the nearby Dean crash site.
>
> Enter Nina Ellington (well-played by Linda Emond), playing that now cliché movie character of a big city woman writer who needs an even bigger life change but doesn't quite know it — in this case, a magazine writer from LA who stumbles upon a forty-year-old mystery that Max has kept secret his entire life.
>
> I'd like nothing more than for this to be a good movie we could celebrate since it obviously has its heart in the right place and is attempting to be a gentle, charming character study. However, the film is undeniably corny and artificial.
>
> The copy on the film's one-sheet notes, "Sometimes losing yourself is the only way to find what you really need." In the case of *Almost Salinas*, the one who lost his way was director Terry Green, and he never got around to figuring out what his film needed.

The movie was a box office failure.

ambulance

The Cholame Ambulance Service was run out of a shed between the Cholame Garage and Cholame Gas Station by burly proprietor Paul Moreno to meet the demands for service in the desolate area highways between Paso Robles and the county line, about seven miles to the east of Cholame. The 1955 Buick ambulance was kept in storage next to the Cholame tow truck. Moreno was also deputized so that he could have some official status in handling the confusion at an accident scene. It is possible, if not probable, that Dean died in the ambulance en route to Paso Robles War Memorial Hospital. Some locals claimed that the ambulance service had an unsavory reputation for robbing accident victims when they were dead or unconscious.

The ambulance in which James Dean died. In the bottom photograph, note the primer paint on the left rear panel from the accident the ambulance was involved in on the way to the hospital. In the background of the upper photograph is Paul Moreno's towtruck and the Cholame Garage (since demolished).

The trip to the hospital from the site of Dean's crash was anything but normal. The ambulance was itself involved in a collision at the halfway point. Moreno did not stop at the scene because it was unsafe, but stopped shortly afterwards to survey the damage before proceeding. Conspiracy theorists speculate that the stop was part of a prearranged plot to either administer the coup de grace to Jimmy Dean, drain his blood, or more thoroughly go through his pockets.

After Dean's Porsche Spyder was towed away from the Cholame Garage, the ambulance itself became an object of grisly fascination to the numerous Dean fans who made the trek to the intersection and other relevant sites. Moreno tired of the queries and of the endless curious requests to see the ambulance in the shed. The less timorous wanted to see inside, and even lie in the berth where Jimmy Dean had been strapped for the final leg of his ride to Paso Robles.

It is not known what eventually became of the ambulance.

A second company, Garges Ambulance Service, was involved in transferring Rolf Wuetherich (who was in the Porsche and injured in the crash) from Paso Robles hospital to Glendale Sanitarium Hospital when Wuetherich's employer, Johnnie von Neumann, decided to have a specialist operate to save his leg.

THE ACCIDENT EN ROUTE

Another accident almost wrecked the Cholame ambulance carrying Wuetherich and the body of Dean: it was sideswiped by a car driven by Llewellyn Hiatt, 23, of Paso Robles. Hiatt told officers the car ahead of him, driven by Carrie Golden, 31, of Herlong, slowed suddenly and veered to the right when the westbound ambulance approached and he tried to pass on the left. The ambulance did not stop and was only slightly damaged.

At the inquest the ambulance driver testified, "I did not stop at the scene of the accident, I couldn't stop there. I proceeded to the top of the hill and stopped and surveyed the damage and seen that I could proceed."

Murder and occult buffs theorize that this stop was staged so that Dean's body could be robbed; Rolf Wuetherich's ring could be removed (*see* ring); Dean could be murdered, finishing what the crash had left incomplete; or Dean's blood could be removed (*see* blood).

The ambulance sustained slight damage but bore the primer in photographs taken over a year later.

ROBBERY?

Dean's friend and fellow actor Bill Hickman was incensed for years by his belief that the ambulance attendants had rolled Jimmy's body after his death. He said there was nothing in Jimmy's pockets by the time he got to the funeral home. The speeding ticket was there, apparently. But the documents from Jimmy's estate say he had about $33.03. That doesn't seem like a reasonable amount for a movie star to take on a weekend trip. Fueling rumors, the Cholame postmistress said that the ambulance service had an unsavory reputation despite the fact the owner was deputized as a deputy. Could this be what happened to Rolf's Pan Am flight ring? (*See* ring.)

Angeli, Pier

Much has been written concerning the relationship between this beautiful Italian actress and Dean. Their ill-fated romance began when they met in 1954 on the Warner Bros. lot where Pier was starring in *The Silver Chalice*.

By all accounts, both were instantly smitten and spent many months together before Pier's mother put an end to the union and arranged for her to marry singer Vic Damone. The mother's intervention into what seemed to be true love between the couple was likely based as much on the fact that Dean was not a Catholic as on his behavior — apparently his eccentricity and "bad boy" antics were on full display when Pier brought him home for dinner one night. It is said that Pier's mother selected Damone because of his Italian Catholic heritage and impeccable manners.

Whatever one makes of the stories, the facts are these: Pier married Damone in 1955 while Jimmy sat across from the church either on a motorcycle or in his car — the versions differ. She had a child by Damone, an event that Dean took very hard. Rumors that Dean was seeing her up until two weeks before her marriage gave rise to questions on the paternity of her son.

Pier and Damone eventually divorced, and after a brief marriage to an Italian film composer ended in another divorce, Pier quietly overdosed on barbiturates, ending her sad life at 39. She left a letter saying James Dean was the only man she ever loved. Some reports say she committed suicide over her fear of turning 40.

Pier's film career was minor and in fact her twin sister, Marisa Pavan, appeared in more movies with better critical acceptance than Pier ever received, winning both a Golden Globe and an Oscar for her role in the 1955 film *The Rose Tattoo*.

See also Damone, Perry Rocco Luigi.

animal symbolism

The bull is important in the symbology of the cult of James Dean. His obsession with bullfighting was taken as a symptom of his death wish.

When Taurus appears in the planetarium scene in *Rebel Without a Cause*, Dean does an uncanny vocal imitation of a cow. Thereafter, he is known by his enemies as "Moo," and "Milk Cow Boogie" becomes his signature song on the car radio.

It all intersects nicely with Dean's Christ iconography. The Spanish bullfight compares the bull to the Redeemer marching towards death. The pass called the "Veronica" consists of holding the cape in front of the bull's face and is named for the compassionate woman of legend who offered her veil to the exhausted Savior on his march to crucifixion.

In ancient times, the bull had the universal character of a symbol of fertility because the shape of its horns resembled the lunar crescent. The bull was one of the symbols through which the supreme god was adored in Thebes. The mysterious cults of Mithra and Orpheus ascribed to the immolation of the bull such a special power of purification and propitiation that the bull sacrifices took on the form and the sacramental liturgy of a kind of baptism of blood, the same function Dean's early death continues to perform for his rapt followers.

Archduke Franz Ferdinand

Could the curse of James Dean's car have its origin in the 1914 assassination that started World War I?

On June 28, 1914, the Archduke Franz Ferdinand and his wife were touring Sarajevo, Yugoslavia, in their 28-foot Graf and Sift motorcar. They were relaxing amidst its sumptuous Aubusson carpets and Venetian crystal bud vases when an assassin began firing, killing the archduke and the duchess of Hohenberg. Blood spattered the African mahogany woodwork of the car's interior. The incident ignited the First World War. It was also the beginning of the bizarre odyssey of the archduke's death car.

General Emil Potiroek succeeded the archduke and commandeered the death car for himself. Five days later, the general was dead. The curse followed the car and nine subsequent owners. In 1923, mechanic Tiber Hirshfeld, who had restored the car, was chauffeuring six people to a wedding when there was an unexplained surge of power that sent the vehicle spilling down a cliff. All passengers were killed.

The car wound up in an automotive history display at the Vienna Museum of Industrial Development, until Allied bombs destroyed the museum in winter of 1944. Dr. Karl Unster of the University of Vienna became interested in the car's enigmatic history and in 1968 traced the remains to a wrecking yard in Stuttgart, West Germany.

According to Ron Smith in his August 1990 *Robb Report* feature story,

"The Car, the Star — and the Curse That Linked Them," this was the same wrecking yard from which Dr. Porsche and son Feery bought recyclable steel for their Porsche Motor Company. Did steel from the archduke's car become a part of James Dean's Spyder?

Smith says that Dr. Unster himself died soon afterwards, but apparently not before inquiring in a letter, "Is it possible for an evil 'spirit' or 'force' to enter into, and become a part of, an inanimate object?"

Archer, Joe

Joe Archer has the distinction of being among the first to report contacts with Jimmy Dean from the beyond. In 1956, he donated to the Marion, Indiana, library his manuscript entitled *Here Is the Real Story of My Life by James Dean as I Might Have Told It to Joe Archer*, which included the following message:

> Dear Friends on Earth:
> From somewhere beyond the veil, which separates the eons of eternity from the hours of time, I am writing to my living friends on earth.
> No, this is impossible, and I am obliged to make contact through the medium of another mind; to a people who grope in the darkness of fiction and make believe, in the hope that some day, the light of hope will shine on them....

Armes, J.J.

A renowned armless detective whom car customizer George Barris claims was retained to help find Jimmy Dean's death car after it disappeared on its return trip from a police safety council show in Miami.

See also Car.

Ashcroft, Ray

The November 1978 issue of *Hemmings Motor News* contained an ad that created quite a controversy in James Dean circles.

Kentuckian Ray Ashcroft advertised for sale a fully restored black '49 Merc coupe, "said to have been driven by James Dean" in *Rebel Without a Cause*. The asking price of $25,000 included life-sized poster boards of Jimmy Dean. The offer aroused the interest of Andy Herman of the Long Island Ford-Merc Club. He believed he had visited the genuine Dean Merc at the Movieworld Cars of the Stars Museum in California a couple of years earlier.

Fascinated by the provenance of the Kentucky car, Herman contacted Ashcroft and was told the car had been bought three years earlier from an owner in Cleveland. Dean's name was still on the keys, and his sunglasses still in the car.

After months of investigation, which Herman detailed in the club newsletter, he finally obtained a copy of the original Warner Bros. registration for the Dean '49 Merc. He traced the ownership of the actual car appearing in *Rebel Without a Cause* from Warner Bros. to a Charles Crail, who sold it to John Whidermann, who sold it to the owner of Movieworld Cars of the Stars Museum.

Confronted with the documentation, Ashcroft apparently dropped his claims.

"Assignment I'll Never Forget" *see* **"Jimmy Dean: The Assignment I'll Never Forget"**

attributes

James Dean was no angel. A perusal of the indexes of his biographies produces a list of unsavory attributes with anecdotal verification: immaturity, inability to take criticism, lack of social graces, need for attention, self-obsession and unprofessional behavior.

auction

In April of 1998, the following articles were advertised for auction in a James Dean newsletter as having been "originally obtained from Winton Dean when he closed out Jimmy's Sherman Oaks home in 1955":

1. From childhood, James Dean's metal mechanical wind-up peacock toy.
2. James Dean's personal clothing brush.
3. Jimmy's tie bar clasp.
4. James Dean's glass and metal cocktail shaker, Art Deco style.
5. Dean's statue of a nude Greek discus thrower.
6. Antique scythe.
7. Curved, Arabian-style dagger.

Bidding on each souvenir began at $995 per item.

autograph

The year 1978 saw the first news account of a sale of Dean memorabilia. It was announced in a UPI story that the star's autograph was purchased at an autograph auction held at the Charles Hamilton Galleries in New York in July. According to the account, Hamilton had expected a top bid of $600 and was surprised to see the bidding rise to $1,000 almost immediately. In the end, an unidentified private bidder paid $10,000 for the signature, which had been the first Dean autograph ever put up for private sale. The prize read simply, "For Howard, James Dean."

Aztecs

"I've always been fascinated by the Aztec Indians," Jimmy Dean told *Modern Screen* magazine — or so *Modern Screen* claimed in an article in September 1956.

"They were very fatalistic people, and I sometimes share that feeling. They had such a weird sense of doom that when the warlike Spaniards arrived in Mexico, a lot of the Aztecs just gave up to an event they believed couldn't be avoided."

Jacques Soustelle wrote in *Daily Life of the Aztecs,* "Human sacrifice among the Mexicans was inspired neither by cruelty nor by hatred. It was their response, an the only response that they could conceive, to the instability of a continually threatened world. Blood was necessary to save this world and the men in it: the victim was no longer an enemy who was to be killed but a messenger, arraigned in a dignity that was almost divine."

For the Aztecs, the sun had to be nourished with human hearts and blood, and if sacrifice was neglected the sun would stop moving and the human race would die in fire. The sun sacrifice was considered a glorious death.

It was appropriate that when a bust of Dean was erected at Griffith Observatory, it prominently featured a quotation from the Aztec "Flight of Quetzalocatl":

> "It ended with his body changed to light
> A star that burns forever in that sky."

B

Back Creek Friends Church

Jimmy Dean attended this church in Fairmount, Indiana, as a boy, and his funeral ceremony was held there on October 8, 1955. Starting in the 1980s, the church became a traditional gathering place for a service commemorating Jimmy. The hymns played at Jimmy's funeral service were often played, and his old drama teacher, Adeline Nall, would speak. From there the entourage of the devoted would form a parade to the cemetery, a cortege led by a black-jacketed man who called himself Nicky Bazooka, with the fragile Adeline Nall sporting one of the colorful scarves Bazooka gave her annually. Bazooka's real name is Terry Nichols.

Baker, Chet

Trumpet player Chet Baker was known as "The James Dean of Jazz." Like Dean, he achieved his fame in the 1950s. He not only looked like Dean, but he recorded an album called *Theme Music from "The James Dean Story"* for World Pacific. The Tommy Sands vocal "Let Me Be Loved" emerged from the cuts on this record. Also like Dean, Baker became a tragic figure. Racing was Dean's downfall; Baker's was narcotics. After his numerous arrests, his fame evaporated except in the memories of hardcore jazz enthusiasts like Bruce Weber, who had just finished a documentary on Baker entitled *Let's Get Lost* when the musician died in 1987 from a fall.

The Baker Boys

This duo is mentioned in an entertaining little book about James Dean and the paranormal, *James Dean Beyond the Grave*, by Texas Dean archivist Bob Rees. According to Rees, the fabulous Baker Boys were two brothers and ex-vaudevillians who performed in the 1930s under the name "Doctor Silkini." By the 1950s they had modified their act to appeal to movie theater owners who, feeling the pinch from television, wished to offer a little something extra to attract customers. Jack and Wyman Baker devised live midnight spook shows, and the craze attending the death of Jimmy Dean gave the entrepreneurs a nifty addition to their hokey illusions, which provided live diversion from Three Stooges and Abbott and Costello double features. They promised to produce the ghost of Jimmy Dean!

Free identification bracelets were affixed to frightened females in case they should become lost in the darkness, and a two-for-one free pass was offered to anyone who survived the heart-stopping experience.

What did the hype amount to? A large portrait of Jimmy Dean covered with glowing green paint and suspended against a backlight. Floating eerily over the stage, the sickly green and glowing head of Jimmy Dean would swoop and swirl above the rapt audiences, who had shelled out ninety cents for a seat. The apparition would also be carried racing up the aisles to much screaming and spilling of popcorn.

Bakersfield, California

This California town 84 miles from the site of Dean's crash has figured prominently in Dean lore, if not his life. In the highway safety public service announcement he filmed two weeks before his death, Dean commented on his racing and mumbled that he "ran pretty good at Bakersfield," though the race was at a track 12 miles north of town. On his last drive, he was ticketed 22 miles south of Bakersfield. He drove through Bakersfield on his last day. Confused reports of his death sometimes claimed he had died near Bakersfield.

Charles Adams, a Bakersfield resident who investigated Dean's death and wrote a report for his family, said Dean often called him at night at the Highway Patrol facility where Adams worked as dispatcher. The second-unit crew of *Giant* came to Bakersfield the month before Dean's death to film shots of oil wells and cattle to be inserted into the film in the section chronicling the impact of petroleum on Texas.

Bakersfield has become one of the stops for the fans who annually retrace Dean's death route. The Bakersfield connection to his last day has resulted in many stories in the local paper, and is often featured in the evening news on the anniversary of his death. Those wishing to retrace Dean's actual route as nearly as possible would take the Union Avenue Exit 17 miles south of town as they head north, and follow this picturesque alignment that was Highway 99 in the 1950s, before being bypassed in the 1960s by a newer highway.

Barhuis, George

His name is sometimes spelled "Barkhuis," and on occasion he is described as a state employee. Whatever the facts of his life, he is possibly a James Dean car jinx victim. Several accounts of the Dean car curse relate how the truck transporting the Spyder to Salinas, California, skidded on a rainy highway and crashed, causing the sports car to roll off the bed and crush the ejected driver. The incident is sometimes reported as having occurred in December of 1956.

Prolonged search by Dean historians has failed to confirm any such event, or indeed any such person as George Barhuis.

Interestingly, his name is almost a cognate for George Barris, who is possibly the origin of the story.

See also Barris, George; curses.

Barrett, Bill

Bill Barrett is the author of the article "The Checquered Flag," which appeared in the *West Coast Sports Car Journal* in January of 1956. An objective and even-handed account benefiting from the direct participation of the two California Highway Patrol Officers who investigated the accident, it is the closest thing to a summary of their investigation to survive. Their testimony at the inquest did not go into detail on the report the officers had prepared. Barrett wrote about Dean, calling him a "star on two horizons—celluloid and track—a bachelor, quiet, sensitive, yet filled with competitive spirit." He went on to explain how Dean had driven in competition with more seasoned drivers on private courses that were well-policed and designated Sports Car Road Races. In verifying Dean's qualifications as a driver, Barrett wrote that if a driver in these private races made a serious mistake, he would be "black-flagged"—forced to pull over and explain his action—and that these mistakes were recorded. Drivers were routinely suspended due to mistakes. Barrett concluded, "There is not much doubt that Dean was qualified, as he had completed or ran in several races and was entered and accepted to race at Salinas."

See also "The Checquered Flag."

Barris, George

A fixture in Hollywood automotive circles for forty years, Barris claims he supervised the Chickie Run for director Nicholas Ray in the film *Rebel Without a Cause*. He also says that on September 27, 1955, three days before Dean died, the actor drove his Spyder to Barris's shop in Compton to have racing numbers applied to doors and hood and the sobriquet "Little Bastard" painted on the back. However, according to Porsche historian and Dean biographer Lee Raskin, race car detailer Dean Jeffers claims that he performed the task. (Other accounts have Dean, in this compressed period of time, taking the car to the shop to repair a ding from a minor traffic accident.)

Most of Barris's claims are unverifiable and subject to dispute. He is the source of the many stories about the curse of James Dean's "death car." (See Curses) His undisputable role in the saga of the car is that he acquired the motorless chassis after the accident, and, after refurbishing it enough that it would hold together, sent it on tour. By some reports, customers could pay 25 cents to sit in the seat. He later claimed that the car vanished en route to Los Angeles from Florida in 1960.

Bayus, Steve

The 25-year-old manager of the restaurant at Cholame at the time of the fortieth anniversary of Dean's death in 1985, he told newspapers, "I guess it's Cholame's claim to fame. The average guy like me isn't into it. You get your hippies, your car buffs. We had one family of Russians come through in a motor home."

The *Fresno Bee* noted, "He happily points out the fatal intersection to all who ask."

Bazooka, Nicky

This colorful fixture, whose real name is Terry Nichols, has for many years shown up at the James Dean Festivities celebrating the icon's death in Fairmount, Indiana. Terry wears a black leather jacket and rides a Harley-Davidson at the head of the procession to Park Cemetery after the church service. His status increased to the point that he eventually addressed the throng. This Bloomington native is a mechanic for pit crews and followed the circuit for years. Each year until her death, he traditionally bestowed a different colored scarf upon Dean's old drama teacher, Adeline Nall. The scarves are on display at the James Dean Gallery in Fairmount.

See also Back Creek Friends Church.

Bean, Art

Bean, who had bit parts in several films, earned his nickname, "Bird Man," because of his lifelong fascination with gliders. He reportedly built twenty-nine of them. His ambitions included gliding off Mt. Wilson into Victory Park and challenging Evel Knievel to a flight across the Grand Canyon. Bean also reported that he had purchased a plot in a Newport, California, cemetery so he could eventually be interred next to one of his idols, John Wayne.

He also had a peculiar fascination with James Dean, as this unattributed newspaper clipping attests:

> Well, this is too much for me. Arthur Bean who is the owner of JAMES DEAN's red jacket from REBEL WITHOUT A CAUSE (there were three jackets used in that film) wore that jacket, Jimmy's motorcycle boots and other James Dean garments while driving a car that was the same as the one that hit Jimmy, driven by Donald Turnupseed. And Art was hit by a PORSCHE, the same type of car that killed Jimmy. Art fractured a leg and had a head concussion resulting in metal plates being implanted in his head. This was the "second" accident he was in while wearing Jimmy's clothes.

The article concluded with the observation that Art Bean was said to have the largest extant collection of property once owned by Dean.

The Beatles

Included on the 1963 best-selling album *Please Please Me* is the John Lennon tune "There's a Place." This poignant harmonica-driven lament with wonderful harmonies was inspired by one of the lines in the film *Rebel Without a Cause*. In need of sanctuary after the knife fight sequence at Griffith Park, Sal Mineo tells Jimmy, "I know a place." He indicates an abandoned mansion — portrayed in a matte shot — nearly hidden in the Hollywood Hills. The Beatles song thematically parallels the symbolism of the refuge from the turbulent teenage world embodied by the mansion secluded in the hills.

The Beatles themselves, perhaps subconsciously, drew their name from the name of Lee Marvin's biker gang in *The Wild One* — a film that was also a seminal influence on a young James Dean. Stu Sutcliffe, the painter who was briefly bass player for the Beatles during their Hamburg days, modeled his stage presentation on James Dean. John Lennon later said, "Without James Dean, there wouldn't have been any Beatles."

bees

Local headlines in the July 27, 1985, issue of *The Bakersfield Californian* announced that killer invader bees had been discovered near the crash site of movie idol James Dean. The deadly Africanized bees had not been expected to reach the United States until 1990. In a scene out of a 1950s horror film, after killing a rabbit, the bees attacked a heavy equipment operator. State food and agriculture officials cautioned the public to take extra precautions while traveling within a 20-mile radius of where the bees were discovered. The bees have been known to chase and sting people within 100 yards of their nest. A task force was formed and fanned out from the site of the first colony of aggressive Africanized honeybees ever found in the United States. An aerial reconnaissance of a 400-square-mile region around the original nest was initiated.

The heavy equipment operator who uncovered the nest was swarmed, but found safety in the glass-enclosed cage of his machine.

Bello, Todd

Todd Bello was a 29-year-old actor and former disc jockey whose Dean-inspired angry-young-man antics eventually estranged him from his father, longtime bandleader Al Bello, who had the distinction of jamming with James Dean in the fifties in an unrehearsed Hollywood ad-lib jazz session. The tape was released in a limited collector's edition record as *James Dean on Conga Drums*.

What brought father and son together in January of 1990 was Jimmy Dean's Porsche Spyder. To promote a documentary film Todd dreamed of, he persuaded his father to put up $25,000 for the James Dean Porsche, or $5,000 for information leading to its recovery. The publicity value was that the rewards would be publicized on a segment of the syndicated series *Missing/Reward*.

The episode was televised, but no one came up with the car.

Belushi, John

Actor and comedian John Belushi died of a drug overdose in Bungalow 2 at the Chateau Marmont on March 2, 1982. Dean biographer Randall Riese claims that this was the same bungalow where Nick Ray hosted Sunday afternoon tea parties during the filming of *Rebel Without a Cause*.

Bernhardt, Sarah

The French stage actress lived from 1844 to 1923 and appeared in a few early silents. Beulah Roth, widow of Dean photographer Sanford Roth, had a wealth of Dean stories, which expanded over the years, and one of the most unlikely was that Jimmy Dean was a great fan of Bernhardt's. Beulah claimed that the Roths and Jimmy visited a Venice hotel where Bernhardt had stayed when she was appearing on the Venice Pier. Jimmy insisted on going alone to the room because "I want Sarah to come to me." Randall Riese quotes Roth as saying Jimmy "lay on the bed where she had slept and he really felt that he had made contact with Sarah Bernhardt." Riese also states that Sarah liked to sleep in a satin-lined coffin and was even photographed in it — just as Jimmy Dean posed in a casket for Dennis Stock on one of his return trips to Fairmount, Indiana.

The Best of James Dean in the Scandal Magazines, 1955–1958

Shake Books published this book in 1988. Edited by Alan Betrock, it culls the most lurid stories printed about Jimmy Dean in the three years after his death.

biographies

Here is a chronological list of biographies and similar Dean books. Note that the publication of books on Dean seems to increase in frequency as the years pass.

1956 *James Dean* by William Bast
1962 *The Rebel* by Royston Ellis
1965 *Continuity and Evolution in a Public Symbol: An Investigation*

into the Creation and Communication of the James Dean Image in Mid-Century America by Robert Wayne Tysl

1974 *The Films of James Dean* by Mark Whitman
James Dean: A Short Life by Venable Herndon
James Dean: The Mutant King by David Dalton

1975 *James Dean: A Biography* by John Howlett
The James Dean Story by Ron Martinetti
The Real James Dean by John Gilmore

1978 *James Dean Revisited* by Dennis Stock

1982 *James Dean: A Portrait* by Roy Schatt

1983 *James Dean* by Beulah Roth
James Dean: The Way It Was by Terry Cunningham
James Dean Is Not Dead by Stephen Morrissey

1984 *The Last James Dean Book* by Dante Volpe
Rebels United: The Enduring by Joe Brean
James Dean: American Icon by David Dalton, Ron Cayen

1986 *James Dean: Footsteps of a Giant* by Wolfgang Fuchs
The Death of James Dean by Warren Newton Beath

1987 *James Dean on Location* by Marceau Devillers

1989 *Wish You Were Here, Jimmy Dean* by Martin Dawber
James Dean: In His Own Words by Mick St. Michael

1990 *James Dean: Shooting Star* by Barney Hoskins
Jimmy Dean on Jimmy Dean by Joseph Humphreys
James Dean: Behind the Scene by Leith Adams and Keith Burns

1991 *The Unabridged James Dean: His Life and Legacy from A to Z* by Randall Riese

1992 *James Dean: Little Boy Lost* by Joe Hyams

1994 *James Dean* by Timothy Jacobs

1996 *James Dean — The Untold Story of A Passion for Speed* by Phillipe Defechereux

1997 *Boulevard of Broken Dreams: The Life, Times, and Legend of James Dean* by Paul Alexander
James Dean: The Biography by Val Holley
Rebel: The Life and Legend Of James Dean by Donald Spoto

1998 *Live Fast — Die Young: My Life with James Dean* by John Gilmore

1999 *Unknown James Dean* by Robert Tanitch
James Dean by William Hall

2001 *The Importance of James Dean* by Walter G. Olesky

Blackwell's Corner

On November 18, 1921, George Blackwell, with some sticks of lumber and a few cans of water, established a gas station and grocery at the intersection of two rural trails. Through the years, the intersection would come to be known as Blackwell's Corner. The trails eventually became the intersection of two major highways, a haven for the stranded motorist and a byword to many people throughout the world.

The curse of Blackwell's Corner first manifested itself when founder George Blackwell was killed in a motorcycle accident in 1924. Thirty-one years later, Jimmy Dean came to Blackwell's some thirty minutes before he was killed. Then the building itself burned to the ground on July 25, 1968, in a mysterious fire. The menu of the rebuilt restaurant boasts that it was not only Jimmy Dean's Last Stop, but the site of the first U.S. colony of killer bees.

See also bees; curse.

Blackwell's Corner as it appeared in April of 1941, when the army practiced maneuvers in the vicinity.

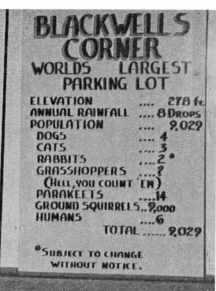

BLACKWELLS
CORNER
WORLDS LARGEST
PARKING LOT

ELEVATION .... 278 ft.
ANNUAL RAINFALL .... 8 DROPS
POPULATION 2,029
  DOGS 4
  CATS 3
  RABBITS 2*
  GRASSHOPPERS .... ?
    (HELL, YOU COUNT 'EM)
  PARAKEETS 14
  GROUND SQUIRRELS .. 2,000
  HUMANS 6
        TOTAL 2,029

*SUBJECT TO CHANGE
  WITHOUT NOTICE.

Top left: Blackwell's Corner circa 1960. *Top right:* Sign at Blackwell's circa 1960. *Bottom:* Blackwell's Corner was destroyed by fire in July 1968.

blood

The California Highway Patrol requested a blood alcohol test on James Dean. According to the coroner's report, "there was not too much blood left in the body for this purpose." But it takes hardly any blood for the test. So what happened to it? The result of this test, if one was in fact conducted, is not known. The report also erroneously gives the date of death as 10–1–55.

Conspiracy theorists have offered that blood is a powerful element in black magic ritual, and the acquisition of Dean's blood could have been a powerful motive for his murder by fanatics intent on generating a designer god for the occult power it would bestow. A historical precedent would be Heinrich Himmler's search for the spear that pierced the side of Christ.

```
JAMES DEAN.
Traffic accident, Cholame, California, 10-1-55
about 5:45 PM.
Dean taken to War Memorial Hospital, Paso Robles by
Paul Moreno, Cholame Ambulance Service.
Dean dead on arrival.  Doctor Bossart pronounced him dead.
He did not examine the eyes.
Taken to Kuehl Funeral Home, and body procuessed by Martin
Kuehl, and states that the left side of the face was
damaged much more than the right side.  Upper and lower
jaws multiple fractures, broken neck, possible basil
skull fracture.  Both arms multiple fractures.  Both legs
O.K., though trousers on one side were ripped off from the
body.
CHP were given the blood for the blood alcohol test, however
Kuehl says there was not too much blood left in the body for
this purpose.  Kuehl also states that there were samll
particles of glass embedded in Dean's face, believed to be
from the windshield.  There were no glasses found on Dean,
and neither Dr. Bossart or Martin Kuehl examined the eyes
for contact lenses.
Body will arrive at the Hunt Mortuary, Fairmount, Ind.
```

This page from the California Highway Patrol Vehicle Accident Report notes the lack of blood in Dean's body.

Many fans who study Sanford Roth's photos of the death car claim they see blood dripping down the side, or on the upholstery, but examination of photos from the original negatives show a staining that is likely motor oil or some other artifact from the crash—though massive loss of blood at the scene must be inferred from the pathology report.

body art

A young Dean fan appeared in Fairmount, Indiana, in 1988 driving a replica of Dean's Spyder and sporting a full back tattoo of James Dean in the "crucifixion" pose from *Giant*. The tattoo had reportedly won first prize at a Biker's Ball.

Bongiovanni, Sylvia

Sylvia Bongiovanni was a legal secretary in Fullerton, California, who became one of the founders of the We Remember Dean International fan club. In the *Los Angeles Times* on September 29, 1985, journalist Rebecca Zahn wrote:

> Sylvia Bongiovanni can instantly recall the moment she fell in love with James Dean: "The movie was East of Eden, and I saw it in a theater in the Bronx when I was 15 with my best friend. He mesmerized us."
>
> Just a few days after Dean's death, Bongiovanni started buying whatever she could find about her idol—books, fan magazines, photos. Today, she has 15 scrapbooks chronicling the actor's life and death, and runs a fan club in his honor.
>
> We Remember Dean International was founded by Bongiovanni in 1978, and its 158 other members, scattered all over the world, are as devoted to the memory of James Dean as she.
>
> "It's nice to be able to share your feelings with people who don't think it's crazy to like a star who's been dead for 30 years," she says.

Bossert, Robert H., M.D.

The doctor who pronounced James Dean dead, he gave the following deposition for the inquest:

> The Cholame ambulance, driven by Mr. Moreno, arrived at the Paso Robles War Memorial Hospital at approximately 6:20 P.M. on September 30, 1955, with two patients. One was Mr. Rolf Wuetherick [sic], and the other said to be by his friends, James Dean. I examined the body of an individual said to be James Dean when he was brought to the hospital following the accident. He was dead and gross examination revealed fractured neck, multiple fractures of forearms, fractured leg and numerous cuts and

bruises about the face and chest. I believe that he died of these injuries and that death came at the time or shortly after the accident.

Bossert lived into his nineties in the Midwest.

Bracker, Lew

The cousin of Leonard Rosenmann, Bracker was the author of Dean's $100,000 life insurance policy shortly before the actor's death. He told *Life* magazine in 1956, "If Jimmy were here and saw what was going on, he'd die all over again without the accident. It's mass hysteria. Somebody has paralyzed the whole country. It's a creepy, almost a sick thing. It's something in Jimmy the teenagers saw, maybe themselves. Everybody mirrored themselves in Jimmy's fame and Jimmy's death."

Bracker and Dean were close friends. "We talked about getting married," Bracker said, then added, "but not to each other."

Brandes, Theresa

Theresa J. Brandes was a New York widow who devoted her life to keeping Jimmy's flame burning bright, chiefly by founding the James Dean Memory Club, also known as the James Dean Memory Ring, and the James Dean Memory Ring Around the World. The door to her East 57th Street apartment was always open to Dean fans. She maintained voluminous correspondence and hounded network execs to show Dean's films on television. Flowers were sent to Dean's grave every year on his birthday and death day. Dean's uncle Marcus Winslow would place them on the grave, then take pictures and send them to Brandes.

She told *The New Yorker* in a September 1969 interview:

> If you're thinking that James Dean is forgotten, you're absolutely wrong. He's not. Sometimes on television these days there'll be a band — today's new type of band — and they'll have a big poster of James Dean, and they're playing this modern music. The young people know about James Dean. And then another time somebody will be talking — like a discussion program, discussing a movie — and the name of James Dean comes up. So James Dean is not forgotten. And with me and the other members of the club, he'll never be forgotten, because we're always talking about him. I always tell people that James Dean will be alive until I die.

Braunt, Robert

Among Dean's effects was the 1955 Ford station wagon that Bill Hickman had been driving behind Jimmy on the day of the crash. When Dean's estate was settled, the car was reportedly purchased by a Robert F. Braunt for $2,200. It is not known what became of Mr. Braunt or the car.

See also Ford station wagon.

Bray, Susan

Jimmy Dean's maid. The documents of final disbursement by his estate after his death note that she was paid $14.72 for services to Dean's Sherman Oaks bungalow the week prior to his death.

Brazil

According to the *Weekly World News*, Jimmy Dean was alive and well in Recife, Brazil, as of January 25, 1990. That was the date he supposedly interviewed with filmmaker Zavro Duarte on a farm near town. The meeting was reported in a *Weekly World News* cover story for March 6 of that year.

As Duarte told it, Hollywood had become too much for Jimmy, so he escaped the tinseltown rat race by duping the public into believing he had been killed in a car crash. Then he headed for an isolated farm in South America to raise chickens and dabble in racing. There was an even chance he might return to Hollywood to make one more film.

In the meantime, Duarte said, "Jimmy tends his animals and hangs out with his buddies, playing cards and passing around a rum bottle all day."

Bridges, James

He was the writer-director of the movie-memoir *September 30, 1955*, which was the story of a young man's experience with the reverberations of the death of James Dean. Bridges also scripted a play that was never produced, *How Many Times Did You See "East of Eden?"*

Bridges was in his twenties when Dean died, but was so moved that he left college for Hollywood to pursue a career in entertainment. Unlike many Dean fans who followed Jimmy's star, Bridges made it: He appeared in nearly fifty films in the fifties, including *Johnny Trouble* and *Joyride*. He was a screenwriter for such prestigious productions as *White Hunter, Black Heart* and directed and co-wrote *The Paper Chase*, *Urban Cowboy*, *The China Syndrome*, *Perfect* and *Bright Lights, Big City*. His Dean picture was also known by the titles *9–30–55* and *24 Hours of the Rebel*.

Brown, Kip

A leading authority on James Dean, Brown is author of the forthcoming book *James Dean: Day After Day*, a self-published chronological look at the life and legacy of the legend (*rarerecords@earthlink.net*, or PO Box

55881, Sherman Oaks, CA 91413–0881). He also served as the official researcher for the 2005 Dean Estate–approved book *James Dean* by George Perry, and he contributed a Dean timeline to that book. In addition, newsletter and occasionally gives personally guided tours of Dean sites in Southern California. A musician (Shock, Little Girls, Weed Patch) and former record store owner (Ear Candy), Brown is the proud owner of a rare, one-of-a-kind acetate recording of James Dean performing an a cappella rendition of the old Eddy Arnold country-western hit "Cattle Call."

Bucholz, Horst

The wiry and intense young German actor and Dean contemporary achieved stardom in his homeland by portraying rebellious teenagers, leading to his brief branding as the "German James Dean." After a modicum of international success, Bucholz moved to Hollywood, where, despite a slight accent, he starred in *The Magnificent Seven*. It probably didn't hurt that Yul Brynner, the star of the film, had a more pronounced accent. Bucholz also starred in Billy Wilder's *One Two Three*, then continued his career in Europe, appearing in TV melodramas as he got older. However, he never achieved the success his early performances augured. He died in 2002 at the age of 69, of pneumonia, while in the hospital recovering from a broken leg.

C

Calaway, Martin C.

Attorney of record for Rolf Wuetherich and member of the legal firm that handled the mechanic's suit against Donald Turnupseed for the injuries he sustained in the car accident on September 30, 1955.

Camden House

In May of 1991, this movie memorabilia auction house sold a black and white charcoal drawing of Dean with a lengthy autograph quotation for $17,000.

candles

Maila "Vampira" Nurmi claimed that on September 30, 1956 — exactly a year after Dean's death — a candle identical to one Dean had drawn in a self-portrait as a corpse exploded and vanished entirely.

See also Nurmi, Maila.

car

Car customizer George Barris claims he advised Jimmy to "buy up" to the Porsche 550 Spyder. Jimmy's friend Lew Bracker, an insurance agent and amateur race car driver, also said he told Jimmy to get the Spyder. Mechanic Rolf Wuetherich said the same thing.

Jimmy's Spyder was shipped from the Porsche factory July 15, 1955, and received at Competition Motors in early September. The engine number was P90059; the chassis number, 550–005; and the gearbox number, 10046. It was one of 75 production models with ladder-type chassis. Dean left Warner Bros. on September 16 and went directly to the dealership to pick up the car, which retailed for $7,000. Dean had traded in the Speedster and paid $3,000 cash. The money had been advanced to him by his agency, Famous Artists, pending final negotiations to do an unspecified film for Italian producer Dino de Laurentiis at a future date.

In the days before pollution controls and safety standards, nearly anything that could be driven could get a license to operate on the street. So it was with the Spyder: It was licensed (2Z77767), and Jimmy drove it around Hollywood hard and fast. Some reports say that Dean dinged his new car in a minor accident with a lady on Sunset, necessitating another return to the shop, and that he returned for the car on Friday, September 23.

The Spyder had an air-cooled flat-4 with four overhead cams, two dual-throat carburetors, a roller-bearing crankshaft, and two spin gears. The engine could expand and contract with temperature changes. The engine was, however, very temperamental. It took an expert mechanic 120 hours to assemble it and up to 15 hours just to set the timing.

What Happened to the Car?

Porsche historian and James Dean expert Lee Raskin wrote the seminal article on the search for James Dean's Porsche 550 Spyder in 1984. His search for information has continued, and his story of the Porsche and of James Dean's racing career will be chronicled in his forthcoming biography *James Dean at Speed*. He kindly updates us on the history of the Spyder and resolves what became of the missing death car:

> After the accident, the wrecked James Dean Porsche 550 Spyder was brought back to Los Angeles and appraised by the Pacific Indemnity Insurance Co. The car was declared a total loss, and the estate received approximately $5,000 from Pacific Indemnity. The estate in turn sold the wreck for approximately $2,500 to Dr. William F. Eschrich, a Burbank, California, orthopedic surgeon, who had raced three times against James Dean

in 1955. Eschrich and his racing friend, Dr. Troy McHenry, a Beverly Hills surgeon, bought the Porsche for its valuable mechanical parts. Eschrich removed the 4-cam Porsche engine, the transmission and running gear, the steering linkage, the torsion bars, and the dash instruments.

Eschrich installed the Porsche engine into his new Lotus Mk9 chassis race car and raced it unsuccessfully several times during 1956. He had an accident in the Lotus at the Pomona Road Races on October 21, 1956.

McHenry used some suspension and steering parts from James Dean's Spyder on his own 550 Spyder. During the same Pomona race in which Eschrich had his accident, McHenry crashed into a tree and died at the scene as a result of his injuries. Purportedly, the Pittman arm failed and McHenry lost complete steering.

As a separate story, about three months after James Dean's accident, the Spyder's chassis remains, which had been stored at Jack McAfee's race car shop in Hollywood, were sold to George Barris for a very small sum. Barris welded up the mangled frame and then loaned the carcass out to the Greater Los Angeles Safety Council for several "Speed Kills" auto show displays. According to George Barris, the James Dean "Little Bastard" exhibit suddenly disappeared while on tour in Florida during 1960, and it has never been seen since.

Raskin believes that the "Little Bastard" chassis was actually losing its fan appeal and that Barris disposed of it because he thought its power as a draw was exhausted. Barris then developed his "mysterious disappearance" story to embellish and perpetuate the James Dean "Death Car" myth (*see* curses).

Raskin's research indicates the following disposition of the remaining parts of Dean's Spyder:

> *The engine:* The estate of William Eschrich, which claims to have "anything which remains which is recognizable as a car."
>
> *The transaxle:* Jim Barrington. Piedmont, California.
>
> *The Nurburgring plaque:* This green and white enameled steel plaque, from the German racetrack called Nurburgring, decorated the driver's side of the Porsche. Purportedly it was picked up by someone who came upon the wreck. It was donated to and resides in the Fairmount (Indiana) Historical Museum.
>
> *See also* curses.

Carter, Lynne

The April 1957 issue of *Rave* magazine promised in an article called "I Learned About Love from Jimmy Dean" that "the shapely photographer's model who was intimately acquainted with the late great idol reveals his romantic secrets." It was a sequel to Carter's article "I Was a Friend of Jimmy Dean," which had appeared in the magazine in January. Many fans apparently took exception to her portrayal of Jimmy, which included such recollections as "He showed me some pictures taken at a party in a friend's apartment in Greenwich Village. One showed him with a big-breasted blonde whom he said was French. He commented on her outstanding features in earthy language. Then he said he was hungry and we went to the Hickory House again...." Carter is herself big-breasted — the article is illustrated with photos of her in a leopard skin bikini, and as a sultan's concubine. The follow-up article that appeared in April was Carter's response to the negative mail the magazine had received after the first story. Despite the accompanying pictures of Carter — bare-shouldered with smoldering lips parted passionately, and one of her in the bathroom brushing her teeth and clad only in a towel — she responded snappishly. "The lack of intelligence displayed in most of these letters is ludicrous. The ignorance and pettiness of Mr. Dean's so-called 'fans' is obvious. I could analyze your illiterate manners, but I'm sure it would accomplish nothing and the lead in my pencil is too valuable to waste on such advice."

cat

On the night before he was killed en route to Salinas, James Dean stopped at the home of actress Jeanette Mille and dropped off the little Siamese kitten named Markie, which had been a gift to him from Elizabeth Taylor. A paper with detailed feeding instructions in Dean's distinctive hand was published in the seventies. There is the embellishment that he dropped off the cat with the cryptic comment, "Who knows, I may not be back."

What happened to the cat? One story that made the rounds at get-togethers of salon maven Samson deBrier was that the cat was passed along to a succession of owners including Yvonne Lime and Tony Perkins. The final owner bought it for its possible worth because of its connection to James Dean, only to become anxious that the cat might run away. He purportedly had it put to sleep and mounted expertly by a taxidermist. Unable to prove the provenance of this treasure, the owner eventually gave it away.

chair

In 1998, it was reported in a fan newsletter that artist Kenneth Kendall had donated to the James Dean Memorial Gallery the very chair that Jimmy sat in when he visited Kendall's Melrose Avenue studio in January of 1955. It would be on "permanent display." Another owner of a James Dean chair was Beulah Roth, widow of Dean's photographer Sanford Roth. The Roth chair had more authenticity, since there were actual photos of Dean sitting in it. The chair was later sold for an undisclosed sum to Seita Ohnishi.

See also Ohnishi, Seita.

Chapa, Damian

Chapa was the winner of several Dean lookalike contests and did an uncanny impersonation. He is the "discovery" of Loren Pike, the Palm Springs investor who at one time owned an option on the authorized screen biography of James Dean. The film was never made, but the events set in motion by Pike's purchase of the rights culminated in the case known as "The James Dean Murders," when con-man Jon Emr was assassinated after bilking investors and associates on the project. Chapa continued to work with Pike's successor, Alan Hauge, and even participated in a trailer for the project "in development."

The actor later appeared in a TV movie as one of the Menendez brothers and also in several Steven Segal films, in addition to the popular *Blood In, Blood Out.* In 2003, he directed himself in the indie film *El Padrino.* He was married to at one time to *Species* star Natasha Henstridge.

"The Checquered Flag"

This seminal article on the Dean crash was the most objective and factual published throughout the fifties and sixties. Written by Bill Barrett, it appeared in the *West Coast Sports Car Journal* in January of 1956.

"In this account of James Dean's unfortunate accident," Barrett wrote, "I do not wish to condemn or condone the actions of the driver or the car he was driving. I am only reporting the series of events as they have been relayed to this magazine." The author worked closely with California Highway Patrol Officers Ernie Tripke and Ron Nelson to produce his account.

See also Barrett, Bill.

chickie run

George Barris, who claims to have been retained by Warner Bros. to supervise the chickie run in *Rebel Without a Cause,* told Steve Roeser in an interview for the June 1990 issue of *Sh-Baam* magazine that Nicholas Ray (director of *Rebel*) had read in the papers about a Pacific Palisades chickie run in which a boy had been killed when he was unable to get out of his car in time before it went off a cliff. Inspired, Ray wrote such a scene into the movie.

Barris said, "We did chicken races in the same manner (in real life).

Of course, losing pink slips was one form of racing. If you lost, you lost your car. But if you were in a chicken race, you could lose your life. We had races where kids did do that. They raced through the streets; they took daredevil chances of losing their lives—either against an opponent or against other vehicles that could possibly be on the streets. In those days—the '40s and early '50s—hot-rodders were considered militants, because we expressed ourselves with vehicles, and we didn't want to conform with the establishment or the police organization that said, 'You cannot do anything to your car; you cannot race.'"

Cholame

Cholame is the California town nearest the crash site. Some say Cholame is a Chumash Indian word for "the beautiful one."

There was a strange meteor shower here in 1974 and a Caltech scientist predicted in 1983 that if a cataclysmic earthquake were really going to rip through California, it would start at Cholame. The town is so tiny it takes less than ten seconds to drive through it. There is only a cafe. Pronounced show-lamb, most of the 65 residents live in the surrounding hills.

In 1977 things changed when Tokyo businessman Seita Ohnishi uncrated a memorial to Dean to be erected at the crash site. The starkly beautiful sculpture twines around an aleanthum, or tree of heaven, symbolically sacred to Asians.

Author Warren Beath, interviewing local citizens, found antipathy to the installation of the monument. "Why make a hero out of someone who was driving 100 miles an hour and then ran into an innocent person?" Alta McMillan, 83, commented. "We needed that space where the memorial is for truck parking." The curmudgeonly editor of the Paso Robles newspaper is more succinct. "Dean was a madman," says Ben Reddick. "He was a brilliant actor and a remarkable young man, but when it came to driving, he was a horse's ass."

Even more outspoken critics have in recent years vandalized the monument with shotgun blasts and sledge hammers.

The Cholame Experience, 1995

"Experience the ride in a car as you approach the intersection," promises the blurb in a fan club newsletter. This two-hour tape by expert Dean writer and archivist Bob Rees was advertised for $38.00. "Classic car rally, James Dean memorial monument. Eyewitness to tragedy speaks for first time. Casper Van Dien appears. Rolf Wuetherich's niece is interviewed for the first time (in-depth, close-up interview, never released)." Also included were video clips from the short-lived TV shows *Missing: Reward,* and *What Happened?* featuring "Transaxle today, computer animation reconstruction of wreck."

Christ

Jimmy Dean created most of his own iconography during his lifetime, and the attitude he assumed in *Giant,* with his rifle across and behind his shoulders, has come to be called the crucifixion pose by his fans. Like Christ, Jimmy had a distant relationship with his own earthly father, and it was with amazement that people tried to accept he could have sprung from the loins of the earthbound dental technician.

A new star bursts across the firmament in *Rebel Without a Cause* during the planetarium scene. The celestial auguries herald the entrance of Jim Stark. Christ was the New Adam, and Jimmy replaces the old Adam, his father, in the distinctly biblical context in which the film *East of Eden* unravels its story.

Like Jesus, Jimmy Dean extended the promise to his followers of reconciling opposites. He was the apparent archetypal rebel on film and in the press stories, but he was also the embodiment of establishment success, a movie star with expensive toys. With his sacrificial death, he broke his body to feed his legions of disciples who could now possess his spirit in a more intimate way than ever they could have communed with the living Dean.

And like Christ, he left behind a church with forms of worship that do violence to his own code and apparent mode of living, canned and homogenized into a bland sacerdotal form. He's even on postage stamps, which is a perverse communion wafer, which his fans place to their mouths, participating in his transubstantiation each time they send a letter.

See also religious symbolism.

Cinemonde

This French film magazine dedicated every September issue to James Dean for four years after his death.

Cisco

Jimmy Dean's palomino horse was named Cisco. After Dean's death, the horse was sold to the Gila Land Company for $130.

clocks

James Dean lends his name and image to a variety of timepieces. The James Dean Triangle Alarm Clock sells for $29.95, while a James Dean Wall

.Clock, with the Rebel's face, goes for $31.95. How about a James Dean Clock Calendar or a James Dean Swivel Alarm Clock for only $29.95?

clones

Many actors over the years have had to bear the title of "new James Dean," "Dean wannabe," or "Dean lookalike." Michael Parks, Christopher Jordan, Aidan Quinn, Martin Sheen, Sean Penn — the list is long, and there are additions every year. With the advent of recombinant DNA they came to be called "Dean Clones." A *Los Angeles Times* columnist was inspired by the cloning of sheep to envision trips to Forest Lawn to extract DNA from dead movie stars. Bioengineers in laboratories could then clone the stars of yesteryear, including Clark Gable and Errol Flynn.

Daft as the idea is, with the extraction of DNA from Egyptian mummies, it is within the realm of possibility that biotic material could be salvaged from the grave of James Dean, and that in a future time he could be duplicated with some cellular integrity. This event has even been imagined in at least one unpublished science fiction short story.

clothes

The bloody haberdashery Clyde Barrow was wearing when he was gunned down has been parceled out for thousands of dollars at auction. What might the torn trousers of Jimmy Dean bring? But according to John W. Stander, who processed Dean's body at the Paso Robles funeral home, they were "probably destroyed."

Clothing from Dean's movies, on the other hand, still exists and is in the hands of collectors. David Loehr paid $2,500 for the shirt and pants Dean purportedly wore in *East of Eden*. He shelled out another $2,500 for the white cotton shirt and striped pants Dean wore in *Eden*. At a Sotheby's auction he paid $2000 for the brown trousers Dean wore in the knife fight scene in *Rebel*. In 1992 he estimated the trousers had appreciated to the $30,000 to $40,000 range.

The Club

It was reported to be a seamy leather bar in East Hollywood and its denizens were the sexual bottom-feeders of tinseltown. Bondage and beatings were the object of the homosexual assignations made there, and it was said that Jimmy Dean frequently dipped his beak in the varieties of sexual experience the Club offered. Rumors have circulated for years that on the evening before his death, Dean attended a homosexual gathering where he was backed into a corner and berated for living a lie. Some versions claim this encounter took place at a Malibu beach house, while others say it occurred at the Club.

cockroaches

At the time of his death, James Dean had an outstanding bill with the Western Exterminator Company. The six dollars due was paid in full by Dean's estate.

Cocks, Harvey H.

Known theatrically as H. Cocks, he is the author of the play *James Dean: The Boy from Fairmount*, which premiered in June 1996 as part of the American Classic Summer Theater Series at Indiana University–Purdue Fort Wayne. Cocks claims to have known Dean when they were both young actors in New York City. The play revolves around the death of Dean, the novelty being the presence of a beautiful "Angel of Death"—à la *All That Jazz*—who provides commentary on Dean's life. Joel Moorman played Dean.

"There were side-splitting lines in this performance," said a reviewer of the first night. "Perhaps the audience didn't laugh because they were all spellbound."

collectibles

"The value of James Dean movie memorabilia has never declined," said Larry Cox, owner of the Nostalgia Shop in Bowie, Texas. Interviewed by Warren Beath, Cox declared, "The Elvis Presley items have always gone up and down. When he was overweight and hadn't made a movie in a few years, sales of Presley items slumped. But just like the Beatles and Marilyn Monroe, James Dean memorabilia has never gone down in price."

The toy monkey Dean fondled in the opening scene of *Rebel Without a Cause* changed hands at auction for $7,000. A high school yearbook, autographed, might draw $3,000 to $4,000. An autographed dance ticket from Dean's high school sold for $2,000. A charcoal drawing which was presented to Dean in the early fifties, and which he signed and inscribed with a few lines of poetry, drew $17,000.

In the 1995 fall issue of *Films of the Golden Age* magazine, Dean archivist Brian Lewis listed the following prices for Dean items he had encountered:

1. Red windbreaker worn in *Rebel*.......................$25,000
2. Musical toy monkey used in *Rebel* $6,500

3. Hollywood contracts or personal letters signed by Dean . . . $6,000
4. Autographed high school yearbook. $4,000
5. One sheet lobby poster from *Rebel* $1,800
6. One sheet lobby poster from *Eden*. $1,000
7. One sheet lobby poster from *Giant*. $500
8. Complete lobby card set from *Eden* or *Rebel* (8 per set) $400
9. 1950s hardcover w/dust jacket bio $150
10. Special issue of tribute LP w/picture on sleeve. $120
11. 1950s one shot tribute mag w/Dean on cover $100
12. Limited edition Dean bust $75
13. Vintage 1950s Dean scrapbook $50
14. Vintage 1950s Dean-related sheet music w/Dean on cover. . . . $25

Collins, Judith *see* **dreams of death**

collision *see* **accident**

Come Back to the Five and Dime, Jimmy Dean, Jimmy Dean

The action in this play by Ed Graczyk takes place on September 30, 1975, at the Five and Dime in the small town of McCarthy, Texas. On this date, the members of the "Disciples of James Dean" gather to commemorate the twentieth anniversary of Dean's death.

The play debuted in New York during the 1980-81 theater season and featured Cher in her breakout role. Her fledgling film career was kickstarted with a Golden Globe nomination for her participation in the movie version. Both were directed by Bob Altman using the same cast, which included Kathy Bates and Karen Black among other seasoned performers.

Graczyk says he was inspired while working with the Midland Community Theatre in west Texas. He visited Marfa, where *Giant* was filmed, and found that the only physical remnant of the filming was the Reata mansion façade. Graczyk drew on his memories of that site, and of the impact that James Dean had on his era, to create his play.

commemorative plates

Curtis Management promised to honor Dean's memory and insure a high quality of merchandise bearing his likeness. Some perceived the upshot as a rip-off. One of the first "official" James Dean products was a set of collector plates to commemorate the 30th anniversary of his death. Sold only in sets of four at a suggested retail price of $60.00, they were individually numbered and limited to an edition of 25,000. "Unwilling to accept hypocrisy," ran the sales literature, "convinced that it was wrong to feel nothing for your fellow man, James Dean's restless strivings for change defined something most admirable in our American character. And a nation was proud to regard him as ... America's Rebel." The pièce de resistance was the "Jim and Spyder" Plate. "Jimmy loved his white Porsche Spyder," the sales literature says. An executive of Dean's licensing agency told Warren Beath, "These are aimed at the 45-year-old female who grew up with James Dean. She won't buy the Schott Bros. motorcycle jacket, but she will buy a porcelain plate."

It's a truism in collecting circles that almost anything can become a collectible except for something that is manufactured to be a collectible.

communist plot

Nell Blythe in the June 1956 issue of *Movie Life Magazine*, in an article "Jimmy Dean Fights Back from the Grave," told of a rumored communist plot in an article that purported to refute the myths that had sprung up in the months since Dean's death.

The rumor was that Dean's death was no accident at all. He was a victim of a fiendish communist murder plot. A mechanic was hired to execute the dreadful scheme, and Jimmy's car had been mysteriously tampered with before he took it out that fateful night. The party wanted to do away with Dean because of his anti-communist activities. And the facts, according to Ms. Blythe, were these: that Jim, like all good Americans, disliked everything that communists stood for, but his anti-communist activities were no greater than the majority of the stars in Hollywood who despise this form of government. None of his friends knew Jim to be politically absorbed in any way.

Continuity and Evolution in a Public Symbol: An Investigation into the Creation and Communication of the James Dean Image in Mid-Century America

A 670-page doctoral thesis by Robert Wayne Tysl.

Converse

It's a shoe — actually, a sort of tennis shoe. Phil Stern took a picture of James Dean wearing a pair of Converse shoes in 1955. And in 1995 it all led to a promotion featuring James Dean, with billboards featuring the photograph mounted atop a building on the corner of Melrose and Vista boulevards in Los Angeles. It was covered by *Entertainment Tonight* and featured an interview with Phil Stern at the site of the old Googie's at Sunset and Crescent Heights boulevards. The campaign was also conducted in San Francisco, San Diego, Seattle and Portland. The accompanying press release stated, "Converse brings two icons to West Coast rooftops this summer in an advertising campaign that highlights the Company's authentic American footwear position with an image of legendary actor James Dean casually sporting a pair of Classic Converse Jack Purcell sneakers."

cookie jar

It was probably inevitable that the likeness of Jimmy Dean, having been featured under the Curtis Management imprimatur on plates and mugs, would find its way onto an authorized cookie jar. What could be more wholesome? The retail pasteurization of Jimmy Dean reaches its temporary nadir in this strangely ghoulish cookie jar. Dean is shown wide-eyed as if startled, fingers splayed and clutching a cigarette. His head can presumably be removed to accommodate the insertion of macaroons and chocolate chip delectables. Manufactured by Happy Memories Collectibles, the licensed James Dean Cookie Jar sells for $275 and is made in a limited, numbered edition of 500. Each jar is made of heavy ceramic and is hand finished with high-fired ceramic glazes.

coroner

Martin Kuehl was the funeral home owner and mortician who, with assistant John Stander, attended Dean's body. He was also deputized to perform as a de facto coroner in lieu of the real thing in the little town of Paso Robles, where Dean's body was taken immediately after the accident. The official resources of the community were spread so thin that the coroner performed as pathologist, just as the ambulance attendants were deputized as sheriffs for reporting purposes on rural accidents. Although Kuehl was the first to receive and examine the body, assistant Stander signed the death certificate.

See also Stander, John.

coroner's report *see page 154*

Coulter and Gray

The law firm of Coulter and Gray was the executor of Jimmy's estate. The firm paid Martin Kuehl's funeral home $982.93 for preparing Jimmy's body for shipment to Indiana, but requested an itemized invoice.

Coyle, Robert E.

The attorney for the law firm of Hansen, McCormick, Barstow & Sheppard who handled the bulk of the legal defense of Donald Turnupseed against the action brought by Rolf Wuetherich. (*See* Lawsuits)

crash *see* accident

Crash

Crash is the title of a 1996 film by director David Cronenberg. Based on a novel by J. G. Ballard and winner of the Special Jury Prize at Cannes, it is the story of a jaded movie director also named Ballard, who is shaken out of his sexual doldrums by the epiphany of a car crash for which he was responsible. Cronenberg's script acknowledges James Dean as the pioneer of this particular sexual pathology. A wacky scientist named Vaughan brings together a 1950 Ford and a Porsche Spyder replica and restages Dean's car crash, refreshing the sexual palates of some assembled thrill seekers. A Spyder replicar customized just like Jimmy's is driven head-on into a 1950 black and white Ford. Vaughan himself assumes the role of Rolf Wuetherich. The driver of the Spyder dies reenacting the highway death of Jayne Mansfield, complete with padded bra and chihuahua.

The interesting idea is the exploration of the eroticism of the automobile and the orgasm of the car crash. Sex hopelessly merges with violence in the lives of the doomed protagonists. The execution is not equal to the vision, and the script takes a wrong turn somewhere between *Smokey and the Bandit* and *Last Tango in Paris*. Maybe somebody will do it better, someday.

crash-scene models *see* Hodgson, Jeff

crash site

The Cholame Valley may have been a sacred place to the Chumash Indians 10,000 years ago, but it remained for the death of James Dean on September 30, 1955, to anoint it with religious import for the twentieth century and beyond. The little postal drop of Cholame consisted in 1955 of a restaurant–gas station and a homely Quonset hut garage that housed a tow truck and ambulance. Within a year of Dean's death, the intersection of Highways 41 and 46 (then 466) was attracting regular pilgrims who placed prayerful personal messages on the wooden fence nearest the spot where

Opposite and top: California Highway Patrol accident photographs. *Bottom, this page:* The intersection in the 1980s.

Dean's car had come to rest. Floral tributes were common, and the locals at the restaurant a quarter mile up the road were deluged with inquiries from mourning fans who needed a focus for their grief.

The numerous fan magazine accounts of Dean's life which were fed to his insatiable public were generalities which in most cases came to a focus and emerged in something like real time with the account of his last day on earth, from his rising in Sherman Oaks, picking up his car in Hollywood, and proceeding to Tip's Diner, to his receiving the ticket at the bottom of the Grapevine.... There was a doomed inevitability to the accounts that lent them the aspect of a Passion. More importantly, they were reducible to psychological graphing in terms of both space and time. They could be retraced and replicated for purposes of spiritual identification, like Christ's last hours.

The publication of photo essays such as "Jimmy's Last Miles" produced a series of successive images of the stops and stations of Jimmy's cross. Like beads on a rosary, contemplation of these images memorialized certain sites from Jimmy's viewpoint. To see them was to relive them through his eyes and be incorporated into him on his final day. Fans became participants in the last drive. The view from the top of the last hill showed the highway stretching beneath to the intersection. The intersection itself was portrayed. The Cholame garage was a sort of ersatz tomb where the car had been taken. The hospital and funeral home became sacramental images because they were stops in the progress of his body.

The 1957 documentary *The James Dean Story* showed a Porsche Spyder on the road, and the windshield-mounted camera showed the approach to the intersection and the fatal sweep of the 1950 Ford in front of the viewer's eye. Filmed at the actual site, it ritualized the mindset of the pilgrim to Cholame: The point was to see what Jimmy saw and, as much as possible, follow him to death. That the film starts with his death was also affecting, if unconsciously. His death was in many ways the beginning of the fan's emotional and spiritual quest. In the film and many magazine articles, his death is the emergence into life. It introduces him biographically in a significant reversal of pop convention, and it also signals the start of the pilgrim's own fascination and quest.

While Dean's friends and family might be unapproachable in a practical sense, anyone could come out and commune with his spirit at the crash site. Inarticulate about the attraction, most felt a hope or promise that the site held resonance of his essence of which they might partake. It was a communion, and after the long drive, the epiphany was to be had at the intersection, if anywhere. With sadness and perhaps catharsis, the pilgrim would go a quarter mile up the road to peer into the garage where the car had been taken, then maybe on to the hospital and funeral home twenty-eight miles up the road.

"We've got Jimmy Dean's car," garage owner Paul Moreno's daughter told Mercedes McCambridge later in the evening of the crash. Within days, the car was ferried under wraps to southern California, but fans still came to peer into the garage where it had for a while resided. And for the next twenty years the fans came with their questions and emotional hunger, but there was no particular place for their religious aspirations to focus. The intersection itself was dangerous to walk around, and the site had been nearly obliterated by improvements, widening, and rechanneling. In 1959 the original road surface of Highway 466 on which Dean had driven had been abandoned by a new route. Still visible from the new highway, it was given over to weeds and wandering cows, and unattainable, unless you wanted to climb through barbed wire fences onto private property. Even the name of the highway had changed, abbreviated to 46. Paul Moreno was long gone from his garage, though it remained, as did the restaurant. A new Standard Station had been built next to the property. The traces of Dean were vanishing and his resonance weakening.

In 1977 a Dean-obsessed Japanese businessman by the name of Seita Ohnishi established a monument around a tree at the settlement of Cholame. Though the crash site was obviously the emotional Ground Zero and therefore his first choice as the spot to memorialize, it would be unsafe to stop there without extensive disturbance of the site, and the landowners were not accommodating. Installation of the $15,000 monument a quarter mile up the road was the best Ohnishi could do, and the resultant publicity and pictures brought a resurgence of religious focus to the site of what was essentially a cenotaph — a monument to someone whose body lay elsewhere. Now the grieving fan had a tangible object for his pilgrimage.

Participation by the owners of the adjacent restaurant was for the most part grudging in the beginning, though by the nineties there was a burgeoning traffic in Dean-related items such as Ohnishi-approved calendars, memorial cards, and a variety of shirts and sweatshirts. Car clubs began to make the monument the object of annual rallies, and the restaurant encouraged it with barbecues and sundry activities. The convocations, usually on the weekend nearest the anniversary of Dean's death, were featured in car magazines and in national write-ups. There evolved a "Cholame Experience," the title of one amateur video, which was offered for sale by the fan clubs. Airline magazines did more than one story on the pilgrimages, with journalists interviewing fans and philosophizing on the import of the phenomenon.

The installation of the monument saw the formalization of the pilgrimage. The inscriptions and invitation to meditation of the symbol of infinity on the chromium surface legitimized and guided the seeker through an experience that recoiled from morbidity. Routes and timetables were printed and circulated, and the number of participants and the ritualization of their communal visitations grew.

crepitation

Crepitation was the grating sound noted by Dr. Robert H. Bossert when he attended to James Dean in the Cholame ambulance. Crepitation produced when the head is moved can denote a broken neck.

cults

"Philosophers of religion tell us that repetition confers a higher, 'mythic' reality on events," write J. Hoberman and Jonathan Rosenbaum in an article entitled "The Idolmakers" which appeared in the December 1982 issue of *American Film*. "Archetypes are archetypes precisely because they repeat themselves. So, of course, do movies—and acolytes return to reexperience their favorites again and again."

Angst-ridden postwar youth in West Germany experienced an underground revolution against Cold War repression, and one manifestation was a James Dean Death Cult. Its probable impetus was the publication in that country of many of the Roth crash photos which were not released in the United States. The photos were copied and circulated as the centerpiece of crude newsletters. A spate of teenage suicides brought the little movement notoriety, as did adherents' penchant for drag racing on city streets. Dean crash survivor Rolf Wuetherich was a source of fascination, though he never deigned to respond to the fan letters his young friends sent him along with innumerable questions about the details of that last day.

A typical club meeting would purportedly involve rock and roll, marijuana, and existentialist discussions on the significance of Jimmy's life and death. In *James Dean: A Biography*, John Howlett writes, "There were clubs in Germany where girls would give themselves unconditionally to any boy who looked like their dead idol."

The fundamental obsession of these young doomsters seemed to have something to do with Jimmy's death wish, which they draped about themselves like a mantle. Sex and drinking parties were held at auto wrecking yards, followed by spray-painting orgies directed against city monuments in Hamburg and Berlin. Pictures of the death car were avidly traded, and accounts of Jimmy's death committed to memory.

Following their publication in Germany, the Roth crash photos were published in France, but no comparable cult phenomenon was reported in that country.

"The Strange James Dean Death Cult"

In 1956 *Coronet* magazine published this little essay by playwright and Lincoln historian Herbert Mitgang. The tabloids and teen mags were boosting sales by exploiting Dean stories, and the more staid publications found a way to jump on the bandwagon by featuring more objective, ostensibly analytical articles which nevertheless allowed them to feature Dean prominently on their covers and in their pages. Journalism devoted to Dean developed into a subgenre in which nearly identical tones of objectivity were adopted by *Life, Look* and, in this case, *Coronet*, who delivered ghoulish anecdote under the aspect of commentary on teenage angst:

> The war years did something even to those who were too young to fight. This "shook-up" generation, bubbling with rebellion, fascinated by violence, speed, raw sensations, took as its symbol a wild one who reflected its restless mood. Psychologists sought clues to adolescent behavior in their weird worship of a dead boy's memory.

The "weird worship" is described:

> A souvenir shop in New York exhibits amateurish oil paintings of Dean that sell from $40 to $200 apiece. Another store bills a long, wicked-looking knife as "The James Dean Special." On the West Coast, a couple bought the wreck of Dean's car and put it on display at fifty-cents admission.
> Besides these macabre touches, there are serious efforts to perpetuate the Dean memory and legend. Pilgrimages are made to Fairmount, where the actor is buried.... On the thirtieth of each month, the day he crashed, flowers are put on his grave anonymously. On his posthumous twenty-fifth birthday, forty baskets and bouquets were found there.

Coronet quotes one mourning cult follower:

> "Is Jimmy still alive? I've heard that, but I don't think so. I don't think he would want to make so many girls suffer as much as we still do pining for him."

Cunningham, Terry

Terry Cunningham is the author of two Dean biographies, *The Way It Was* and *The Timeless James Dean*. The latter purports to be "a detailed account of the life, career and mysterious death of a Hollywood and international cult figure whose popularity has lasted over 50 years. The other driver in that fatal crash claims Dean was not driving and reveals all on the cover-up after Dean's death."

The interesting thing is that Cunningham claims to draw upon an exclusive interview with Donald Turnupseed that was offered him by a female journalist named Moretti. In the interview, Turnupseed allegedly claims that Dean was not the driver of the Porsche at the time of the accident.

In 1985, while researching his first book, Cunningham claimed to have talked to Turnupseed himself. He claimed that he had traced Turnupseed to his home in California and that Turnupseed agreed to see him based on Cunningham's promise to tell Turnupseed's side of how the crash happened. Cunningham says he called at the house and that although someone was inside, no one would answer the door. Eventually he got Turnupseed on the phone and the reclusive figure "really opened up," saying he did see the Porsche and thought he could make the turn in front of the Porsche.

Cunningham claimed his publisher would not print the interview because it had been conducted on the phone and there was no proof it was Turnupseed on the other end.

curses

THE CAR

The "curse" of James Dean's death car has become an element of American cultural mythology, recounted first in tabloids and then absorbed into biographies and broadcast on innumerable movie and television documentaries. If there is an historical model for the phenomenon, it would be the curse of King Tut's Tomb.

The source of the myth is car customizer George Barris, who purchased the wrecked chassis and placed it on public display. He likes to describe a series of accidents involving the chassis, resulting in injury to spectators and even to a truck driver hauling the car to an exposition. In one version, it was December of 1956 and the Spyder was being transported to Salinas, California, when the truck skidded on a rainy highway, crushing the driver when it rolled off the bed. The driver's name is sometimes given variously as George Barhuis or Barkhuis, and he is identified as a State of California employee.

No news reports of such an incident have been found.

Another story claims that in Oregon in 1958, the truck carrying the Porsche chassis slipped its emergency brake and rolled into a store. Also in 1958, en route to Oakland on a truck bed, the car supposedly broke into two pieces and fell to the pavement. This event is also ascribed to October of 1959, with the addition that the falling pieces caused a fatal accident. A variant describes a separate event in November of 1959, with the car breaking mysteriously into 11 pieces.

According to writer Ron Smith in an August 1990 *Robb Report* article, "The legend gained momentum. In Detroit, on September 30, 1959, four years to the day after Dean's wreck, a 15-year-old youth who had come to see James Dean's car, and was dressed just as Dean had been in *Rebel*—blue jeans, white T-shirt, red jacket—was standing 12 feet from the display. Three bolts snapped and the car rolled over on him, crushing both legs. According to the *Detroit Free Press*, 'Witnesses claimed that the car seemed to just move by itself.'"

Legend also holds that the chassis mysteriously disappeared in 1960. According to one story, the Spyder was sealed into a truck trailer and hauled across the country. When the trailer was unlocked, the car was gone. George Barris also reported that the car had been shipped not by truck but by train; the Porsche, he said, had been packed in a sealed boxcar and escorted by a team of Pinkerton detectives. Upon the train's arrival, Barris said, he signed the manifest and verified that the seal was intact—but the boxcar was empty.

Porsche historian and James Dean expert Lee Raskin, who has spent years researching the Dean car, believes that Barris simply disposed of the chassis when he felt it was losing its fan appeal. The "mysterious disappearance" stories were Barris's way of perpetuating the Dean myth.

On the other hand, some of the stories associated with the car are apparently true. For example, news reports corroborate the story that the chassis was damaged by fire. (In less trustworthy variants, the Dean car is the only one *not* damaged in a mysterious fire.) The March 12, 1959, edition of the *Fresno Bee* reported that the car was damaged on the night of March 11 in a fire at 3158 Hamilton Avenue, where it was stored "awaiting display as a safety exhibit in a coming sports and custom automobile show." Two tires and the paint—or whatever remained of the paint, considering that the car was already a wreck—were damaged in the fire, whose cause was unknown.

It is also true that a man was killed in a race car equipped with salvaged parts from Dean's Spyder. This story, which may be the tale that gave rise to the whole "curse" legend, was reported in the *Pomona Progress-Bulletin* of October 22, 1956. According to this article, plastic surgeon Troy McHenry, 45, was killed fifteen minutes into an hour-long race for modified sports cars under 1,500cc when his Porsche Spyder spun out of control and hit a tree. The October 24th edition of the same paper carried a follow-up story headlined, "Parts Used in Fatal Crash Here Came Off James Dean Car." The article noted that "several pieces of equipment from the sports car in which actor James Dean crashed and died 13 months ago." (Lee Raskin reports that these were suspension and steering parts.) The paper also reported that McHenry's friend William Eschrich, who had bought Dean's engine and placed it in his own racing car, was also involved in an accident at the same race, but he was not injured. "Asked if he was superstitious," said the *Progress-Bulletin*, "Dr. Eschrich said yesterday, 'Not a bit.'"

An odd footnote: Eschrich had competed against Dean in the Bakersfield Sports Car Meet in Bakersfield on May 1, 1955. Jack Drummond, an Arizona driver, died that day in a separate race.

FIRES

- Beverly Wills was one of James Dean's dates before he made it big. The daughter of Joan Davis, she died in a fire in 1963 in Palm Springs. Also claimed by the fire were her two sons and grandmother.
- James Dean's Sherman Oaks cottage was destroyed in a fire.
- Blackwell's Corner, the small restaurant where James Dean stopped for a bite some 30 minutes before his death, was destroyed by fire in 1968.
- The wreck of Jimmy's Porsche was also scorched in a mysterious fire. (*See* THE CAR, above.)

466

There is something lulling about the seemingly endless expanse of arrow-straight road once known as 466 — the unbroken monotony of tumbleweeds and dry flatlands.

Dusk was falling on the evening of Thursday, April 3, 1998. The young Loma Linda woman felt herself nodding. Thirty-year-old Jenny Moon, in her westbound 1996 Ford Mustang, probably did not know that in 1955 this same highway 46 had been known as 466. Still, only her drowsiness could have kept her from noticing the route's connection to the death of James Dean. Placards and billboards announced "James Dean's Last Stop" as she approached Blackwell's Corner.

Ten miles past the rest stop, and some twenty miles from Dean's fatal intersection, she apparently became hypnotized by the sameness of the desolate plains. Sleep overtook her. The Mustang drifted across the center line at 65 mph and smashed into a Chevy pickup driven by Shannon Pierce of Little Rock.

The horror was not over even as the dust cleared: A westbound Toyota 4-Runner smashed into the shattered Mustang. Highway patrol officers raced with sirens howling to the site of the highway carnage.

Jenny Moon, Pierce, and a passenger in the pickup were dead at the scene in the horrendous head-on smashup. Another passenger in the pickup was taken to a local hospital.

Local television stations prominently featured footage of James Dean in their reporting of the highway deaths.

Curtis Management

Curtis Licensing founders Mark Roesler and Greg Thomas closed a deal with the heirs of Jimmy Dean's estate for the exclusive rights to sell manufacturers the use of Dean's name and likeness. Retail sales of items including collector plates, Stetson hats, jeans, sunglasses, leather jackets, sweatshirts, posters, buttons, satin pillows, puzzles, greeting cards, and calendars are said to exceed $100 million annually. The licensing agreement sent a chill through the cottage industry revolving around Dean, as Curtis Management slapped those who infringed with cease-and-desist orders.

Debra Zahn, in the *Los Angeles Times* feature article entitled "Rebel with an Agent," says it took the lawyers four months to close a deal with the family. The clincher was reportedly that the family had been particularly hurt by a book on Dean that featured "lewd pictures." Marcus Winslow and other heirs constitute a legal entity called the James Dean Foundation, which passes or rejects anything bearing Jimmy's name or likeness. Mylar balloons were rejected. Zahn says that an attorney who typically wears suave Nino Cerruti suits would don jeans, boots and plaids to pay a call on the Winslows. The family finds the attorneys "down-to-earth and sincere."

Vice president Greg Thomas told the reporter, "Jimmy didn't grow old and fat like Elvis. From a marketing perspective, that plays very well. He died that glorious dramatic death that seems to appeal to the people he speaks to."

D

Dada

In the years since his death, James Dean has provided inexhaustible inspiration for painters, poets, musicians and writers. In 1982 a group of Dadaist artists from Union City, California, went to the crash site on Dean's birthday disguised as Cal Trans workers. They placed a cutout format on the point of impact, and painted a four-color portrait of Dean as Jett Rink from *Giant*. The portrait survived for some months before the tires of coastal-bound traffic obliterated it.

Dakota, Bill

William Dakota's fascination with Jimmy Dean brought him to Hollywood in the year after Dean's death. His identification with the star led him to befriend Nick Adams, who was himself busily befriending Natalie Wood and Elvis Presley in his quest to identify himself as the preeminent Dean Friend. Dakota became editor and publisher of *Hollywood Star Newspaper*. He eventually founded the James Dean Memorial Foundation with the ostensible purpose of installing a Dean monument at decrepit, and eventually bankrupt, Hollywood Memorial Park Cemetery. He envisioned not only a monument to Dean in the moribund lawns where Valentino reigned for nearly sixty years as the greatest interred screen god; he went to Fairmount, Indiana, and sent out tentative feelers to Dean's remaining family: Wouldn't it be a nice idea to have Jimmy transplanted to the City of the Silent at Gower and Santa Monica, alongside Tyrone Power, Douglas Fairbanks, and Virginia Rappe? The family did not warm to the idea, and the townsfolk of Fairmount could have been expected to put up a fuss before relinquishing their greatest tourist attraction.

But it turned out to be the least of Dakota's problems. Curtis Management Group of Indianapolis, claiming the Dean licensing rights and authorized by Dean's family, filed injunctions and blocked Dakota at every turn. Dakota published a newsletter through which he threw down gauntlets to CMG and their authorized products, specifically Levis and the authorized sunglasses.

> James Dean didn't wear Levis. He wore LEE RIDERS, for those of you that collect Dean tid-bits. And his waist was 33". Levis is using Dean's image in Japan to sell Levis, which is false! Other less-than-true ads are for sunglasses like Dean wore. Well, Dean wore clip-on sunglasses over his prescription glasses. They *weren't like* the ones being promoted as "those like he wore." And those leather jacket ads state: the type he wore in *Rebel Without A Cause.* He wore a red nylon jacket in *Rebel,* not a leather jacket, although the jacket being sold was made off a pattern supposed to be like the one he wore in *Giant.* Wrong again. It's like his personal jacket, but he didn't wear it in *Giant.* These people are selling "licensed" lies, licensed through Curtis Licensing Company. And the small Dean figure from *Giant* looks nothing like Dean. Where do they dig up the artists? Of course it was made in Taiwan.

Beleaguered, Dakota opened a hot dog stand downstairs from his Vine Street offices and began selling Coney Island Red-Hot Dogs.

Damone, Perry Rocco Luigi

He is the son born to Pier Angeli and Vic Damone, on July 21, 1955 — eight months after their wedding. In *The Unabridged James Dean*, writer Randall Riese comments, "It is interesting to note that Pier had still been seeing Jimmy as late as two weeks before her marriage." Dean biographer Joe Hyams wrote in 1973 of seeing a devastated Jimmy two days before the actor's death. The actor said he had just discovered that Pier was pregnant. Hyams' account fueled speculation that Pier Angeli had a son from her liaison with Jimmy Dean. Perry Damone is indisputably the son of Vic Damone but has had to deal with the conjectures attending his parentage. He is a disk jockey in Phoenix, Arizona.

See also Angeli, Pier.

Darin, Bobby

The irrepressible song stylist famed for "Mack the Knife," Darin died tragically young at age 37, his heart damaged by a childhood bout of rheumatic fever. Al DiOrio describes in his Darin biography *On Borrowed Time* how Paramount Studios asked Darin to make a screen test after catching his nightclub act. "Bobby had eagerly agreed, and veteran film director Norman Taurog had been assigned to direct it. Taurog had given Bobby two scenes— James Dean's opening scene from *East of Eden* and a bit from an old Fred MacMurray movie, *The Gilded Lily*. Bobby had impressed the director with his skills, and Paramount had signed him to a nonexclusive, seven-picture, million-dollar deal."

Unfortunately, when Bobby's big break came with an assigned role in *Cry for Happy*, he had to pass because of his loyalty to George Burns, for whom he was the opening act. When he asked to be released to do the picture, Burns rebuked him for unprofessionalism, unaware that Bobby was passing up an increase of $17,500 a week to continue to open for the old ham. Darin, who regarded Burns as a father — he never knew his real dad — never mentioned it.

date of death

The coroner's report on James Dean erroneously states that he died on October 1, 1955. Dean died on September 30.

"Date with Death"

David Browne wrote this magazine article for *Confidential* magazine (January 1958). It focused on the interesting memento of Jimmy's copy of Hemingway's *Death in the Afternoon*. In the front of the book, Jimmy himself had written, "God gave James Dean so many gifts to share with the world, has he the right to throw them away in the bullring?" He had also color-coded passages in the book. Green meant "disability," red was "death," and yellow was "degradation."

"The Day James Dean Died"

This article by Dean fan Brian O'Dowd was printed in the September 1987 issue of *Hollywood Studio Magazine*. Typical of the spate of articles Dean fans were producing into the 1990s, it relies heavily on the apocryphal recollections of Rolf Wuetherich's "Death Drive" and Sanford Roth's "Assignment I'll Never Forget."

To O'Dowd's credit, he did visit the scene of the accident and did interview retired highway patrolman Ron Nelson, who said, "It only took me about 15 minutes or less to arrive at the scene in my new '55 Buick patrol car. As I pulled up I could see the ambulance driver, Paul Moreno, was putting Dean's body into the wagon.... Maybe if Dean's car had lights on it might have saved his life. Officer Ernie Tripke was in charge of the investigation and was already taking control when I arrived. I don't believe that Dean's car was going that fast, maybe about 65 miles an hour at the time as there were very few skid marks."

Dead Famous

This British series features model Gail Porter and ghost hunter and "sensitive" Chris Fleming searching out the spirits of some of Hollywood's brightest stars, including Marilyn Monroe, James Dean and Frank Sinatra. Scheduled to premier in April of 2005, the debut episode features California ghost hunter Richard Senate in a visit to the site of James Dean's auto accident. A visit to the home of Dean biographer Warren Beath is included.

See also Senate, Debbie.

Dean, Ethel

Ethel Dean was the Wicked Stepmother to many Dean fans, the remote replacement for the artistic and fragile Mildred Dean. After Jimmy's death, his father and stepmother went about rather ruthlessly liquidating his estate. Among the items converted to cash were some that one might have expected to have some sentimental value, such as his horse and his racing helmet.

But Ethel Dean did emerge from her seclusion when some item of Dean memorabilia appeared to be at stake. The following letter was printed in *The James Dean Anniversary Book*:

> Dear Mr. Delacorte:
> I believe one of the longest hours that I've ever sat through, was the night *MODERN SCREEN* was presenting their awards, at the Cocoanut Grove.
> I knew the program could never have ended unless Jimmy was mentioned.
> Mr. Dean and I would like to thank you and the people who made it possible, from the bottom of our hearts for our Jimmy's award.
> I do not know how these things are handled, but nothing could make us happier than to be able to have his award to treasure forever. Do you think this would be possible? Do you know who has it now?
> Sincerely,
> Mr. and Mrs. Winton A. Dean

The *Modern Screen* plaque was presented to Warner Bros., where it was placed in the studio trophy case. But the magazine requested that that plaque be sent to Dean's parents.

Dean, Winton

Winton Dean, to his credit, married Jimmy's mother when she turned up pregnant. He later falsified the marriage certificate, backdating it two years out of consideration for Quaker sensibilities. But his behavior was not always kind. After Mildred's death, he shipped Jimmy to Indiana. He didn't even go to Jimmy's funeral. For years, family apologists claimed he was broke after his wife's illness and didn't have time to care for a child. But it wasn't true. His insurance through the federal government, of which he was an employee, paid for Mildred's medical expenses.

He seemed to disown Jimmy almost immediately. Some have interpreted all of Jimmy's subsequent life as a futile attempt to get the attention and approval of his father.

Bill Dakota reported that Winton Dean used the money from Jimmy's estate to buy a motel in Bakersfield.

Beulah Roth, widow of Dean biographer and photographer Sanford Roth, described to Warren Beath in 1990 an encounter she had had with Winton Dean. She said she had a self-portrait in clay that Jimmy had done at

·the studio of Pegot Waring. "For months, I had a wet towel on it. Until Mr. Dean called me and he said, 'You have a self-portrait of my son, Jimmy.' I said 'Yes, Mr. Dean, and come get it. Because I don't want it.' And he talked to me as though I was trying to keep it. I didn't want it.... So he came over — a very unpleasant man, I thought. And he grabbed that thing as though I was trying to keep it from him. I was so glad to get rid of it! What was I going to do with it? And he took it away, and I hear he had it cast and sold the cast."

Dean Con

The year 1984 saw the first official Dean Con — James Dean convention — at the Holiday Inn in Burbank, California. Besides showing all the Dean films and some rare TV appearances, it featured a Triviathalon, Blue Jean Social, Dean Art, Poetry and Song Fest, James Dean Dress-alike contest, "Friends of Dean" speaker panel, memorabilia expo and dealer's room. Ads claimed, "We're celebrating a life!"

Dean Widows

Beulah Roth, wife of Dean photographer Sanford Roth, bestowed this name on the women who called on her in hopes of feeling some connection with Jimmy. She found their behavior spooky: Always wanting to sit on a chair if Jimmy had sat on it. Gazing vacantly at the walls that had once enclosed him. For these women, Dean has become a sort of husband in absentia. Their devotional intensity is reminiscent of the cloistered nuns of the Middle Ages who wrote about their mystical yet sexualized encounters with the Savior. Ravished by Jimmy in their dreams, awash in his blood, the Dean Widows dedicate bankrupt lives to collecting Jimmy Dean memorabilia and even baking him birthday cakes. They mourn for him on his deathday and get together on his birthday. They find meaning and communion in gatherings with other like-minded ladies, sharing the contents of their scrapbooks. They cry at Jimmy's gravesite and rail against those whom they see as attacking their dead Jimmy.

Deaner Theology

Deaner theology received its first scholarly investigation courtesy of Dean fan and academic Jim Hopgood's essay "Back Home in Indiana: The Semiotics of Pilgrimage and Belief in an American Icon," included in the book *Explorations in Anthropology and Theology* (by Frank Salamon and Walter Adams). He waded in among Dean fans on pilgrimage to Fairmount, Indiana, for his research on topics such as "Genesis of the Dean Image/Icon and Deaner Theology," "Deaners: an 'Iconic Movement,'" and "Semiotics and Pilgrimage."

Deaners

They go into service stations to use the restroom and don't buy anything. They go to the cemetery and light candles, or leave Jimmy's tombstone besmirched with red lipstick kisses. They ask incessant questions. They buy second-hand reminiscences wholesale and breathlessly, clogging sidewalk traffic while they take innumerable photos of Dean sites. Who are they? They're "Deaners," the less-than-affectionate name the locals of Fairmount, Indiana, use to designate the rabid fans that descend on their town throughout the year.

Antipathy has been mitigated over the last couple of decades by a keen commercial sense, which the chamber of commerce promotes by sanctioning "Dean Days" on the anniversary of Jimmy's death. It is partly an attempt to focus and control the outpouring of fascination while exploiting it to swell the coffers of the little town. Town residents hope that activities like the Rock-Lasso Contest and Dean Lookalike Contest will channel the energies that tend to run rampant through the sedate little Quaker community.

Deaners — The Band

"The Deaners" was a band apparently formed as a tribute to James Dean. They gained some local fame in Los Angeles in the 1980s.

Deaners — The 'Zine

This cyberzine, helmed by Sandra Weinhardt, is subtitled "James Dean Fans Speak Out." It's unclear what, if anything, they have to say. There are sections devoted to car runs, rockabilly weekends, the endless merchandising of the Curtis Management Group — treated in reverential tones like the Spirit of Dean on the Earth — in addition to the Marfa Ghost Lights, Cholame, cars, and the annual festivals where Dean fans gather.

Deanmania: The Man, the Character, the Legend

This 1991 book about Dean collectibles by Robert Headrick was the first serious treatment of the phenomenon of Dean memorabilia and collectibles.

"Dean's Eleventh Dream"

This is a tune by a rock band called the James Dean Driving Experience, a 1980s group from the UK whose influences included the Smiths.

"Dean's Lament"

James Dean participated in an impromptu jam session that was recorded on a home tape. After his death, it was released as a limited-edition collector's record. The sleeve explains,

> It all came about when James Dean, like many other greats of show business, would visit a Sunset Strip nightclub called Tablehoppers to listen to a unique jazz pair, Bob Romeo on flute and Al Bello on bowangos. The weird rhythms so fascinated Dean, he returned night after night. Soon they became close friends and at Romeo's invitation, Jimmy would sit in a have a "ball."
>
> One night after the show, Bob brought in his tape recorder to record some of his work. Noting Dean's great interest, Bob invited him to sit in. Jimmy accepted and stayed practically all night, playing, relaxing and talking. Fortunately, two of these ad-lib sessions were recorded on Bob Romeo's tape recorder.

The two tunes were "Dean's Lament" and "Jungle Rhythm." Originally it sold for $1.29. By the mid–1990s, the asking price was $150.

Dean's Men's Stores

"His spirit of independence in Dean's Men's Stores everywhere" is the slogan of this chain of stores. But they're to be found only in South Africa.

death certificate *see page 133*

"Death Drive"

The magazine was *Modern Screen* and the first-person story appeared in October of 1957 under the byline of Rolf Wuetherich. Rewritten into third person by John Lindahl, it reappeared in *Pix Annual* in the fall of 1958. Lindahl was probably the author of the original version.

This poignant and sun-drenched saga is responsible for several misconceptions which were incorporated into the Dean legend in nearly every subsequent account: the story of the Pan Am flight ring, Dean's last words ("He's gotta see us. He's gotta stop"), and Turnupseed's tearful words at the scene ("I didn't see him, by God, I really didn't see him").

In the original article, Rolf recollects, "A 1950 Ford was coming at us." The second article says Rolf did not see the Ford, and Jimmy's last words are omitted. The reason for this pointed and interesting emendation might be that Rolf was attempting to sue both the Dean estate and Donald Turnupseed within this time frame. To say that Jimmy and Rolf saw the Ford might bolster the defendant's contention that Dean assumed risk and also responsibility for the proximate cause of the crash. His attorneys were contending that Dean was reckless and exhibiting wanton disregard.

Of course, in the hospital after the crash Rolf claimed that he remembered nothing immediately before the crash, and specifically that Dean said nothing prior to impact.

It is not known how much money Rolf got for the use of his name and recollections.

See also lawsuits; ring; Wuetherich, Rolf.

Death in the Afternoon

Reportedly "Jimmy's most cherished book," Hemingway's *Death in the Afternoon* is a paean to dusty death in the bullring. Jimmy's copy was found after his death to be color-coded for passages dealing with death, disability and disfigurement.

See also "Date with Death."

death mask

Chopin had one, so why not James Dean? According to a story circulated among high school students in the county where James Dean met his death, a seventeen-year-old girl crept into the room in the mortuary where Dean's body was awaiting shipment to L.A. Her father was an attendant at the establishment, and she was motivated by a dare, and by her own Dean-worship. She got some mortician's wax. After opening the casket, she made a mold of Jimmy's face in the repose of death. This she transferred to plaster from which she made duplicates which were circulated.

This story cannot be confirmed, but even today in the vicinity of Paso Robles where Dean's body was taken after death, you may meet people who were teenagers at the time who claim either to have seen one of these masks, or to have known someone who saw one, or knew someone who knew someone who...

The Death of James Dean

The Death of James Dean by Warren Newton Beath is a 1986 book about the James Dean car accident. It drew heavily on inquest documents and the private investigation of Charles Adams, plus the previously undiscovered deposition Donald Turnupseed gave to an insurance attorney in the aftermath of the crash. The second half of the book was a thinly disguised account of the author's experiences as a fan and Dean researcher.

"Death on the Highway"

The rumor was persistent throughout the seventies: There existed grainy amateur 16 mm color film footage of the aftermath of Dean's car crash taken by a man on vacation who happened upon the wreck. The action was grisly and showed graphically the extent of Jimmy's injuries. Where might such a tasteless cinéma vérité exercise ever see the light of day? High school campuses! The film was supposedly incorporated into California Highway Patrol safety films and shown as an admonition to would-be reckless drivers. It was also reportedly shown to new recruits at Fort Hood in 1962.

People investigating this story have encountered adults who vividly recalled seeing the clips of Dean shattered behind the wheel of his Porsche. In some versions, the Highway Patrol had taken the film. Never verified, the story nevertheless achieved the status of a minor urban legend.

An investigation with the Highway Safety Films Project — an organization devoted to preserving and distributing those nostalgic highway safety films shown in driver's ed classes in high schools in the 1960s and 1970s — has convinced Dean fan and college professor Dr. Barbara Inman Beall that she has identified "Death on the Highway" as the title of a since-lost scare film she saw in high school that featured footage of James Dean in his car after the accident.

Inman Beall told Warren Beath, "I contacted them a few years ago. They didn't know that they once had James Dean in their program. But based on my memory of some of the pictures in that film, they were able to identify the name of the film I saw, which was 'Death on the Highway,' produced by the Suicide Club out of Fort Myers, Florida. I don't think Jimmie was in their program much beyond that semester. My sister took driver's ed in the summer. She once remembered seeing a close up of his face after the accident (but has no memory of that now. I asked her)."

Inman Beall had nightmares of the grisly segment.

There are no verified reports of any color footage taken at the time of the accident, but Inman Beall is far from alone in her recollection that there was a highway safety film featuring the aftermath of Dean's car crash.

death ride

A list of people who at one time or another were reported to have declined Jimmy's invitation to accompany him on September 30, 1955:

Nick Adams, Ursula Andress, Bill Bast, Lew Bracker, Jane Deacy, Bob Hinkle, Charlie Nolan Dean, Winton Dean, Mercedes McCambridge, Beulah Roth, Steve Rowland, Bill Stevens (real name Bill Tunstahl), Dennis Stock, and Jane Withers.

They would have needed a bus, anyway.

death route

Many of Dean's fans find the ultimate experience of identification with their fallen hero is the retracing of the route he took to his death. The pilgrims made the route in an unorganized fashion until the 1980s, when a series of organized car rallies put the Dean death drive on an annual agenda. Today many of the cars are vintage and provide a colorful parade on the highway as they wend their way from Los Angeles to the monument at Cholame, usually stopping at checkpoints along the way that have significance to the student of Dean's last hours.

Dean started his final day on Sutton Street in Sherman Oaks and went to Competition Motors at 1219 Vine Street. But there the tale gets confusing for the zealous death route retracer. Did he have a doughnut at Farmer's Market or the Ranch Market? And a legion of his friends, including Jane Withers, describe him as stopping off to say goodbye or give them one last chance to ride with him. (*See* death ride.) Other accounts have him stopping off at Jack McAfee's garage on Beverly Glen. He did get some gas at 14321 Ventura at the corner of Beverly Glen before he got on the freeway. He stopped for a treat at Tip's Diner, where he slipped a ring on Rolf Wuetherich's finger, then continued on Highway 99. The original Tip's is no more, so this stop must be omitted from today's Death Route Parade. The pilgrims then stop at the Ticketing Site at the foot of the Grapevine, then into Bakersfield and onto Route 46. The next stop is Blackwell's Corner, rebuilt from the little stand where Dean stopped; for miles leading up to Blackwell's, billboards hail it as "James Dean's Last Stop" and promise souvenirs. The journey continues onto the monument at Cholame, for refreshments and check-ins. Many drive back to the intersection, and some make sure they are standing at the hallowed spot near sunset at the exact time Dean met his fate.

death wish

Did James Dean have a death wish? It is regarded as a commonplace that many car accidents are actually suicides in a more socially accepted form, and the relationship between Thanatos, sex, and the culture of the automobile has been investigated with interesting results by many writers, including J. G. Ballard, author of *Crash*. Dean's extraordinary exhibitionism on both bikes and automobiles, obvious from a very early age, has been said to evince a love of risk that implied self-destructiveness. But when an eighty-year-old former president jumps from an airplane, we call it *joie de vivre*. Where is the truth?

The difference may reside in Dean's own confirmed fascination with death, specifically his own. The wasting death of his mother to cancer, and the consequent identification of death as the abode of the maternal, seems to have been the beginnings of his interest. Immortality was an insistent theme of his more profound ruminations, and he seems from an early age to have had his eye on eternity in addition to stardom. Many of his friends—including film composer Leonard Rosenmann—believe he had a death wish. And at least one of those who thought he did not—Beulah Roth—refused to drive with him.

Dean was photographed in a coffin at his own insistence and to the discomfort of the photographer; his eventual residence as an actual corpse in that same funeral home—Hunt's in Fairmount, Indiana—would seem to imply the fulfillment of some sort of dream or unspoken wish.

He was also photographed with a noose around his neck—and he was to die from a broken neck. He made rambling meditations about death on his home tape recorder, and he identified himself with the existentialist pose of a constant awareness of his own contingency, even if an understanding of the actual tenets of the philosophical movement was beyond him.

But in the final analysis it is recklessness on bikes and in racecars that gives the most weight to the argument that Dean wanted to die on an unconscious level. The myriad stories of risk-taking, his speeding on city streets, his need to constantly test the boundaries of himself and his luck, argue that he felt a compulsion to put at risk not only his exquisite features and his career, but his very life.

decapitation

"Head Missing from Bust of James Dean," heralded the "head" line of the April 1, 1959 *Chicago Tribune*.

See also vandalism.

Dekker, Albert

On May 5, 1968, Albert Dekker, who appeared with Dean in *East of Eden*, was found in his locked bathroom at 1731 Normandie in Hollywood, hanging by a rope harness he had tied around his neck and thrown over a shower pipe. Handcuffed and tightly bound all over in ropes, his body was marked by hypodermic needles, and his nudity was besmirched by obscenities in red lipstick. An apparent incident of autoerotic asphyxiation, his death was listed as "accidental."

"Delirium Over a Dead Star"

Veteran Hollywood journalist Ezra Goodman, who would later pen *The Fifty Year Decline and Fall of Hollywood*, a corrosive history of the studio system, weighed in on the posthumous Dean craze near the first anniversary of the actor's death. His forum was this article for the *Life* magazine issue of September 24, 1956. His tone is disturbed, and he writes with the mingling of relish and disgust which helped articulate even as it embodied the attitude of the older generation toward the necrophilic hoopla in which America was awash a short year after Jimmy's death.

Del-Mar Cleaners

Jimmy died in 1955 before he could recover his tan sweater from this Hollywood cleaners. Today it resides, with a plastic cover, in the Fairmount (Indiana) Historical Museum, having been donated in 1998.

deposition *see* Turnupseed, Don

Depp, Johnny

Wrote the *New York Post*, March 5, 1998: "Even former hotel wrecker Johnny Depp always behaved himself when he stayed in the James Dean Room at the Iroquois Hotel. Like other guests, Depp held Dean in awe and treated the room — where the "Rebel Without a Cause" star stayed from 1951 to 1953 — as if it were a shrine. But now the Iroquois management has refurbished the 75-year-old hotel on West 44th Street, and Jimmy's room has been trashed. It's now a luxury suite with just a number on the door, instead of the old brass plaque celebrating its famous former occupant."

Der Tod des James Dean

A German stage recitation (translation: *The Death of James Dean*) which debuted in February of 1981 near the time of Jimmy's birthday. Gunther Geiermann and Hanni Stadler were the stars in this production at Munich's Bliss Theatre.

Devil's Den *see under* ghosts and hauntings

DeWeerd, James

James DeWeerd, a sophisticated Wesleyan and decorated war hero, was in his thirties and living with his aged mother when Fairmount, Indiana, high school senior James Dean became his protégé. Dean friend Joe Hyams conducted interviews with DeWeerd in 1956 for a *Redbook* feature on Jimmy. What he did not disclose until his 1992 biography of Dean was that the reverend Mr. DeWeerd had confessed to a homosexual relationship with Jimmy that lasted for several years. It purportedly began with long drives in the minister's convertible on which he would invite young Jimmy to insert his fist into the hole in his stomach, the remnant of the wound DeWeerd had received and been decorated for at Monte Cassino.

According to Maila Nurmi, when someone told Dean's Aunt Ortense that DeWeerd wanted to teach Jimmy Greek, Ortense replied, "That's what I was afraid of!"

DeWeerd died on March 28, 1972. His grave is not far from Jimmy's in Park Cemetery.

diary

The Sunday *New York Times* of April 10, 1994, reported in a review of Paul Alexander's *Boulevard of Broken Dreams* that James Dean "kept a diary which is owned by his family and has never been released. Dean's father, who is still alive, has not allowed it to be removed from a safe. It is not known how revealing it is about his private life."

See also Hauge, Alan.

"Did James Dean Really Die?"

This uncredited fan magazine article, which appeared in the May 1956 issue of *Rave*, considers the title question and quickly introduces a second subject for investigation: "*Why the luscious dolls he left behind won't let the handsome ghoul rest in peace....*" But this inquiry, too, is quickly abandoned in favor of a comparison of the slavish female devotion inspired by the cult figures of James Dean and Rudolph Valentino, although *Rave* quickly admits that "impartial laboratory tests reveal that the greatest difference between Rudy's ghoul and Jimmy's is the superior quality of the latter. To put it mildly, the dames who revere Valentino are the choicest collection of fruit and nuts outside a Christmas plum pudding."

Dig Magazine

From 1957 to 1962 this teen-oriented magazine published several stories about James Dean, including "James Dean," "The Life of James Dean," "The Miracle of James Dean," and "The James Dean Story, A Legend Revisited."

disk

Christie's auctioned an acetate disk purporting to feature James Dean singing cowboy tunes for around $500. It contains good-natured laughter, and Jimmy Dean crooning, "I'm brown as a berry, from ridin' on the prairie...." It's not known how the disk came to be made.

disfigurement

The one-shot *The James Dean Album* magazine announced in 1956, "We see it very clearly, now: James Dean is not dead. He is not going to die. We know, because we have the evidence — in many ways. Most poignantly, in the letters and phone calls that are pouring into our office every day. Of course, a certain amount of such interest was to be expected. But, after an interval of mourning, it would normally stop. *It hasn't stopped.* And, much more significantly, *the people do not speak of Jimmy as if he were dead.*"

A British fan magazine said it was rumored that the grave contained the remains of a hitchhiker whom Jimmy had picked up just before the accident.

"Dear Jimmy," a typical letter would go, "I know you're not dead, but in hiding. We don't care what you look like, it's you we love. Please return to us!" Unable to accept the death of their idol, the fans let their grief find expression in the belief that Jimmy Dean had not died in the crash but been horribly disfigured. Swathed in bandages, these stories went, he was in gloomy convalescence in a series of mystery houses in the Los Angeles area.

From *Private Lives*, June 1957:

> Now it can be told: JIMMY DEAN WAS NEVER KILLED! Based on information from authoritative sources, the editors of *Private Lives* believe that Jimmy is really secretly hiding somewhere in NEW YORK CITY. A reward of $50,000 is offered for information leading to the actual person of Jimmy Dean! Informed sources, whose names we cannot disclose, say that Jimmy was horribly mangled by that "fatal" accident last year. He is said to be afraid for the world to see his now-marred face. So to you, Jimmy, we write this open letter: Come out of hiding. Your fans love you — will always love you — no matter what you look like!

In October of 1961 an Australian paper reported that "many thousands believe he still lives— dreadfully disfigured and hidden away in a home for incurables."

Author John Howlett wrote in his biography of Dean:

Refusal to believe in his death had led to wild rumors that Dean was alive but so terribly disfigured that he had been shut away. Fans picketed the sanatoriums where they believed him to be. Other rumors had Dean escaping from the publicity he hated, having swapped identities with a dead Wuetherich: he had entered a Buddhist Monastery or the Roman Catholic church; he had defected to Russia; he was hiding in downtown Los Angeles, tracking down his enemies with his switchblade and his gun; he would pay visits if girls left their photographs and addresses at a box number in a local newspaper.

A member of the James Dean Death Club submitted to an interview with Lee Belser in 1956, saying, "We know where he is, and we've got a lookout there. They keep all the shades down, but one night we got close enough to look through a tear in the blind and we saw him sitting there swathed in bandages. He acted like he wasn't quite in his right mind."

In 1973 the *Enquirer* published an article, "James Dean Did Not Die in Fatal Car Crash Auto Accident. Paralyzed and Mutilated He's Hidden in a Sanatorium." Even up to the 1980s, tabloid journals ran stories that he was alive in South America, alongside portraits that aged his image via computer so he could be more readily identified.

Private Lives had said, "He lives on, maybe right next door to you! And someday soon, perhaps Jimmy, in his own way and in his own good time, will once more come back and face the world that waits for him."

Mark Kinnaman, who keeps a website dedicated to Dean and corresponds with people from all over the world, reports on this phenomenon:

I had a salesman tell me that his company had purchase a large quantity of plastic milk jugs — several semi trucks' worth — and they were stored in a warehouse in New York City. The salesman went along to make sure the transaction and the paperwork went smoothly. As he was ready to leave and the last of the trucks were loaded up, the night watchman was just coming on duty. The older gentleman could barely walk and the left side of his face was disfigured as if it was smashed in. The salesman talked for several minutes with the older guard and found out that the old geezer was from the Midwest and had had an automobile wreck that ended his highly paying career. He didn't say what his career was. He said that he moved back to New York because he loved the energy of the city. His eyes, the salesman told me, were so penetrating, and he spoke so low — almost a mumbling whisper — that he was convinced that he was talking to the one-time youth movie idol.

I have had people tell me that they met Jimmy on a farm just north of his hometown of Fairmount, Indiana; that they saw him working as a night desk clerk at a Los Angeles hotel, a doorman in NYC, a cowboy in

Arizona. One lady met him at an estate auction in Florida. I've heard many other stories of strange places and occupations.

Dr. Jekyll and Mr. Hyde

The Robert Louis Stevenson horror story had been filmed three times, the classic role assayed by actors of the caliber of John Barrymore, Spencer Tracy and Frederic March — who won an Academy Award for his portrayal. After Dean's death, Hollywood friends said he had dreamed of starring and directing in another version, which he would also script.

doll

In 1985, the International Toy Fair in New York saw the unveiling of a James Dean doll which could cost as much as $2000. It was part of the aggressive Curtis Management invasion of the James Dean marketplace. Curtis attorney Mark Roesler announced, "The Dakin people, the largest 'plush' manufacturer in the nation, introduced their new James Dean collectible doll at the toy fair today." "Plush" is the industry designation for stuffed animals.

The basic 18-inch-tall James Dean collectible doll came equipped with an outfit consisting of the red windbreaker, white T-shirt and blue jeans that made up Dean's ensemble in *Rebel Without a Cause*. This doll would cost $100. The skin would be made of a new porcelain-vinyl material, and Roesler promised it was "the most lifelike doll I've ever seen."

The $2000 version, planned for release three months after the basic doll but never produced, would be dressed in blue jeans, a suede fringe jacket and a small Stetson cowboy hat. "The expensive version will be a limited, numbered edition," the attorney said. "Probably only 500 will be made."

The doll came with a replica of Dean's trademark cigarette. When the American Cancer Society raised hell, Dakin offered a doll without a cigarette.

Don't Destroy Me

British playwright Michael Hastings dedicated this play to James Dean in the 1970s with the words, "This play is dedicated to the thought of James Dean. There is no other actor, and there never has been since the end of the war, who has so wholly represented my generation, here in England; but strangely he is American. This play, in its entirety, I give to Dean. But he is dead now."

Dooley, Don

According to an AP bulletin of October 12, 1955, Don Dooley and Thomas Fredericks testified at Dean's inquest that they believed Rolf Wuetherich, rather than Dean, was driving the Porsche at the time of the crash. Their claim rested largely on the fact that Wuetherich was wearing a red T-shirt while Dean's was white; they recalled seeing a red-shirted driver in the car before the crash.

"Eyewitness to accident says mechanic was driving," was the heading of an October 1992 *Bakersfield Californian* interview with Don Dooley. He was fifteen years old when he witnessed the accident that killed James Dean.

"The headlight ring of the Porsche flew over our pickup, that's how close we were," Dooley said in that interview. He was a passenger in a 1952 Dodge pickup driven by his brother-in-law, Tom Frederick, whose five-year-old son, Gary, was also in the truck. They were headed east on old Highway 466 en route to Bakersfield to see relatives. "Donald Turnupseed, the guy in the '49 [sic] Ford, passed us. He was between 75 and 100 yards ahead of us, if that far. He tried to turn off to Avenal. I guess he saw the Porsche coming and tried to get back. About that time, the left front of each car hit. What I remember is the rear end of the Ford going up in the air and going perpendicular to the road.

"The Porsche, as I can best remember, went airborne, made a complete circle in the air and landed next to a barbed wire fence." Dooley said it looked like Dean was struggling to keep from being thrown out. His upper body hit the fence then bounced back. Frederick stopped his pickup. He and Dooley went over to the wreck.

Dooley said he helped Turnupseed out of his Ford, told him to lie down because of shock, and gave him his coat or something to cover himself.

"All I could see was wrong with him was blood on the bridge of his nose." Dooley went over to the mangled Porsche. Dean's mechanic was on the ground near the driver's side, seriously injured. He was bleeding from the mouth and trying to say something Dooley could not understand. It sounded like "Where's Jimmy? Where's Jimmy?"

Dooley said he found Dean on the ground between the fence and the passenger side of the silver Porsche.

"I looked at him. You couldn't tell who it was because of the blood and dirt on his face. I tried to find a pulse. I couldn't detect anything.

"Later a station wagon pulling a car carrier comes up and this guy comes running out of there, saying 'Oh God, please save Jimmy! God, please save Jimmy!'"

Dooley insisted that, based on the color of their shirts, the mechanic was driving. He said he was at the scene for about an hour. Among his prized possessions were three slightly curled black-and-white snapshots with "Sept. 1955" in the scalloped borders. Two were overexposed shots of the mangled Porsche; someone on a stretcher is visible in the photographs. Another photo shows the wrecked Ford. In 2003, he sold the photos to David Loehr of the James Dean Gallery for $900, and they reportedly will appear in a forthcoming book.

Dooley, despite his youth, spoke up at the inquest into the death of James Dean, saying he had seen an earpiece to some glasses on the roadway. He was the youngest person to speak at the inquest. In his later years he was a resident of Bakersfield, California.

Douglas, Jack

Comedy writer, racer, and bon vivant Jack Douglas shared his recollections of James Dean's last day in a letter to Warren Beath dated August 30, 1982:

> First time I met Jimmy was in Palm Springs races—he raced in what was termed a novice race.... He won this event and seemed very happy about it.
>
> The only good car he had was the Porsche, which apparently was brand new—and in which he got killed. The morning of the day he got it, some of us, Dean included, met at Jack McAfee's garage-shop on Ventura Boulevard at Studio City—or maybe in the Van Nuys district.... As I remember, Dean was quiet—unobtrusive as usual. All it was was 'Good morning—how do you feel" and that was about it.... I left first.... I was towing my race car on a trailer.... The other drivers were going to follow a little later. We were all on our way to Salinas. I turned off the highway.... Dean and his mechanic passed me somewhere along 46, going pretty fast ... and then I came upon the accident which apparently had taken place not long before. There were a couple of cars there so I didn't stop.... On the way to drive in a race it is not good to stop and look at smashups.... I didn't know it was Dean or I would have stopped.
>
> I think Dean would have been a good race driver—if he had more time—and naturally, a better car.

draft board

"They ought to draft that guy and teach him some manners," said a disgruntled Warner Bros. employee as he watched Dean's self-absorbed shenanigans on a movie set. Dean's problems with the Selective Service has been most thoroughly researched by biographer Val Holley, who had the advantage of years of familiarity with Dean's hometown folks, especially Adeline Nall. Holley's research discloses that the former Indiana state director of Selective Service, Robert Custer, said that Dean requested a deferment as a conscientious objector, with reinforcement of an attached letter from a minister. The former state director also said that Dean wrote a letter citing his homosexuality as a reason for deferment. When the appeals were rejected, Dean took his case to a national board.

Nelle Hines was the clerk of the local draft board in 1951, and her discussions with Custer are evidently the source of this information. Adeline Nall was apparently told by Hines that Dean had told the local board, "You don't want me in your man's army."

Rogers Brackett apparently said that he paid Dean's psychiatric bill so his friend could obtain a letter certifying him as a homosexual. Dean had two physical examinations, which was unusual, and the upshot of the second was that he was rejected for the service. Perhaps it was at that visit that he delivered his psychiatrist's letter.

During the last months of his life, *Daily Variety* reported that Dean had been called to an Army physical. Sheilah Graham of the *Hollywood Reporter* said that Nick Adams would replace Dean as Jett Rink in *Giant* if Jimmy were drafted. "He won't be called into the Army for about two years," Graham wrote. "If the Army knows what it's getting into, they'll let Jimmy alone."

dreams of death

Judith Collins was the name of the girl who supposedly authored *Jimmy Dean Returns*, a 1956 magazine article which described her love affair with Dean which persisted beyond the grave. In these memoirs she recounts sitting in a small park overlooking the East River in the fog when a moody Jimmy broke his silence about something troubling his sleep.

She wrote of how Jimmy recounted to her a dream he had —"A very vivid dream, more vivid than any he could remember." In the dream, he watched a small car tearing around curves along a winding road. The car took the curves at such amazing speeds that Jimmy thought there must be an expert driver at the wheel. She wrote, "He tried to see who this driver was, for usually the people who appear in a dream are well known to the person having the dream; but the dusk was falling and perhaps because of this or because the car was going so fast, he could not see."

Jimmy's perspective in the dream suddenly changed so that instead of looking at the car from above and behind, he was now lifted high above it so that it was merely a dot on the highway. According to Collins, "As he stared at it and wondered again who the driver was, he became aware that there was a purpose behind his having been lifted to this great height. For his point of view had widened enormously and he could see, not only the road with the racing car, but *another* road — a road that lay behind some low hills."

The article describes how Jimmy told Judith he could see another car racing along this road but that the driver of the first car could not, as it was behind some hills, and that he also saw where the two roads met.

As Jimmy saw this in his dream he tried to shout a warning to the driver, and even though he did not see the person, "he felt some kind of curious, sympathetic connection with him and interest in him."

The dream, of course, ends with the two cars colliding in a "hideous tangle of tearing metal," while Jimmy tries unsuccessfully to warn the unknown driver. Collins also reports that he could see a crumpled, motionless figure — the unknown driver — in the ravaged wreckage.

Collins commented that after having told her the dream Dean asked her "what was the meaning of the dream ... why should it have been so vivid? Why should he have felt that curious attachment to the driver of the first car?"

Her conclusion was that Jimmy himself was the unknown driver.

drinking

In an interview with Warren Beath, film composer Leonard Rosenmann said, "He was an abusive drunk, all right. When he got drunk he got very abusive. That was one of the reasons we didn't speak for a year, he came in drunk and started to really carry on horrendously and I threw him out physically. Then I went down to his place and woke him up the next day and told him 'I don't know you any more.' And he felt terrible — I did too, but he was just too unstable.... I just didn't like him drunk and skulking around the place and he took one drink and slid under the table. He licked the cork and went berserk. He was not really a drinker.... Jimmy just got kind of evil when he drank."

See Rosenmann, Leonard.

driver's license

In 1998 the James Dean Memorial Gallery began to offer for sale a novelty James Dean driver's license, laminated and actual size, with a photo and an expiration date of "9–30–55."

Drummond, Jack

Arizona race car driver Jack Drummond died in the Bakersfield road race in which Dean had also participated when his car spun out of control and into a bale of rain-soaked hay. Witnessing this death was an experience that troubled Dean. "I think it got to him," Dean's friend Bill Hickman said in an interview with Warren Beath. "He had a nightmare or two about it. The kid [Drummond] would come and talk to him.... or something."

The date of the race was May 1, 1955. The place was the Minter Field airport race outside Shafter, California north of Bakersfield.

Squalls and cloudbursts had made the track muddy and treacherous. Turn number three had been especially dangerous. Soaked with rain, the bales that channeled and buffered that corner had become hard and heavy. The outer edge was spongy turn. Instead of sliding into a safe spin-out, drivers who oversteered would trip and roll.

Three cars crashed on the curve that day. Jimmy was entered in the San Luis Trophy Race, a six-lap event for 750–1,500 cc cars. He placed third in his white Speedster, after an MG Special and a Panhard.

Drummond was crushed underneath his car when it flipped. His death cast a pall over the day. Dean's nearness to the disaster was something he did not brag about at the studio where he was filming *Rebel Without a Cause.* If not prohibited, racing was certainly discouraged in the middle of a project.

Hickman had no idea what happened to the tapes into which Dean recorded long and rambling meditations on death, but he thought that Jack Drummond was a persistent theme. "He wouldn't really talk about it, plus it's bad luck. But he would dream the kid would show up at his door late at night, all broken up from the wreck. Like it was maybe a warning, or something."

It was rumored that Dean at one time had several of his charcoal drawings on display in his Sherman Oaks bungalow, depicting Drummond's wreck and its aftermath. It was the occasional theme of idle and cryptic cartoons he would draw upon napkins in restaurants, then crumple and jam in his pockets before he left.

Dylan, Bob

LeRoy Hoikkala, a drummer for Dylan's early band, told an interviewer from *On the Tracks* (issue 18): "We'd go down to the newsstand and get all the magazines that had any articles at all on Dean. He was kind of our idol. This is one thing for sure, that Bob dug James Dean. We idolized him both as a person and an actor. We felt, including Bob, that his acting was actually himself. He wasn't just acting the roles he was in. The roles were him."

On July 15, 1988, Bob Dylan visited Fairmount, Indiana, at midnight after playing a concert. He and his entourage of about 15 walked the streets, a local policeman showing up shortly to act as escort. The Fairmount museum was opened, and Dylan viewed the memorabilia. He also visited the farm of Marcus Winslow, Dean's uncle, where Dean spent his boyhood. Young Chuck Winslow, another of Dean's relatives, was waiting at the farm when Dylan showed up. After a conversation with Marcus Winslow, Dylan let Chuck show him the barn and basketball hoop. Dylan looked at the farm's hay truck and meditated at Dean's gravesite for a half hour, leaving at about 3:00 in the morning.

E

ear

In a 1964 *Borderline* article entitled "The Ghost of James Dean," Maila "Vampira" Nurmi recounted to Sidney Omarr how shortly before his death James Dean left her a mutilated photo, which she had tacked to the wall with a dagger. Dean had cut this calling card carefully to leave only his eye, nostril and ear. Jimmy's cryptic comment was, "You may have need of these."

On September 30, 1955, Nurmi was sitting around with Tony Perkins when the picture began to swing over Tony's head. A phone call informed them that James Dean had just died. Nurmi immediately contacted mediums, who told her Jimmy wanted her to pray for him. She began to talk to the picture. "Is it true, Jimmy, that you are in pain?"

The top part of the ear wiggled, just as the radio began to play the cowboy song, "Dig Me a Hole and Bury Me Deep and I Will Lie in Peace."

A startled Nurmi continued, "Jimmy, if you were talking to me, wiggle the ear three times."

The ear wiggled three times!

"Is what the cowboy sang true?" she asked. "If so, wiggle two slow and three fast — the same as your favorite drum beat."

Ten persons reportedly saw her converse with the paper ear and witnessed its responses.

Perhaps the least likely part of the story is that Tony Perkins was listening to a country station.

earthquakes

In recent years, metaphysics and geological science have been merging in theories regarding the effects of the extraordinary forces and pressures exerted in the vicinity of earthquake faults. Investigators for an emerging science speculate that strange events magnetizing along fault lines are consequences of little-understood forces generated by the grinding of continent-sized tectonic plates beneath the earth's surface. Lightning emanations from the ground and widespread neuroses and incidence of violent crime have been statistically verified.

James Dean's death at the intersection of two highways lying almost directly upon the San Andreas fault is only one of many deaths that have occurred there since the 1920s—and perhaps much earlier. The intersection of the highways as seen from satellite cameras reveals a significant design—an angle known astrologically as the Finger of God, which denotes bad luck and malign influence from above and below.

Physics, medieval cosmology and American Indian lore coincide in depicting the earthquake fault as a "hell mouth" that emanates bizarre radiations and comprises an egress from the underworld or hell. Electromagnetic waves form an invisible corona inflicting hallucination, hysteria and personality aberration. Time and space are bent by fluctuations in the planet's gravity, and batwing nightmares darken the sky like a plague of starlings released from the bowels of earth—according to the new theorists.

Ghostly sightings, spectral occurrences and poltergeist activity are reported at the intersection of the highway on the fault line. Extraordinary events magnetize to these spots, hallowed by the ancient Indians and studied by geologists and physicists. In this context it seems like more than accident that James Dean should have died on the fault line, a spot of such intense geological history and strange activity.

The death of James Dean on the active fault may prefigure the ultimate disaster that would break California and destroy the West Coast as we know it. A study remains to be done on the activity of the fault on September 30, 1955.

A geology professor from the California Institute of Technology says that Cholame may well be the epicenter of the ultimate killer California earthquake. Kerry Sieh predicts that a quake of a magnitude of 6.0 on the Richter Scale will hit a 13-mile-long segment of the San Andreas fault, toppling the hills like geological dominoes to detonate an even greater quake of 7.0 or even 8.0 along a 62-mile crack in the earth. The fault moves, or "creeps," about one-tenth of a mile per year in the Cholame area near Highway 46.

In fact, the fault line crosses the highway just yards to the west of the spot where Dean's crash took place, almost directly under the bridge spanning Cholame Creek. The Cholame Valley itself is a depressed block between two active branches of the fault zone. Expert Robert Iacopi writes in his book *Earthquake Country*, "The eastern branch is difficult to trace in the valley, but the western branch is visible as a low, discontinuous scarp at the base of the ridge bordering the valley. Where the main road to Parkfield follows this ridge, the scarp and sag areas show up at the edge of the roadway."

A scarp of the eastern fault line becomes visible east of the road as it enters the hills north of Cholame Valley. The roadway assumes a very straight course for 1.5 miles along the very edge of the steep side of the escarpment.

On March 10, 1922, the Cholame Valley experienced a major quake of a magnitude greater than 6.0. The shock was centered in the thinly populated area of Cholame Valley, but it damaged several houses at Parkfield to the north and threw down chimneys throughout the area. Within the valley, cracks 6 to 12 inches wide and a quarter-mile long were opened in soft ground. There was heavy shaking at Shandon, Hollister, and San Luis Obispo.

A quake hit California's central coast on December 22, 2003. Measuring 6.5, it was felt from San Francisco to Los Angeles. The temblor was centered seven miles beneath the surface and 24 miles northeast of Paso Robles, where two women were crushed to death by falling debris and 40 other people were injured. More than 40 buildings in the downtown area were leveled or severely damaged, including the historic clock tower, a landmark that had stood since 1920. The Paso Robles Chamber of Commerce vows to rebuild and restore the devastated structures.

EARTH ENERGY LINES

The Indians were the first inhabitants of the Cholame Valley by 10,000 years. The primitive shamans of the Chumash Indians appointed settlement locations by dream and divination along lines of energy beneath the earth. Ancient peoples apparently sensed a pulsating force coursing underground and made stone monuments where it was strongest. These lines became ancient tracks that linked their sites of sanctity. Route 46 follows this ancient path through the Cholame Valley.

So-called earth energy has been researched both physically and psy-

‑chically. Weird occurrences and supernatural happenings have been reported along these invisible lines, which form a grid in the vicinity where James Dean met his death. The fundamental tool for detecting these lines of energy is the dowsing rod, usually made from the branch of a green tree. Dowsers are still employed by farmers in the area to detect underground water sites.

In the early 1980s a feature story in the *Bakersfield Californian* likened the route on which James Dean drove to his death to a "time bomb for a tragedy which is due to go off." Pockmarked with chuckholes and crumbling pavement lipped at the outside edges, the highway offered no turnouts or passing lanes for motorists.

It was reported, "In the past five years, 28 people have died and 492 traffic accidents have occurred on Highway 46 between Highway 99 and the San Luis Obispo County Line.... From that point to Highway 101, a distance of 52 miles, there were 269 accidents, and 19 fatalities, in the same 1978–82 period." Driving the decrepit road surface was "a dangerous and nerve-wracking experience."

Some James Dean crash site visitors today report the physical presence of a strange force that they cannot see but that lifts them from the ground, strikes them, shoves them, or causes unexplained mood swings and depressions.

Ebon, Martin

Ebon is the author of "American Fascinations," an article that was featured in 1956 in the occult journal *To-morrow*. Ebon wrote that the cries of Jimmy's heartbroken fans recalled the lamentations of Nefertiti, the Egyptian queen who mourned for her dead brother: "I long to breathe in the sweet breath of your mouth. I long to hear your voice, the wind that will restore life to my limbs. Hold out to me your hands in which your spirit dwells so that I may have the power to receive it and live in it."

effects

In the fall 1995 issue of *Films of the Golden Age* magazine, Dean archivist Brian Lewis listed the following items found in Dean's apartment after his death:

1. A Rolex watch
2. Four sports car-racing trophies
3. An electric blanket.
4. A large wardrobe of his clothing.

5. Two pairs of silver spurs.
6. A pair of cufflinks with an oil well design.

Court documents enumerate some other personal articles including a pair of bull's horns and a matador's cape, a red leather suitcase with Leonard Rosenmann's monogram, silver cuff links, a traveling clock with Dean's name inscribed, a perfume flask, a wristwatch with a gold dial, gold cufflinks, ID bracelet and chain, two gold cup racing trophies and one silver cup trophy, a Marlin .22 rifle, and bongo drums.

See also auction.

Elvis

A tremendous Dean fan, Elvis Presley was the subject of a *Movieland* article of August 1963 that boasted, "Elvis Hears from James Dean!" The interview posed the question, "If someone who is dead is still influencing the present, might we not think of him as being a live spirit?"

Said Elvis?

"Yes."

Fan magazines also said that Elvis was tapped to play Dean in a biography in 1958, but that the project turned into a documentary. But Elvis' fascination with Dean was real and passionate. He screened *Rebel Without a Cause* countless times in his private theater and could recite the dialogue along with the actors. He ingratiated himself with Dean friends and hangers-on such as Natalie Wood and Nick Adams. He sought out Dean's Hollywood haunts such as Googie's and Barney's Beanery. He had intense conversations about Dean's death with Bill Hickman on the set of *Jailhouse Rock*, in which Hickman is seen briefly as a guard who flogs Presley. When Elvis was tapped for his first picture, *Love Me Tender*, he told producer Hal Wallis that his only stipulation was that he did not want to smile, because Jimmy didn't smile in his roles.

Presley of course had immeasurable resources and since the mid–1990s it has been rumored that his fascination with Dean and the car accident led to an obsession to obtain the ultimate relic — the smashed Porsche. This scenario has Elvis procuring the car privately and for a great deal of money, secreting it in the bowels beneath Graceland.

Emr, Jon

He claimed to be a Hollywood player, this Scotch-guzzling Clark Gable lookalike, with projects "in development" with titles like *Magnum Thrust* and *Feet of Death,* and to be a black belt who had taken martial arts classes from no less than Chuck Norris. Somehow, the smooth-talking Emr managed to con millions out of gullible investors lured by his promise of becoming Hollywood producers. It was a projected James Dean authorized film biography that led to Emr's murder by a former bodyguard. After purchasing the rights from the management of Dean's estate, Emr proceeded to sell the idea to investors, and then steal the money.

After his death and the resolution of all the loose ends— the body of Emr's murderer had been found in the Mojave Desert, along with the body of Sue Calkins, his girlfriend, in a murder-suicide — the police called a press conference that featured a large poster of James Dean as an exhibit. Chief Ted Cooke announced, "The fact that the film actor James Dean is involved makes this real interesting for you folks. You see, there were two competing interests for the rights to the James Dean story. They clashed and that led to all the bitterness that led to this murder."

See also Hauge, Alan.

Erb, French, Picone & Griffith

This Beverly Hills law firm represented Dean's mechanic, Rolf Wuetherich, in his suit against the estate of James Dean, alleging in their complaint filed August 20, 1956, that

> as a direct and proximate result of the willful and wanton misconduct on the part of the defendants, and as a result of the collision aforesaid, the plaintiff sustained severe personal injuries and was thereby made sick, sore, lame and disabled and sustained a severe and profound shock to the nervous system, all of which said injuries have caused and will continue to cause this plaintiff great pain and discomfort; all to his general damage in the sum of $100,000.

See also lawsuits.

F

failure analysis *see* **simulation**

Fairmount High *see under* **ghosts and hauntings**

fan clubs

Young girls at Immaculate Heart High School in Los Angeles formed the first Dean fan club in 1951. Inspired by one of Jimmy's earliest television performances in a religious drama, they called their club the Immaculate Heart James Dean Appreciation Society. Biographer John Howlett offered some figures on the growing trend. A club called Dedicated Fans claimed a membership of 430,600. Dean's Teens boasted 392,450 members, and Lest We Forget, 376,870. Other clubs included Laura Dale's James Dean Fan Club, Dedicated Deans, the James Dean Memorial Club, and the James Dean Widows Club. By 1957 there were 3,800,000 dues-paying Dean fan club members in America.

British journalist Gilbert Harding took ghoulish Dean fans to task in a January 5, 1957, issue of *Illustrated:*

> I believe the morbid and the mawkish have launched "Lest We Forget" clubs in the name of this unfortunate young man. The utterly tasteless are prepared to rock 'n' roll to a tune called "Jimmy Dean's Christmas in Heaven."
>
> Girls— perhaps they should be pitied rather than despised —fought for blades of grass from Dean's grave on the first anniversary of his death. He was too good for this.
>
> Can't the young — the "Dean-agers"—find themselves a better hero, a real hero?

He proposes, as an alternative icon, Group Captain Cheshire, V.C.

Bill Lewis of Anderson, Indiana, was president of the Indiana Connection James Dean Fan Club, which had about 50 members. Annual dues were $8, for which members received a newsletter. The club's funds were used to put flowers on Dean's grave on his birthday, Memorial Day, and the anniversary of the accident in California. Lewis, who lived about 30 miles from Fairmount, Indiana, decorated the grave and always participated in the ritual walk from Back Creek Church to the cemetery each year. "It's a happy get-together," he said.

A typical "News Flash" ran, "On Feb. 6th. At the municipal building they were showing the film 'Giant.' Ortense Winslow along with 15 other fans of Jimmy's stayed for the whole showing and they said Ortense is doing real good. After the movie Bill served cake and punch."

"Far from Eden"

Dean's Deathday had rolled around again and *Car and Driver* commemorated it with an article in their October 1985 issue. Writer Brock Yates went out to the death scene and produced a nicely written article which emphasized Dean's racing career and his highway death. It includes the recollections of race driver Phil Hill:

Phil Hill was about two hours behind. He came upon the accident site long after the Porsche and the Ford had been hauled to a little Quonset-hut garage in Cholame. Dean's body had been taken to the Kuehl funeral home in Paso Robles while surgeons at the local hospital were deciding whether or not to amputate Wuetherich's left leg. Turnupseed told the police he simply had not seen the Porsche, and he was not charged. Hill recalls seeing parked cars and masses of smoking flares and flashing lights arcing in the desert night. After being informed of the crash, he and Pickett drove on to Salinas.

Yates writes very evocatively of the highway and the crash itself:

> Welcome the silence. Break for a moment your bonds with time. You'll hear it first — the frantic growl of a four-cam Porsche. Unmuffled. Running hard. Look into the brown-weeded hills, where the old road winds around the edge of the ravine. A tiny silver Spyder squirts into sight, lashing through the apexes, its impudent snout nipping at the wooden guardrails. Stand back as it rushes past, scrabbling for traction on the scarred macadam. Follow its raucous exhaust. The two men in the cockpit — a slight young driver with clip-on sunglasses and a beefy passenger — lean slightly as the Porsche clears the final bend. It powers clean and straight, speed building, toward the valley...

Farmer's Market

A moody James Dean emblazoned the flyers distributed to draw customers to a "commemorative brunch buffet" at Farmer's Market, where Dean is misreported to have had a doughnut on his last day on earth. According to the flyer, "James Dean ate his last brunch at Farmer's Market on September 30, 1955, before wheeling off on his fatal journey."

In the promotion on September 30th by the Kokomo Cafe, participants were offered the possibility to "win a black leather jacket in our 'Spirit of James Dean' look alike contest — separate winners for men and women!"

Unfortunately, Dean ate at the Ranch Market that morning. The confusion between the names has evolved into a cottage industry for Farmer's Market — itself the scene of a horrific traffic accident some forty-five years later when an elderly driver became confused and mowed down nearly sixty people in the market, killing thirteen.

fatal injuries

Dean's injuries were a broken neck, multiple fractures of upper and lower jaw, multiple fractures of left and right arm, and internal injuries. The body was nearly evacuated of blood. The left side of his face was much more damaged than the right, a circumstance due to his position in the car as it struck the Ford from his left. The trousers on one side were ripped from the body. Small particles of glass were embedded in his face. Presumably, they were from the windshield. Gross examination revealed fractured neck, multiple fractures of forearms, fractured leg and numerous cuts and bruises about the face and chest.

No eyeglasses were found. Neither Dr. Bossert at the hospital nor mortician Martin Kuehl examined the eyes for contact lenses. (*See* glasses.)

favorite possession

Maila Nurmi told Warren Beath in an interview: "Jimmy made a big thing of giving me a present once — it was his favorite possession. It was a small gray object that at first looked and felt like a pumice stone with a hole in the center, but upon closer scrutiny caused speculation. It might have been a spinal disc, slightly petrified, from some long-gone animal. Jimmy had found it in the earth in Salinas and claimed that by holding it to the eye and looking through the hole, one could see anything one chose to see. He presented it to me with much fanfare and I cherished it. I had it strung on a chain and dangling from my neck in *First American Teenager*. Through much of my narrative I fondled it as I hoped Jimmy would speak to his friends through me. I guess nothing special happened, though, and I've lost the magic 'stone.' I retain the memory of the giving — so joyful. But at the last minute, having built to a great crescendo, Jimmy threw it at me across the room. Shy, shy, shy."

fertility

The James Dean death site has for years attracted faithful hoping that contact with the essence of their idol will cure ills both emotional and physical, apparently even including infertility. One man was drawn to the site by a woman he had recently begun to date. Not a particular Dean fan, he let himself be guided by her through a tour of the intersection and the monument up the road. Then she drew him toward the abandoned garage that still existed in the late eighties. His recollections are quoted here with his permission, though the reason he wishes to remain anonymous is evident.

> I followed her into the abandoned garage, and she pointed out where Jimmy Dean's car had been brought. It was dark and musty. Then she turned to me and gave me a kiss like she never had before. She took off her sweater and put it on the concrete foundation. I was worried about spiders and rats, but she was peeling off all her clothes. She pulled me onto

the concrete and we made love, right there. I was shocked. Back out in the sunlight, she acted like nothing had happened.

I found out later that she had dreams of having a baby. She was nearly forty, and she'd had a couple of surgeries. I guess they left her eggs intact, but she had some sort of female complications which left childbearing an iffy proposition. She had even considered trying to find a surrogate mother, but it would cost about $30,000 bucks. What she said was, that she felt that making love on the site would be good luck. But later she said that if a baby was conceived on the anniversary that Jimmy died, his spirit would go into it. I ran across some reading, later, that said that the Japanese believe that a baby born on its father's birthday will inherit his spirit when he died. Maybe she had this mixed up, I don't know. It was a Japanese guy that installed the monument there, and the garage was full of these sacks of polished stones he had spread around the base. But it was wild.

And, no. She didn't conceive.

figurine

"Fully sculpted and exquisitely detailed in pure bisque porcelain, this Special Edition figurine captures all the good looks and magnetism of the late, great star," read the sales material on the Jimmy Dean Special Edition Figurine. Each was hand painted and numbered on the base. They came gift-boxed with Certificate of Authenticity (authenticity of what?)? Looking more like Barbie's boyfriend Ken than James Dean, this Curtis-licensed item featured the new, wholesome James Dean. Suggested retail: $65.00.

A musical figurine was produced by PSC International Corporation in a limited edition of 7,500. This nine-inch figurine, showing Dean with a cigarette in his mouth and a jacket draped over his shoulder, played the song "California Dreamin.'" It retailed for around $25.00.

Fisher King

From the vast and ancient body of Arthurian folklore comes the figure of the Fisher King, part of the Grail legend, whose central theme can be traced as far back as ancient pagan fertility rituals and the restoration to life of the dying god of vegetation. Beneath the legend are the rites and symbols of a secret cult that had translated primitive fertility ritual into an initiation in the secret of Life. Some have connected the Fisher King with such rites. The underlying motif is that the fertility of the land depended on the life and sexual potency of the ruler. Because the Fisher King is sexually wounded — in Eschenbach's *Parzival*, the Maimed King is pierced through the testicles by a poisoned spear — his kingdom is a wasteland.

James Dean came full circle in the mythic cycle of his pictures to become at the end the ailing elder King, the father figure he had vanquished in *East of Eden*. Jett Rink, Dean's character in *Giant*, is the ailing Fisher King in the Texas wasteland. And in real life James Dean was to die a death in a wasteland milieu, a death which was revivifying for a legion of fans and gave rise to a ferocious cult following.

Highway 466 ran across the wasteland, the desert. Ahead was the crossroads. It was emblematic of the condition of America. It was a land wasted and fallen asleep, the desolate realm of the Fisher King. Dwight Eisenhower had suffered a heart attack on September 24, 1955, and on September 26, the stock market crashed more than 30 points. More potently, among that new phenomenon, the youth culture, there was a pervasive materialistic complacency and disaffection with the petrified religious dogmatism. The time was right for a savior.

Flexidisc

"At Last the Voice of Jimmy," was the come-on from *Hear Hollywood*, which boasted that it was "The World's First Talking Magazine!" The insertion of thin, inexpensive records called "Flexidiscs" allowed readers and subscribers to hear a recorded message from the late James Dean.

Ford sedan

The fatal Ford sedan involved in the accident which killed James Dean had License No. 6A48142 and was purchased by Donald Turnupseed on October 26, 1953. Thirty years later, Turnupseed claimed not to know whatever became of it after the collision. *See* accident.

Ford station wagon

James Dean's 1955 Ford station wagon, driven by Bill Hickman, was following behind the Porsche, with racing trailer in tow, when Dean was killed on September 30, 1955. The car is seen in one of the photographs taken outside Competition Motors by Sanford Roth, who was Hickman's passenger on the fatal day. When Dean was stopped for speeding, Hickman also received a ticket from Officer O.V. Hunter, for doing 55 in a 45 zone — exceeding the speed limit for a car pulling a trailer. When Dean's estate was settled after his death, a Robert F. Braunt purchased the station wagon (engine number M5RY 167 500) for $2,200. It is not known what became of it.

Forever James Dean

This 1988 documentary featured some previously unseen material, including Dean's soft-drink TV commercial. The film boasts interviews with his childhood and Hollywood friends, including Adeline Nall, Dennis Hopper and Jim Backus, as well as a wealth of archival footage. It was released to coincide with the 35th anniversary of *East of Eden*.

France

Dean's popularity when he was alive wasn't limited to the United States, but in death, his iconic status grew exponentially both in America and abroad. Every country needed its "James Dean"; in France there were actually two. The first was Gerard Blain, born on October 23, 1930. Debuting in films in 1954, by 1958 he was the sympathetic lead in Chabrol's *Le Beau Serge* and *The Cousins*. His acting career evaporated in the sixties, but he reinvented himself as a director. His other films include *Deadlier Than the Male*, *Crime and Punishment*, *The Hunchback of Rome* and *The American Friend*, in which he appeared with Dennis Hopper.

In the sixties, Alain Delon was also called "the James Dean of France." He appeared in *Is Paris Burning?* (it was) and *The Concorde — Airport 79*.

Francis, Robert

Twenty-five-year-old actor Robert Charles Francis died in an air crash July 31, 1955. His death followed close on the heels of the death of actress Suzan Ball, who died of cancer at age 21. When Jimmy heard about Francis's death, his ominous comment was "They always come in threes." He was right — within two months he was dead. Robert Francis, the young man who inspired the morbid bit of reflection, had appeared in *The Long Gray Line* but will probably be remembered as "Willie Keith" in *The Caine Mutiny*.

See also premonitions of death.

Frederick, Tom

Witness to the fatal collision. *See* Dooley, Don.

From Tom Mix to James Dean

Raymond de Becker produced a mythological study of the Jimmy phenomenon in his 1959 book *From Tom Mix to James Dean*. He wrote:

> But this god is closer to Dionysus, Wotan, Attis and Antinous than Christ. James Dean died at twenty-four, and as with the murder of Adonis, the sacrifice of Mithra, and the suicide of Antinous, he could not have lived on without destroying the myth on which his cult is founded. Undoubtedly the same psychological structures are recreated throughout

history on different levels and adapted to different forms; it is the archetypal solution for an age of confusion. Gods who die young possess the universal power to express the themes of adolescence; at the crossroads of life they are signs of the future. The god of American youth surges up from the depths of the earth; in the delirium of a sullen energy he offers himself up to immortality. He is a dark god crying out, with a craving for power and resurrection. He is not an ascetic and scarcely a martyr; he is the Divine Dancer, and by his death he brings on the spring once more.

G

gas station

On the day he died, James Dean filled his tank at 14321 Ventura, at the corner of Beverly Glen. In recent years the site has come to house a flower shop. The islands where the pumps stood are still visible.

Gearin, Richard

A minor repairman in Dean's hometown of Fairmount, Indiana, he claimed to have lived with James Dean in New York. He was eventually sponsored by Dean's relatives, the Winslow family, and nearly moved in. In frail health, he died in 1987 at 60.

Gerhart, Gary

An Indiana schoolteacher and the author of an unpublished manuscript, *James Dean: Remembrance*, which is an account of James Dean's boyhood that includes extensive interviews with people who knew Dean. Gerhart's proximity to Dean's boyhood haunts, not to mention relatives like aunt Ortense Winslow and his old schoolteachers, naturally suggested this project.

ghosts and hauntings

Many of the people who perform various pilgrimages to sites identified with Jimmy Dean's life seem to have a need to walk away with a supernatural anecdote. Visiting a place with a connection to Jimmy Dean, they frequently encounter his ghost. Sometimes the apparition is manifested as a mere "feeling" or "presence" signified by chills, goosebumps, and a prickling of the hairs on their arms. Other times, an actual spectral form appears.

The following is a list of some of the places the "ghost" of James Dean has been experienced, ranked in order of the frequency of his visitations.

1. Park Cemetery, the James Dean grave in Fairmount, Indiana.
2. Grave of Mildred Dean in Marion, Indiana.
3. The fatal intersection outside Cholame, California.
4. Griffith Park Observatory, Los Angeles, California.
5. The barn at the Winslow Homestead, Jonesboro Pike in Indiana.
6. Anywhere Maila "Vampira" Nurmi is.

Here are some other ghostly anecdotes:

"THE BUSIEST GHOST AROUND"

Dean devotee Mark Kinnaman compiles Dean sightings and hauntings on his website in a department called "The Busiest Ghost Around": "By far, the most often-told tale is that they saw Jimmy driving his Porsche in the desert. One lady wrote me and told me that she and her husband were driving through the California desert when a silver sports car pulled up right behind them and stayed on their rear end for a few miles. There were two men in the car, both wearing sunglasses. Without a warning, and [with] no place to turn off, the car and its occupants completely disappeared. They were not James Dean fans and only later when they saw a photograph of Jimmy taken in his Porsche on the day that he died, did it hit them that it was James Dean following them that day. Her husband went into therapy, convinced that he had an experience with a spirit."

COPS NAB JAMES DEAN'S GHOST!

"Suspicious Cops Roust a 'Ghost'" was the title of a 1956 *Mirror News* article. Young Frank Anthony Horton was arrested after a robbery and identified by the victim because he looked like James Dean. The arresting officer had to let him go. "After all, there are thousands of kids who look like James Dean and they seem to be out here."

He noted that none of them were working, either.

DEVIL'S DEN

Wrote Sam Schaeffer in "James Dean, the Ghost Driver of Polonio Pass" (*Whisper*, December 1957):

> Not far from this junction (where Dean died), about 18 miles due east to be more exact, is a supposedly haunted place called The Devil's Den. Polonio Pass itself is in the Diablo (or 'Devil's') Range of mountains, a sec-

tion of the California Coast Range. Many of the valley towns, I soon learned, are inhabited by people of strong Indian, Mexican and Filipino ancestry. Many of the native whites of the region have a touch of Indian blood in them, too.

The entire locale is a place replete with legends of old massacres, of lovers killed by thwarted suitors or vengeful relatives— of violent death and the restless dead.

So perhaps it's not strange that among such people one would hear whispers of a Ghost Driver of Polonio Pass.

FAIRMOUNT HIGH

"The ghost of James Dean haunts the old Fairmount High Auditorium. The building is now the town's middle school. Several years ago, a sixth-grade teacher photographed her students during a play. After the photos were developed and returned, a strange circle of light was seen in the upper right-hand corner of each picture." —*Indianapolis Star*, September 22, 1985.

FLOATING DEAN HEAD

Doris Danielson was a Trenton, New Jersey, stewardess in March of 1957 when she woke up in the middle of the night to find a mysterious red circle forming in her bedroom door. James Dean's head appeared in the center, then floated across the room. It vanished as mysteriously, and the stewardess devoted herself to prayer. At last report, she lived in Texas and had had no other visitations from Dean's head.

GHOST DRIVER OF POLONIO PASS

In *Whisper* magazine, December 1957, author Sam Schaeffer describes a sentimental journey to the crash site on Highway 466. He recalls standing with his friend Jim on the Great White Way two years earlier when the young star saw his name in lights for the first time. Now he sees a different, macabre marquee: the weird shrine Jimmy's fans have dedicated to the dead star.

To Jimmy — now only in death shall we meet.

Jimmy, you'll always be remembered, you were the greatest, the absolute greatest.

Why did you leave us, Jimmy — why were you in such a hurry?

Whisper is the magazine, and it was whispers that brought Schaeffer out to this lonely spot. Whispers of a ghost car racing through the night. Noises of screeching brakes and an ear-splitting collision where there are no cars. A phantom ambulance careening out of nowhere, disappearing into nowhere.

He meets a superstitious Mexican who tells him, *"This is the place —
this is the very place where that young señor Dean was killed. It is a very bad
place!"* The Mexican crosses himself. *"It is bad, very bad! He drives that
road every night between sundown and sunrise. It is as though he is looking
for someone."*

GRAVEYARD GHOST

Dean biographer Donald Spoto tells the story of a twenty-five-year-
old Virginia woman by the name of Debi Bottigi who slept on James Dean's
grave on the thirty-fifth anniversary of his death. She reported that the
sound of footsteps gradually became audible through the darkness and the
sighing of the tall cypress trees. "It was Jimmy in his boots," she recounted,
"walking back to his grave."

Spoto says that for months following Jimmy's spectral visitation, hundreds of fans slept at his grave in hopes of his return.

HAUNTED STUDIO

Movie Life magazine published an article by Jane Williams entitled
"Did Jimmy Dean's Spirit Haunt the Studio?" It's a breathless chronicle of
the supernatural events attending the production of Robert Altman's 1957
The James Dean Story. The manifestations include a ghostly cat that appears
on the editor's shoulder in the cutting room; the discovery of film in which
Dean is playing the first four notes of the posthumous documentary's
theme song, two years before it was written; and the rattling of a window
screen. Nerves are understandably frayed by the time the production goes
to the site of Dean's death:

> For months the group working on the picture had been so immersed
> in the Dean saga that when it came time to recreate the scene of the fatal
> car crash, they all felt jumpy about it.
>
> Without intending it, as they neared the actual crash scene it was
> growing dusk. It was just about the time of day that Dean's accident hap-
> pened. Nobody let on to the others what he or she was thinking. The only
> show of outward tension was Judy George's periodic requests, "Please,
> drive slower."
>
> As they neared the corner, that country intersection where the life of
> James Dean was snuffed out in a split second, they could see an old jalopy
> approaching. It came closer, its noisy motor shattering the peaceful twi-
> light. Then, as they reached the corner, the jalopy turned off onto the side
> road.
>
> Bob Altman heaved a great sigh. "Turnipseed's [sic] early tonight,"
> he quipped, easing the tension a little.

THE HIGHWAY UNDER THE LAKE

James Dean left Los Angeles on the day of his death and traveled US Highway 99 along a route that has since been circumvented and rerouted with successive improvements due to the need for an expanded inland route. A driver attempting to retrace the route today would find the old highway ending mysteriously in the deep watery expanse of Pyramid Lake. The lake was created in 1974 and put a significant stretch of the old highway under millions of gallons of water. Few of the skiers and fishermen suspect that beneath the lapping waves of the scenic lake is the route that Dean traveled to his death. To those in the know, however, the fact offers an explanation of some strange apparitions on the emerald waters.

The 1970s and early 1980s were the years of the most common sightings, a haze on the water at dusk or early evening, or the materialization of a glimmering figure walking across the lake. After dark, strange lights coasting or darting across the water were commonly reported.

"Ghost traffic" was the jocular expression of one Pyramid Park ranger shortly before his retirement, in reference to the streams of lights that were sometimes visible atop the water late at night. More objective observers speculated that the dancing lights were actually the reflection of the beams of traffic passing on Interstate 5 on the eastern boundary of the lake. The Pyramid Park resort area is tremendously popular with fishermen and jet skiers from southern California, and the number of recreational visitors gave rise to a frequency of sightings that accelerated in the late summer and fall months of the twentieth anniversary of Dean's death.

"JAMES DEAN SPEAKS FROM THE GRAVE"

So reported Robert DeKolbe in *True Strange* magazine (September 1956):

> Last night I actually talked with Jimmy Dean, and his message was not to me but to all of his present-day mourners. "Tell them," he said, "to stop mourning for me. I am very happy where I am. Here, there is no confusion, no unhappiness, no cold, no hunger. And I have my mother with me, whom I lost when I was only seven years old."

The medium in this case was 33-year-old "sensitive" Anna M. Van Deusen. According to DeKolbe, a séance was arranged in Van Deusen's studio. "Mrs. Van Deusen is a college graduate and anything that smacked of phony or fake would be an insult to her intelligence." Dean's spectral approach is announced by Van Deusen: "Wait! Energy. I'm coming upon great, massive amounts of energy. This will be it, but I'll have to search for him."

The interview has an inauspicious start when Dean misidentifies his birthplace as Marion, Ohio. The death of his mother was a signal event, according to Van Deusen. "Idea of death was planted in his mind. These were the seeds of destruction, which he nursed all his short life. His thoughts were preoccupied with death. But death is nothing more than a cessation of a particular body, the energy lives on...."

Questioned as to the meaning of life, Dean says he believes he was put on earth to symbolize the confusion of young people. Why did he die so young? "That's just it," Van Deusen says. "If he had lived to be older, there would have been no symbol. He'd have just lived in vain. An older person cannot symbolize humanity's suffering, then there might have never been any such thing as Christianity. Dean had to die while still young."

Regarding the death itself, Van Deusen says, "On the fatal day, some-one suggested that Dean 'ride' his racer to the track on a truck. More especially, there was the motorcycle cop who stopped him and gave him that ticket. These were actually energy forces trying to prevent him from dying. But Dean knew his time had come."

JIMMY DEAN RETURNS!

This was the title of a delirious one-shot 1956 magazine from Rave Publishing recounting Jimmy Dean's posthumous confessions psychically transmitted to a shop girl named Judy Collins. No doubt the name disguises the real author. It reportedly had a run of half a million copies.

The turning point for the shop girl turned psychic is the discovery of a book called *You Do Take It with You* by one R. DeWitt Miller, "one of the world's foremost authorities on psychic phenomena," who espoused the bizarre theory of "the second body." Collins wrote, "But what does Mr. Miller's theory of the 'second body' have to do with Jimmy Dean — and with me! ... But I could believe in this new, thrilling idea that the body we see in this existence is not our only body; that, when what we call "death" happens, our physical body is discarded and our other body, our second body, takes over."

Jimmy begins to communicate through her by automatic writing, apparently possessing her hand.

"Yes, Judy, I can speak to you in this way.... The crash itself was nothing. I felt no shock. No hurt. I could see myself lying there. This was what we called death. But it wasn't Death. The other body that lay down there was only a shell. I, the real I who inhabited it, was still alive...."

LARRABEE HOUSE

The Larrabee Street home of Maila Nurmi in West Hollywood was haunted by James Dean, according to an article she wrote in *Borderline* magazine (Volume 1, no. 4, 1964). During a séance at which eight people were present, including actor John Franco, the phone rang. But Nurmi herself had cut the lines several days earlier. One woman fainted, and everyone was frightened. Wrote Nurmi, "Jimmy often visited me after this incident — and continued to make his presence felt for about four months," usually by starting a spontaneous fire in an ashtray. She says she eventually moved to get away from it all. In the same article, she also predicted Tony Perkins would be the "new" James Dean. *See* "Black Madonna."

THE PHANTOM HITCHHIKER

Sometimes the coastal fog sweeps inland, resulting in prime conditions along Highway 46 for the sighting of the Phantom Hitchhiker — James Dean. This apparition has been reported on the lonely stretch of the highway between the little settlement of Lost Hills and the intersection where the crash occurred. In most versions of this story, a family station wagon coast-bound on vacation sees a dim figure on the roadside, apparently the victim of a breakdown on the desolate road. The father at the wheel of the wagon passes the figure and then is persuaded by his wife to go back and help. When they slow to talk to the person, they see a young man in bloodied clothes and with severe head injuries— whom they nevertheless recognize as James Dean. He promptly vanishes.

In a more grisly variant of this story, the family picks up the hitchhiker and is ferrying him to a gas station. The father at the wheel of the car inquires whether he was hurt badly in the accident. At that point the hitchhiker tells them that he has a broken neck. His head falls sickeningly backwards, and the wife and children begin to scream. The wagon careens off the road and overturns. In the aftermath, the hitchhiker is nowhere to be found. A helpful police officer tells the family that their passenger was James Dean, who frequently appears on the road looking for a ride into town.

Dean devotee Mark Kinnaman reports, "I had a truck driver write me and tell me that he passed a hitchhiker in the same California desert that looked just like James Dean, complete with white T-shirt, jeans and red jacket. But when he stopped to pick him up, he was nowhere to be found. The trucker got out of his truck and searched, but had no explanation as to where the young man had gone. He told me that he had an eerie feeling that he had just seen a ghost.

...I get many of the same stories. Usually, in the California desert, a silver sports car with racing numbers painted on the side passes people driving along at 75 mph; the sports car passes them and then disappears about a mile ahead of them. I personally have received at least 20 accounts of this same scenario and not one has brought any tangible proof or sent me any pictures."

POLTERGEISTS

The sleepy Texas town of Marfa came briefly to glamorous life when the crew of *Giant* came to town. A huge mansion was built on the flats outside of town, and miniature oil derricks dotted the plains. Every room in the Hotel El Paisano was booked. The little ranching town of almost four thousand souls was never to see the likes of such activity again. A pile of rubble marks the site of the mansion constructed for the film. The Old Borunda Cafe, where Liz Taylor had a few meals, is closed down, as is the Palace Theater, where locals viewed released Dean films during the shooting.

But it is still a mecca for intrepid Dean fans because it is where he spent the last two months of his life, making the film that garnered him an Academy Award nomination. The Clay Evans ranch, where the mansion stood, is private property, but Dean fans have occasionally finagled private tours.

One such female visitor came to Marfa with the intention of driving out to the filming location. Her problems began the night she checked into El Paisano, whose lobby boasts some of the movie memorabilia — autographed pictures and articles — commemorating the time when the army of technicians came to town.

The woman experienced strange pressure zones within the room, and she felt someone next to her in the dark. Dogs barked mysteriously all night — mysteriously, because there were no dogs below the window. En route to the bathroom, the guest encountered a strange mass, which did not want to let her pass.

Needless to say, she cut her visit short and checked out first thing the next morning. The lady at the register said she had had no other reports of such occurrences, and seemed a trifle annoyed.

SEX WITH A GHOST

TV Star Parade magazine (1970) did a feature article on "Mod Squad" television starlet Peggy Lipton that described her unique problem. "Peggy Lipton's Dilemma: She's in Love with a Dead Man!" recalled her hippie days when she moved into a commune in Topanga Canyon. The article stated, "One night, after an evening spent with a close friend of Jimmy's, Peggy went to bed and had what seemed like an extraordinarily vivid dream in which Jimmy came and made love to her. But it was not exactly a dream, because when she 'woke up' Jimmy was still there, sitting in her bedroom speaking to her.

"This was the first of a long series of nocturnal visits in which Jimmy came to her bedroom, made love to her, and conversed with her as a friend and as a lover."

SPIRIT LIGHT

In *Borderline Magazine* (Vol. 1, no. 4, 1964), Maila "Vampire" Nurmi told the story of hearing of James Dean's death, and the accompanying "unearthly light."

She said that in her house on Larrabee Street in Hollywood, one day at about 5:45 she witnessed an "unearthly" light filling her living room. Jack Simmons, who was with her, was spooked by the light and wanted to leave. Nurmi and Simmons left, although Nurmi didn't want to; she said the light was "excruciatingly beautiful."

They returned in 15 minutes with the actor Tony Perkins. At 6:12, Nurmi got the phone call that Dean was dead. She immediately thought of the light: "I was later told that the light is classic and is called a 'spirit light.' That light had a roseate incandescence I cannot define ... but it was noticeable, distinctive and stirring." Nurmi explained that her drapes were closed in the living room as usual so where the light originated from physically she couldn't say.

However, she said, "Believers in the supernatural say that when a person is about to experience a bereavement, a spirit guide arrives shortly beforehand to speak to the subconscious mind of the about-to-be-bereaved. This spirit is called a teacher and brings with him a beautiful supernatural light." Nurmi said that the light, which occurred in her house at the exact time of Dean's accident, frightened Jack Simmons because he was a highly materialistic person who did not have the spiritual development to appreciate it. "I marveled that anyone could find such an obviously beautiful thing unpleasant," she added.

Giant, the record

This is the musical soundtrack of the film released by Capitol Records in 1956 and composed and conducted by Hollywood legend Dimitri Tiomkin, whose evocative and powerful work supports dozens of films from *It's a Wonderful Life* to *Rio Bravo*.

Gilman, Aaron

He is the Grant County deputy sheriff who broke the case of the third theft of James Dean's tombstone, when he smashed into it in the dark on State Road 28, tearing the transmission out of his patrol car. One of the Dean websites reported on the recovery of the marker, warning, "Remember, people could have been killed hitting that stone on the highway. You never know what might be out there and we don't want to lose a Dean fan, ever."

Gilmore, John

Gilmore's first book on James Dean was *The Real James Dean,* which was touted, against Gilmore's wishes, with the words "a lover of both women, and men." Gilmore is also the author of *Cold Blooded,* about Tucson Pied Piper murderer Gary Schmidt; *The Garbage People,* on the Manson family; *Severed,* the story of the murder of the Black Dahlia; and *Laid Bare,* Hollywood memoirs. With *Live Fast — Die Young: Remembering the Short Life of James Dean,* he returned to the subject of James Dean and wrote,

> It was a period of exploration. It wasn't so much a physical thing. Jimmy said it was probably possible for him to have a relationship with a guy, too — to have a physical exchange without it being labeled "homosexual," because he felt it was simply an extension of the friendship. "Just going to the edge of the friendship or sort of beyond it," Jimmy said.

"The Girl James Dean Was Going to Marry" *see* marriage

glasses

An extraordinary to-do was made at the James Dean inquest over his glasses. Extraordinary because there was no groundwork laid for the inquiry in a proceeding notable for its lack of interest in the actions of the driver of the Ford. The driver of the Ford invaded Dean's lane in an illegal left turn without a signal, yet the focus of the questioning returned again and again to the issue of whether Jimmy was wearing his glasses. The subject came up more than twenty times in the inquest.

For instance, when the attending physician testified as to the cause of death, the coroner immediately turned the questioning over to the assistant district attorney, who asked, "Doctor, there were no signs of any glasses or anything on Mr. Dean at the time you examined him, were there?" From the leading way this question is framed, it's obvious that the DA's office planned to make the case that Dean was not wearing his glasses.

The next police officer to testify told about Dean's restricted driver's license and that he had to wear corrective lenses. The assistant DA asked, "Did you see any physical evidence of glasses?" The cop had seen a piece of glasses at the crash site, the stem which attaches over the ear, but had not saved it and did not know where it was. Tom Frederick had been driving behind the Ford, and he was also asked whether he saw any glasses in the area of the crash. The officer who had ticketed Dean was asked whether Dean was wearing glasses. Wuetherich, in his hospital bed, was asked whether Dean had worn glasses as he drove and answered that he had.

Donald Dooley caused a stir when he piped up, "I seen some glasses near the Porsche." He was promptly sworn in and told about seeing some yellow glasses on the pavement after the accident. Under questioning, he said they were more like goggles.

The coroner's report on Dean's death also made the point that no glasses were found on Dean, and neither the mortician nor the doctor had examined Dean's eyes for contact lenses.

Candid photograph of James Dean wearing his glasses (courtesy Marfa Public Library, Marfa, Texas).

glue

The Marion, Indiana, *Chronicle-Tribune* of June 1985 reported that a monument company would donate a headstone to replace the one stolen from James Dean's grave two years earlier. This one would be more high-tech. It would be "bolted with steel rods and attached to the base with a space-age glue." The new stone's lettering would also be etched more deeply, making it more difficult to chip off.

Nonetheless, the stone was stolen again in July of 1998.

See also Gilman, Aaron.

GMT Studios

The initials stand for "Great and Mighty Things," which reflects the born-again Christianity of studio owner Alan Hauge. Located on Buckingham Parkway in Culver City, the studio has been headquarters to Hauge's long-standing attempt to bring to the screen an authorized biography of James Dean. The first incarnations of the project were hampered by con man Jon Emr, Hauge's partner, who skimmed investor money from the project's accounts. Since Emr's 1991 murder by a disgruntled former bodyguard who had also invested in the project, Hauge has continued on alone, and persistently. He makes frequent trips to Indiana, and claims to have traveled 4,000 miles alone on the quest to find a suitable location site for the filming of Jimmy's rural car crash. (He decided on a spot outside Taft, California.)

See also Hauge, Alan.

Golden, Carrie

This Herlong, California, native was thirty-one years old in 1955 when she encountered the racing ambulance carrying Dean's body to the hospital in Paso Robles. She slowed suddenly and veered to the right. The driver behind her, John Hiatt, foolishly tried to pass on the left and sideswiped the ambulance.

Gore, Christian

Author of a one-shot magazine entitled September 30, 1955 Never Happened, which appeared in 1988.

Grant, Lilly

Lilly Grant was postmistress at Cholame, stationed in the tiny little office that had been the foreman's shack when the road crew had built Highway 46 in the twenties. Because of her stationary position, many of the people who visited the Dean crash site brought their questions to her. Seita Ohnishi, the Japanese businessman who eventually erected a Dean monument at Cholame, wrote her: "Dear Mrs. Grant, It is with great pleasure to inform you that you would understand my thinking about Jimmy Dean Memory establishing in your town." She really didn't understand what he meant, but his letter became the first entry pasted into the scrapbooks she began to keep.

She wrote back to Ohnishi and encouraged him with his project. She told Warren Beath in an interview: "At first, he wanted to have a garden around the monument, but we have mineral water here and we don't have flowers as such. So he settled on a rock garden. The rocks were shipped here from Tokyo in 50 pound bags."

With the uncrating of the 1,863-pound memorial came a peculiar kind of national and international recognition for the postmistress of Cholame. She received letters and phone calls from all over the world. "People write me and ask me about the monument," she said. "What am I supposed to do, drop 'em into the wastebasket?" At least 10 people visit the monument daily, she remembered. Some leave mementos: a single red rose, a license plate, a pebble from Fairmount, Indiana.

"Even musicians come.... They must be into rock, from the way they look. But they speak just like you and I."

grave

After Dean's burial in Fairmount, Indiana, the James Dean Foundation received numerous letters begging for a mere blade of grass or piece of sod from the grave. As many as 500 people a day were visiting the cemetery a year after the funeral. Visitors included a young, pre-stardom Jean Seberg. The tombstone was stolen twice from the grave in the 1980s, and again in the 1990s. Bob Dylan made a late-night pilgrimage to the grave when he was playing in Indianapolis.

In 1993 a Japanese family and six friends came from Japan to perform a ceremony, replete with pictures, mirrors and incense, to unite the spirit of their son, an actor who had been killed in a filming accident, with that of James Dean. Several locals attended the ritual. The Japanese then reportedly donated $10,000 for Fairmount's monument to James Dean, which was eventually erected in town.

grave robbing

In his 1958 novel *The Immortal*, Walter Ross imagined a news release:

> AP Bulletin, January 1, 1959:
> An epidemic of teenage violence and law-breaking that began on New Year's Eve culminated early this morning with the opening of the grave of John Preston, late motion-picture star, and the near-fatal beating of the cemetery watchman, 70-year-old Mr. Goldsmith.
> The violence began late yesterday, according to local officials, when a caravan of hotrods and motorcycles, driven by leather-jacketed and blue-jeaned teenagers from at least six States, descended on this small town.
> According to the eyewitness account of Mr. Goldsmith, now in a critical condition in hospital, the entire group gathered at Preston's grave and began a ceremony whose meaning has not been interpreted.
> The ringleader, an unidentified youth of about 19 or 20, held a large knife, and, as each boy or girl walked by the grave, he or she bared the right forearm, which was then slashed enough to draw blood.
> Each then waited until several drops of blood fell to the ground, then walked on. The witness overheard a statement that this was "Johnny's knife."
> When Goldsmith came up and asked what they were doing, one boy said: "Go away, pops, before the spirit moves us and behooves us."
> Goldsmith remonstrated, saying that they were desecrating hallowed ground. "Why don't you let the boy rest in peace?" he asked.

A pony-tailed girl in black skin-tight jeans and a black turtle-neck sweater jumped in front of Goldsmith and screamed, "Because he ain't dead, that's why." She then attacked Goldsmith with her fists, and the others joined in.

By the time Goldsmith came to, the grave was empty.

Ross's novel was purchased by Metro Goldwyn Mayer but never brought to the screen. George Hamilton had been proposed in the title role of self-absorbed, self-destructive actor "Johnny Preston," who dies a premature and violent death that elevates him to cult status with his bereaved fans.

Dean biographer John Howlett wrote:

There are still those who claim that the grave in Fairmount is empty: that Dean was not buried; or if he was buried, that his body was stolen by night soon after the funeral when the earth was still freshly dug. The intention had certainly been expressed, and the local police mounted a night and day guard on the cemetery for several weeks after the funeral. Later, when a memorial was put up to Dean outside the cemetery, the plinth was cut down and stolen.

"The Great Original"

The title of an article by Charles Robinson which appeared in the December 1957 issue of *The New Statesman*. It concerns a Briton who had his name legally changed to James Byron Dean. Robinson wrote:

Mr. Dean, who comes from Catford, recently changed his name by deed poll, since he believes most sincerely that he is controlled by the spirit of the late actor. Something very remarkable has undoubtedly occurred to him, he would be the first to agree. Mr. Dean is shortly off to Fairmount, Indiana, the Birthplace, where he hopes to open a home for juvenile delinquents. About fifteen years older than his namesake, with a shock of bright yellow hair, Mr. Dean is not a person one forgets easily.

Griffith Park

A prominent setting in the movie *Rebel Without a Cause*, Griffith Park was a gift to Los Angeles County from Colonel Griffith J. Griffith in atonement for his attempted murder of his wife in a Santa Monica motel room. He believed she was under the control of the pope and the Catholic Church, that all of them were plotting to poison him and get his fortune. He handed her a Protestant prayer book, made her swear that she had been faithful, then shot her in the eye. He then tossed her out the window. She survived to testify at his trial. He was sent to San Quentin for two years. To rehabilitate his civic image, he donated the observatory to the townsfolk. Construction commenced in 1935. The site is the second highest peak in the Hollywood Hills. The Colonel's bust is in the lobby.

See also curses.

Grundell, Herbert

Herbert Catherwood Grundell was the district attorney of San Luis Obispo County at the time of the inquest into the death of James Dean. He participated in the questioning of witnesses. He died in 1976 at the age of 79.

Gunn, Bill

Bill Gunn was Jimmy's friend in life, and perhaps even beyond. After Dean's death, Gunn was fighting a high temperature when Jimmy returned to him in a dream with a message: "Beware of Death. He has sharp teeth."

Guzak, Eddie

Retired policeman who in 1990 told journalist Ron Smith of a late-night encounter with James Dean outside Competition Motors on September 16, 1955. Guzak was responding to a concerned citizen's call about a break-in in progress when he found James Dean before the chain-link fence, admiring the Porsche Spyder.

Guzak told Smith, "I asks him what he's doing there, and all polite-like he answers me that he wants to buy a car, and I says to him that he has to wait until they open. He wasn't drunk or nothin' like that, and just as polite as he could be, but he just had to see his car. You work as a cop in Hollywood long enough, you see everything. But this was totally different. I give him a ride up to Hollywood and Vine and tell him to get on home."

H

Haffey, Chester

Chet Haffey was twenty-two years old, recently out of the service and en route to Bakersfield from San Miguel, when he came upon the results of the James Dean car accident at the intersections of 41 and 466 on September 30, 1955. Though he was at the scene only five minutes, he was captured in three of the famous Sanford Roth photos of the wrecked car. In black shirt and Levis, the blond Haffey is visible standing before the injured Wuetherich. It had long been assumed by many that the figure in the black shirt was Donald Turnupseed.

Haffey drove on and thought little more of that day until nearly fifty years later when he saw a picture of himself at the scene in a car magazine. He recalled the wreck but had not known it was the collision in which James Dean had died. His daughter came forward, interested only in obtaining a copy of the photo for her father.

Haffey worked as a teamster and in special effects for MGM for over thirty years, working on countless television shows. His last assignment was *Baywatch*.

hair

Art Bean claimed to be the owner of a black leather jacket that Dean bought to impress Marlon Brando. While going through the pockets of Jimmy's jacket he found a four-inch strand of Dean's hair. Bean, who claimed to have also found a pack of Chesterfields in the coat, said the hair had been cut off by Dean himself as a keepsake for Pier Angeli. He said he declined the offer of $1,000 to buy the priceless artifact.

See also Bean, Art.

Hampton Inns

The Hampton Inns have a Web site listing hundreds of offbeat American landmarks that are near their hotels. Among the landmarks mentioned is the Dean crash site near Cholame, California. By logging on to hampton-landmarks.com, travelers can search for spots of interest in several categories including music, celebrities and American History. In addition to the Dean site, there are other death places to visit such as the Tennessee forest where Patsy Cline's plane crashed, Kurt Cobain's Seattle suicide house and the motel where Sam Cooke was shot to death.

Hansen, McCormick, Barstow & Sheppard

The Fresno, California, attorneys who represented Donald Turnupseed in his defense of the suit brought by Rolf Wuetherich. McCormick attended the deposition of Turnupseed held in Fresno in 1958.

Harvey, Xen

Harvey gave the eulogy at Dean's funeral on October 8, 1955 — a eulogy entitled "A Drama in Three Acts." The closing line was "The career of

James Dean has not ended. It has just begun. And remember, God himself is directing the production."

Hauge, Alan

A born-again Christian and owner of GMT Studios in Culver City. The initials stand for "Great and Mighty Things," a biblical quotation that aptly describes his epic campaign to bring to the screen an authorized biography of his hero, James Dean. Perhaps "autobiography" might be more accurate, as Dean's cousin, Marcus Winslow, has made Hauge privy to Jimmy's private Hollywood diary. As Hauge tells it, Winslow allowed him a peek at the diary as a test to see whether he was honorable enough to be trusted with the project—for which Hauge had already bought the rights anyway. Hauge did not release the contents of the diary to the press, so presumably he passed the test.

Not that he had anything to worry about, really. Alone among those vying for anointment by the family, Hauge promised to deliver to filmgoers what author Rod Lurie called, in his account of the entire saga, "the heterosexual, father-loving Jimmy."

Hauge met originally with would-be producer Loren Pike, who believed he could round up investment money if he could secure Hauge's studio as distributor. Hauge became fascinated with the Dean project and paid Pike $25,000 for the distribution rights to the film — which Pike had already lost to another man for failure to pay back the loan with which he had originally bought the rights from the management group controlling the Dean estate.

Hauge eventually traveled to Indiana and tried to quell Marcus Winslow's fears that a film might portray Jimmy as a homosexual and show him "flailing around" in a depiction of the car accident. According to Lurie, Winslow also said to Hauge, "I'm going to give you twenty-two letters that Jimmy wrote home. I don't want to see them in the *National Enquirer*. I don't want you to spread them all over Hollywood. I just want to give you more insight into Jimmy."

Hauge lived up to the confidence reposed in him, not even showing the letters to his wife. Hauge also made a trailer for the proposed film, featuring young Dean lookalike actor Damien Chapa, and, as extras, members of the James Dean fan club. The trailer was market-tested in Arizona, Florida, Nevada, and Los Angeles, with apparently positive results. Hauge felt the results justified his own request that he direct any proposed project, despite his lack of directing experience.

Relations soured when a payment for retention of the option came due, but eventually Pike signed over option rights to a con man named Jon Emr, who had insinuated himself into Alan Hauge's dream project. In addition to paying what the family said Hauge owed them on the other option, Emr paid $150,000 for a new option. Unhappily, Emr's involvement was only his oft-pulled scam to skim money off investors he brought in. The Dean family became quickly disillusioned with the volatile Emr, who was eventually assassinated by his own bodyguard on a street in broad daylight.

Hauge emerged unscathed from the debacle, and since that time has continued to cultivate relations with the family, pay for the option on the story, and scout locations for the proposed film, despite its unhappy record to date.

Hawaiian aloha shirt, "The Rebel"

Produced by Reyn Spooner, this 100 percent rayon shirt was produced in size XL and featured James Dean in a variety of poses among Hawaiian floral motifs.

Hayashi Family

The family of a young Japanese actor who was a great James Dean fan before he died while filming a picture. The Hayashi Family gave $10,000 toward the monument to James Dean erected in the James Dean Memorial Park on Main Street in Fairmount, Indiana. At one side of the brick wall at the entrance is a bronze plaque to commemorate the young Japanese actor. The Hayashi family came to America to perform a ceremony over Dean's grave, involving mirrors, incense and incantations—plus a red windbreaker—to unite their dead son's spirit with Jimmy's.

hearse

Maila Nurmi claimed that Jimmy liked to do stunts in the headlights of her Cadillac hearse as they cruised at night. She told Warren Beath in an interview:

> Jack Simmons and I would ride up Sunset Plaza Drive on our way to Jimmy's apartment of a night. It would be midnight or later—empty streets—Jack and I in the front seat of the Caddy hearse—Jack driving—leading the way was Jimmy on his red motorcycle (Indian, I believe) right on the white line center divider. Hands above his head—Jimmy would "hula" his hips to make the cycle dip from side to side—Jimmy's thighs scraping the road. If a car came around a curve, on its way down—Jimmy had no control over his cycle—or of us—directly behind him. I would

scream for him to stop. He would turn his head back and laugh. We had to pull over and stop to force him to stop. The open road was a stage for him, we were his audience and our headlights his footlight. He fumed when we closed the show.

Hell-Fire Club

The original hell-fire clubs were aristocratic Satan-worshipers in the eighteenth century who met in abandoned monasteries to perform forbidden rituals as a prelude to sexual orgies. King George denounced them in an edict of 1721. The Bold Backs, Demoniacs, Dublin Blasters, and the Edinburgh Sweating Club kept up their activities despite royal disapproval. Membership included the Earl of Sandwich and the First Lord of the Admiralty, plus sundry members of Parliament. Some eventually rose to the highest levels of government, including prime minister. Their ceremonies were based on the Black Mass.

Hollywood, as one of the hedonistic capitals of the world, saw the descendants of these clubs as the inevitable import of European expatriates, starting in the twenties. In the forties, the sex ring of Lionel Atwill was disclosed when a young female participant from the Midwest turned up pregnant. But the popularity of these rings, where young and not-so-young men with jaded palates sought forbidden experience, survives to this day. The fifties saw them take on a bohemian cast as the revels of the likes of Errol Flynn recovered some of the darker satanic cast that had excited the Victorians.

Persistent Sunset Strip rumormongers over the decades had enlisted Jimmy Dean, who boasted, "Why live with one hand tied behind your back?" as a member of a beatnik Hollywood Hell-Fire Club composed largely of young artists and actors. Driven more by caffeine than by alcohol, they carried out satanic dawn patrol. Existentialist in philosophy, their rationale was that life was short, so one should live it to the hilt. Experience everything, for your art.

Meeting in the Hollywood Hills, or in parking lots after hours, they tried to exceed one another in a quest for bizarre experience which often led them to Hollywood Memorial Park Cemetery for sloppy Black Masses—which usually terminated with pissing on prominent graves of movie moguls and Hollywood pioneers—or to partner-swapping parties at someone's pad.

Stump-rubbing with amputees was an experience at a premium, despite a shortage of amputees. Dwarves figure prominently in some of the sexual adventures. The Venice Beach pier was a popular rendezvous, and readings from occult texts provided a pseudo-intellectual veneer to activities that really seem like a lot of young wannabe ne'er-do-wells blowing off steam and trying to impress each other.

Jimmy Dean had a penchant for recording people secretly with a small microphone, and legend has him taping some of these sexual sessions—which tapes were later stolen from his bungalow after his death, for obvious reasons.

helmet

After Dean's death, his racing helmet was purchased by a Pasadena woman, Mary Moron. She paid $30, but today it would fetch possibly seven to ten thousand dollars.

Heroic Love

James Dean's best film experience was with Nicholas Ray, who allowed him to be virtual co-director of *Rebel Without a Cause*. Near the end of his life, according to John Francis Kreidl in his biography *Nicholas Ray*, the dying director claimed he and Dean had a project in development at the time of Dean's death.

"The last time I saw James Dean," recalled Ray, "was when he arrived without warning at my Hollywood home, about 3 o'clock in the morning.... That evening we had met for dinner. We talked for several hours of many things, of future plans, including a story called *Heroic Love* that we were going to do."

What was this story?

A boy (James Dean) returns from the war. He's standing on the train platform in a small western town, and there to meet him is his hero, a distinguished attorney. Dean's father and mother have died during the war, leaving him a ranch in which he has no interest. He wants to become a lawyer and study under this man. The attorney is moved by this, and invites Dean to stay at his home. The attorney is married to a much younger woman, who tries to seduce Dean, who rejects her. In revenge, she makes love to the attorney's junior partner in the law office — and Dean catches them in the act.

But he doesn't say a word about it. Instead, he begins a rampage of seducing every young girl in town. All the local mothers are up in arms, but they're secretly jealous if their daughters have been passed over by Dean.

Meanwhile, a Chinese cook goes berserk, kills three men, but is saved from lynching by Dean and the attorney.

Eventually, the wife accuses Dean of trying to seduce her. The husband—knowing she's been having an affair with *someone*—assumes she's telling the truth. He calls Dean to the public square and horsewhips him out of town. Dean stoically maintains his silence.

Kreidl believes this bizarre plot derived from the emotionally complex relationship between Dean and Ray.

Hiatt, John

Hiatt was driving eastbound on 466 when the car in front of him (driven by Carrie Golden, 31) slowed for the approaching ambulance bearing Dean's body to the hospital. Hiatt tried to pass that car on the left and sideswiped the ambulance, causing only slight damage.

Hickman, Bill

Dying of cancer in the early eighties, the affable Bill Hickman still experienced intense emotions whenever he thought about two particular events from the day James Dean died. Hickman was driving Jimmy's 1955 Ford wagon behind the Spyder when he came upon the crash. Over twenty-five years later he was still incensed that Jimmy's body had been rolled by the ambulance attendants, and by the fact that Sanford Roth had taken pictures at the crash site rather than attending to the victims. He said that he had yelled at Sanford Roth, "Stop, you sonofabitch! Help me!" when he saw Roth unfurling his camera. Hickman also said that Dean had died in his arms, that he had felt the breath leaving his nose.

Bill Hickman's family was involved in the motion picture industry. His father was the director Charlie Hickman, who had made pictures as early as 1927 and was 20 years with MGM. His father's cousin was character actor Howard Hickman.

Bill played Clark Gable's mechanic in the racing picture *To Please a Lady* in 1950, and he continued to do stunts and develop into a leading stunt driver. He was coordinator of stunts at NBC for two years. His closest industry friends were Jane Deacy, Dean's former agent, and actor George C. Scott, to whom he had become close during the filming of *The Flim-Flam Man*.

Despite the risks he took in cars, he said the worst injury he received was during the making of *The Red Badge of Courage*, when a straw pierced his inner ear after he fell into a haystack. He wouldn't work with horses after a bad experience on the television show *Bonanza*. "Don't mess with horses," he told Warren Beath in an interview. "You can't control them!"

But he could control cars. He drove against Steve McQueen in the classic car chase in *Bullit*, and followed that astounding sequence with the astonishing car chase in *The French Connection*. He largely withdrew from the industry after *The 7-Ups*. "Three films with Phil d'Antonioni, and him taking all the credit," he explained as his reason.

He was in semi-retirement when, on a speedboat off Catalina, he hit a wave at 60 miles per hour. The seat hit his tailbone. "I lost my back," he said of the result. It was the end of his stunt driving.

He said that Jimmy called him Big Bastard, and that he had warned Dean to slow down at Blackwell's Corner — to watch out for the cars turning in front of him in the dusk. He followed the ambulance with Dean's body on its way to the hospital, and then to the funeral home after Dean was declared dead. The death of Jimmy Dean was something from which he never completely recovered.

He never saw Sanford Roth again.

Hickman contracted cancer in the early 1980s and had difficulty speaking, his tongue burned by the radiation treatments. Even in such ill health, he was a gentleman and unfailingly kind, and it speaks well of James Dean that he had such friends.

highway patrol investigation

In 1970 patrolman Ernie Tripke sent Warren Beath an account from *West Coast Sports Car Journal*. He said, "It is authentic."

> At approximately 5:45 P.M. at the intersection of Highways 41 and 466, about 28 miles east of the City of Paso Robles, the checkered flag dropped for Jimmy Dean. Westbound on Highway 466, he collided with a Ford driven by Mr. Turnupseed, eastbound on 466 and making a left turn off Highway 41. Neither vehicle had headlights on — they were not required at this time. The Spyder was equipped with one safety belt, which was not in use at this time. The passenger seat had no belt. The mechanic, Rolf Wuetherich, was thrown out of the car — Dean's feet became entangled in the clutch and brake pedals, preventing him from being thrown, even so, he was lifted from the seat and thrown backwards over the car, his right hip was resting on the cowl, lying on his back with his head hanging over the right door. Wuetherich was found about five feet from the left side of the Spyder. It was unknown how far he was thrown as the Spyder traveled 45 feet after the point of impact.

According to testimony taken at the inquest, both Dean and Hickman, pulling the trailer, were cited for 65 mph in a 45 mph zone on Wheeler Ridge (US 99 south of Bakersfield) at 3:30 P.M. The distance from Wheeler Ridge to the scene of the accident is 108 miles. When one figures in the time required for Dean to pass through Bakersfield at peak traffic plus about a 15-minute stop at Blackwell's Corner and the time consumed in writing the ticket by Officer Hunter, the timing works out.

Hinkle, "Texas" Bob

"The man who taught James Dean to use his lasso," he calls himself. *Giant* includes a memorable scene where Dean toys with a lasso in a bit of shameless scene-stealing, and Hinkle says he's the one who gave Jimmy his chops on the rope. He was dialogue and technical director of the set of *Giant*. He used to go rabbit shooting with Dean on location. At the end of filming, Dean gave Hinkle an honorary Oscar engraved with his name. Hinkle is a sunny presence, feted at fan get-togethers. His "Oscar" is in the Fairmount (Indiana) Historical Museum.

"His Love Destroyed Him..."

The venerable William F. Nolan published the first, and still the best, article on Dean's love affairs with cars in *Modern Screen* of February 1957:

> He loved the cold, swift rush of wind against his face, the blur of road under the spinning wheels of his Porsche, the intoxicating breath of danger as trees and rocks and brush blended into a single dark line to either side; he loved the high, rich music of the straining engine, the steadiness of the racing wheel under his hands, the free, soaring sense of power over time and space as he drifted along sweeping curves. James Byron Dean loved the world of speed, and...
>
> HIS LOVE DESTROYED HIM...

The biographical parts are de rigueur and pedestrian, but the article is a near contemporary account of Dean's racing career, promoting the actor's identification with cars and racing.

Hodgson, Jeff

Jeff Hodgson sells his unique James Dean crash-scene models on the Internet. They are faithful reproductions of the legendary intersection complete with crumpled cars, asphalt, road signs and topographical detail. Jeff is a California fire captain whose interest in Dean began in high school, but it was when he visited the Cholame crash scene in 1989 that he was inspired to create his unique memorials. Jeff says, "I have the need to express and create and what I create may seem dark, macabre, or in bad taste to some, but I find that others embrace it. I do it to keep his image and spirit alive in people's hearts and minds."

Fans who are interested in one of Hodgson's crash scene models can reach him at harleyhodge@adelphia.net.

Hollywood Forever

This gothic necropolis in the heart of Hollywood at Santa Monica and Gower is the final resting place of screen immortals Valentino and Douglas Fairbanks Sr. It's also home to such ne'er-do-wells as Bugsy Seigel. Bordered by the industrial-looking soundstages of Paramount Studios, it is a stop on the Gravelines tours. Few realize that if one intrepid entrepreneur had had his way, it would also have been the resting place of a relocated Jimmy Dean, and home to an extremely interesting monument.

"Help Build Jimmy's Memorial" went the entreaty circulated by Bill Dakota in the 1980s in his quest for donations. Lamenting that there was no Hollywood monument celebrating Dean's achievement, he set about correcting the situation by raising money for a most unique project. The James Dean memorial would be "a bronze statue, seven-feet tall, finished in 23 carat gold leaf. It will be on a black granite base, with Jimmy's name etched in gold. Three black granite curved columns will form a backdrop for the statue and on each column will be etchings relating to the three films he starred in. The memorial will be located in Hollywood at the Hollywood Memorial Park Cemetery, near the Douglas Fairbanks crypt and memorial."

The artist for the project was to have been four-time national high jump champion Ernie Shelton, the creator of the dinosaur for the film *Baby, the Legend.*

"Jimmy has been gone thirty years," Dakota's flyers read. "Don't you think it's about time we did something?" He said he had raised money from Dick Clayton, Burt Reynolds and Sammy Davis, Jr. On a trip to Fairmount, Indiana, where Dean is buried, he also pursued the idea of relocating Jimmy's remains. The family evinced no interest. But it was the intervention of Jimmy's licensing agency, Curtis Management, that put an end to the visionary project. They objected to anyone raising money using Jimmy's name. The project foundered in the ensuing lawsuit.

In recent years, Hollywood Forever has fallen under hard times, receding into serious disrepair and bankruptcy.

homosexuality

Dean's sexuality is the most hotly contested topic of his brief life. Joe Hyams in his biography *Little Boy Lost* says that Dean was initiated into homosexuality at an early age by the Reverend DeWeerd, his mentor and a local eccentric who was into bullfighting, yoga and yogurt. Dean reportedly announced his homosexuality to the Draft Board to avoid conscription. (*See* draft board.) Hollywood producer Rogers Brackett claimed (in an interview with Ron Martinetti for the book *The James Dean Story*) that Dean was sexually involved with him. Dean had several homosexual roommates and one of them — Jack Simmons — reportedly performed necrophilic sex on him after his death. (*See* Necrophilia.)

The most explicit claim of Dean's homosexuality comes from writer John Gilmore, who has made a minor literary cottage industry out of his friendship with James Dean. In 1976's *The Real James Dean* and in 1997's *Live Fast, Die Young* he describes in great detail his friendship with James Dean, and their sexual encounters, which commence as a sort of extension of friendship.

The problem is there is little to indicate that Gilmore knew Dean, and aside from his own claims, no verification of any sexual relationship. There are no pictures of the two of them, though Gilmore has claimed to have pictures taken by Dean. Gilmore also claims to have had sex with Janis Joplin. His books, in fact, contain extraordinarily entertaining encounters with any celebrity that seems to pop into his mind — including Jim Morrison, Hank Williams, Elvis and the Black Dahlia.

The weight of reliable evidence indicates that Dean was bisexual. He had relations with both men and women.

honeymooners

In late August, a couple of honeymooners visiting Indianapolis hired a taxi to transport them on a 130-mile round trip to Fairmount just to see James Dean's grave and the Fairmount Historical Museum, which houses Dean memorabilia. One local cab firm estimated the cost of the trip at more than $100.

But the trip to Fairmount was a small hop compared to their original point of departure — Kyoto, Japan." — The *Indianapolis Star*, September 22, 1985.

Hord, Clifford

A local farmer who, with his wife and two children, was on his way to a football game when Dean's Spyder forced his car off the road. Dean was trying to pass slower traffic and misjudged the speed of oncoming cars. Hord was forced onto the shoulder in a maneuver that shook his family. He was interviewed by the authorities because the incident happened shortly before Dean's fatal collision.

November 21, 1981

CLIFFORD HORD: "We were on our way to the football game in Bakersfield. I was driving a Pontiac. Had seven of them in a row. The two younger kids were in the back, the boy and the girl. The older one, Phil, was behind us. After they passed, I thought first thing, I'm glad Phil's behind us. He was the first one to stop at the crash.

"I saw him (Dean) coming down the hill. There's two hills. It was at the second one. Where there are four trees. He was going west, coming around this other car. I said, 'Look at this Son of a Bitch! I ran off the side of the road, onto the dirt. There were three of us abreast."

MRS. HORD: "I was sewing this black lace shawl for my daughter. It was fine points, with hooks and detail. I couldn't go back to it. You don't forget something like that. You remember every detail. The thing I never will forget was that Dean and the German boy were grinning at us from ear to ear."

MR. HORD: "It was less than a mile east. It was just behind us that he crashed. Phil was the first one to stop. There was a nurse in the second car. She looked at him and said, He's dead."

MRS. HORD: "We drove on to Lost Hills. Phil drove up, honking, and told us about the accident."

MR. HORD: "Word got around that he'd run us off the road. So I was subpoenaed to the inquest."

MRS. HORD: "The insurance underwriter came with him. He was just in town, and he said, "I'll go with you to visit the Hords' — to the sheriff. He said, 'Boy, if you think my name isn't mud.' He'd just had Dean sign a policy. Cliff talks with his hands, so they got a chalkboard for him to draw what happened. (At the inquest)"

MR. HORD: "They booed when I came off the stand. The people from Hollywood. Movie stars. All I did was tell the truth. State the facts. After the verdict, the young man in the other car came up to me. He asked me how fast I thought Dean had been going when he ran me off the road. One hundred, one hundred and forty miles an hour. Turnupseed said he had stopped, then started to pull out. But the other car was coming so fast, he couldn't go ahead, or go back.

"We passed forty or fifty of the racers, but most of them had them on trailers, or were driving like they should be."

Officer Ernie Tripke recalled that there was a "large crowd from Hollywood at the inquest, but I do not recall any booing at Hord's testimony."

Hotel of the Stars

Switzerland boasted a Hotel of the Stars in the mid–1980s. There was a James Dean Suite which had replica's of Dean's awards from *Eden* and

Giant, three big color pictures, photos, posters, and autographs. The bathtub was in tesserae with the embossed initials "J.D."

"human ashtray"

The delightful sobriquet applied to Jimmy by Kenneth Anger in *Hollywood Babylon II*:

> Dean had taken to hanging out at the Club, an East Hollywood leather bar. The predatory night prowler, who dug anonymous sex, had recently discovered the magic world of S and M. He had gotten into beating, boots, belts, and bondage scenes. Regulars at the Club tagged him with a singular moniker: the Human Ashtray. When stoned, he would bare his chest and beg for his masters to stub out their butts on it. After his fatal car crash, the coroner made note of the "constellation of kerotoid scars" on Jimmy's torso.

The coroner did not actually file a formal report. What passes for a coroner's report was a memo writen by the morticians, who were deputized to perform that function. In their memo there is no mention of any such scars. During a Dean retrospective in the eighties, a fan asked Dean biographer Bill Bast about the report and he responded with a loud raspberry.

Hunter, Otie Valero

The patrolman who gave Dean a speeding ticket shortly before the fatal accident. Hunter testified at the inquest. He was nicknamed Buzz, and his wife's name was Judy. California Highway Patrol officer Ron Nelson, who was present at Dean's crash site, says that Otie Hunter once won $15,000 on *Jeopardy*. He's an expert on comic books.

Hush, Hush

This Hollywood gossip magazine reported in 1956 that Jimmy's death was a suicide precipitated by recently being dumped by Ursula Andress. Beulah Roth, wife of photographer Sanford Roth, claimed (in a 1985 interview with Warren Beath) that Ursula rushed over to her house hysterical, and stayed to sleep in the other twin bed. She wanted "to be with somebody who was close to Jimmy," according to Beulah. Ursula, Beulah remembered, blamed herself for Jimmy's death because she had broken up with him.

Ursula Andress was soon to become the wife of starmaker and actor John Derek. Later she bore a son to actor Harry Hamlin, whom she had met on the set of *Clash of the Titans*. Her other film credits include *Dr. No* and *The Sensuous Nurse*.

I

I, James Dean

This Popular Library paperback by T. T. Thomas was published in 1957 and told Jimmy's story in the first person.

> I, Jimmy Dean, never knew who I was or what I was... I was the hopes and dreams of my farm-girl mother, for when the years had broken her of any real hope for herself; she passed on to me the dusty dreaming of her youth. I never had a chance to be Jimmy Dean....

> "He's gotta stop!" Jimmy yelled at Wuetherich.
> The Ford's brakes were jammed on, hard. Screeching tires on the road... A wailing of rubber... Then the Ford slowly, inexorably, began to turn left, directly in front of the onrushing Spyder.
> *Now, the Ford was no longer a small black beetle; it was the huge black hull of Death — and Jimmy's mother was riding it, beckoning to him ... beckoning ... as he swerved to the right to avoid the crash...*

> ...Just as, one hundred years before, a different generation of youth was chilled by the death of Lord Byron at Missolonghi.
> *Do not judge me as James Byron Dean. I am the man you dreamed me to be. I am the parts I played throughout my meager yesterdays. I am the young and the lonely and the lost. I am a part of every one of you who know of me!*

"I Miss You Jimmy"

A tune recorded by a singer named Varetta Dillard and released on Groove Records. An Internet site still sells her music.

> "There's also an intriguing tribute piece, I Miss You Jimmy (Tribute To James Dean), prompting speculation as to whether the song was Dillard's idea or a company ploy to exploit Dean's tragic demise in 1956. Dillard makes most of these songs entertaining, and sometimes turns in a triumph." — Ron Wynn, *All Music Guide.*

The *Encyclopedia of Popular Music* comments on Dillard's choice, writing that the song was released in spite of Valetta's distaste for her record label's venal motives.

"I Owned James Dean's Death Car!"

He not only owned it, but he customized it. He's George Barris, and the title is of an interview he gave to Steve Roeser which appeared in the June

1990 issue of *Sh-Baam* magazine. It's another entry in his ongoing promotion of his connection to Dean's Porsche Spyder. This occasion was to hype the proposed $15-million movie *The Legend,* for which he was contracted to supervise the car crash in the Dean biopic.

images, use of

In July of 1996 *Variety* reported, "A duel between two James Dean Web sites in cyberspace has spilled into the courts for what could be a landmark case involving copyright law on the Internet."

Ron Martinetti is the author of the estimable 1974 biography *The James Dean Story.* This lucid and insightful book is often underestimated for its contribution to Deanology, though it predates David Dalton's paisley masterpiece *James Dean: The Mutant King.* In the nineties Martinetti had the foresight to reissue his updated biography and establish the American Legends website, which promoted his book and prominently featured James Dean.

In 1996 CMG filed a lawsuit in Indiana against the American Legends website, charging them with copyright infringement, defamation, unfair competition, and conversion. CMG hired a New York City public relations firm to publicize its lawsuit.

CMG had earlier alleged that it represented the James Dean Foundation — a trust that allegedly owned the "right of publicity" on James Dean — and objected to "the tenor of the alleged personal information regarding James Dean's past relationships." Translation: homosexuality.

But in Ron Martinetti they had taken on a worthy opponent. He is also a Glendale-based lawyer. He quickly responded that if the court wanted to adjudicate whether Dean's relationship with another man "was meretricious, then be my guest."

Martinetti obtained high-powered legal counsel which stated, "The historic value of a person's image cannot be diminished by the truth." Martinetti's website added, "The Internet is the ultimate medium to bring the truth forward. In suing our new Web site, those who make millions from Hollywood legends may have gotten more than they bargained for." The *High Point* (North Carolina) *Enterprise* noted, "Thousands of Web sites around the world feature information and pictures about actors ... and practically anyone else in the public eye. This suit could affect how or even if those Web sites are allowed to continue." The issue was also raised about the James Dean stamp. It would be interesting to know about CMG's dealings with the Postal Service, whether they were willing to pay CMG every time they say Dean's name or show his face.

The Web site was quoted as saying, "The Web is much like the Old West used to be — an exciting, still unexplored frontier.... But now the powerful net sites are trying to squeeze out the smaller net sites, just like the huge ranchers squeezed out the small ranchers out West around the turn of the century."

The Curtis lawyer explained CMG's position by claiming, "If people out there are using Dean's name and image in a commercial manner without our authorization, that's going to lead others to wonder why they have to pay."

See also Curtis Management.

Indonesia

In 1957, *The New York Times* reported that a group of Dean worshipers had turned up in the unlikely locale of Bandung, Indonesia (about 100 miles from Jakarta). There, teenage boys and girls paid homage to Dean — whose movies had been playing in Indonesia — by strolling through town in blue jeans and red jackets, upsetting conservatives who disapproved of such nontraditional attire. Reportedly, the teenagers shrugged off the complaints of their elders and continued with their plans to commemorate their idol, not only through their fashion statements, but through regular Dean-worshiper meetings.

inquest

If James Dean had not died in the crash, Donald Turnupseed would have been cited at the scene for an illegal left turn and perhaps other negligence-related charges, such as failure to signal, failure to see safe movement, and unsafe speed. But because the crash involved a fatality, the authorities made an investigation and turned the information over to the sheriff-coroner whose job it was to call an inquest and determine whether the death was caused by a criminal act.

The inquest into the death of James Dean was held at the council chambers in San Luis Obispo. Turnupseed appeared with his lawyer and his parents. Because of the crowd of curious, the sheriff moved the proceeding to the old U.S.O. building at nearby 10th and Park streets.

On October 11 the jury of nine men and three women was sworn in at 10:15 A.M., and ambulance driver Paul Moreno was called as the first witness to be questioned by under deputy district attorney Harry Murphy. The deposition of Doctor Bossert, the physician who pronounced Dean dead, was read and the injuries described. Doctor Bossert was asked whether there was any evidence that Dean had been wearing glasses. Highway Patrolman Ernie Tripke was called to the stand and introduced the diagram of the accident:

> MURPHY: Now, considering the color of the car, the height of the car, the time of day and the amount of sunlight, do you have any opinion as to how hard or difficult or easy it would be to see this car coming up the highway?
> TRIPKE: Well, it would blend in pretty well with the highway color and the horizon, it being silvery gray. There were some red stripes on the rear of the Porsche, but they couldn't be seen from the front of it.

Because of the damage to the car, Tripke probably couldn't tell that there had also been large red lettering on the front hood and the side doors. Murphy also had Tripke discredit his own diagram, by eliciting testimony that the skid marks he portrayed could have been made by another car, despite the fact that they tied in perfectly with the point of impact.

Witness Thomas Frederick was called and described what he saw, which included the assertion that the victim in the red shirt — Rolf Wuetherich — had been driving. Highway Patrol officer O. V. Hunter was called to the stand and testified that he couldn't remember whether Dean had been wearing glasses when he cited him for speeding about an hour and a half before the crash. He produced Dean's copy of the ticket, which had been found on his body and mailed to Bakersfield Highway Patrol headquarters.

Witness Clifford Hord testified about being run off the road by the Porsche just before the accident. Don Dooley, Thomas Frederick's nephew, was also a witness; he piped up to offer he had seen something like plastic goggles on the pavement. He did not mention, nor had the investigation disclosed, that he had also taken some Polaroid pictures of the accident scene. He also testified that the man in the white shirt, Dean, had been sitting on the left side of the car as it came towards them.

After noon, the jury left to deliberate and quickly returned a verdict that they found no indication James Dean met his death through the criminal act of another. The entire proceeding had taken two hours and fifteen minutes.

inquest exhibits

The inquest into Dean's death included the following exhibits, numbered as shown here.

1. Photograph of the 1950 Ford Tudor after the accident. The photo shows the last set of skids terminating in a scuff mark at the point

where the Spyder struck the left front fender. The photo is looking east, and shows the depth of the point of impact in Dean's westbound lane. The "stop" line is in the right-hand lane of Highway 41. The Ford was originally traveling the direction of the car to the right.

2. Photograph of the Spyder after the impact. The left front fender of the Ford is in the foreground, and Rolf Wuetherich's detached seat is near the Porsche.

3. Photograph looking east to the hills down which the Spyder came toward the camera. The picture was taken the day after the crash by California Highway Patrol officer Ron Nelson at the approximate time of the accident. The man to the left is ambulance attendant Paul Moreno. The photograph shows the 22-foot skids immediately prior to the point of impact.

4. Regarding numbers 4 and 5, there is some confusion. They are not mentioned by number in records of the inquest. However, a notarized letter from Sanford Roth identifying the deceased as his friend James Dean appears in the court file with the numbered exhibits listed here, all of which were entered into evidence. Missing from the file, but read in court during the reading of the deposition of Dr. Robert Bossert, was Bossert's letter to the coroner affirming that James Dean died of his injuries incurred in the accident and that "death came at the time or shortly after the accident."

5. It seems likely that the doctor's letter and Roth's letter were exhibits 3 and 4, as they seem to have been introduced into evidence after the photos numbered 1–3. There are only eight exhibits on file in the county recorder's office.

6. A closer view of the Porsche.

7. Photograph showing the highway looking west on US 466.

8. Photograph showing the highway looking east, again. Taken from further back, it depicts both sets of the Ford's skids.

9. Highway patrol diagram of the accident.

10. The ticket Dean received for speeding not long before the fatal crash.

intersection

For many Dean fans, the intersection of Highways 41 and 466 is Ground Zero. Many report supernatural experiences at the site, as if Jimmy is somehow reaching out to bond with them. An angelic choir comes over the radio. The weather changes suddenly. One fan reported seeing a rattlesnake suddenly at his feet. Another saw a strange dark cloud suddenly form the image of Dean's face overhead. True believers have been healed of chronic maladies. Strange temblors rock and roll the earth beneath some fans, while others report faintness as if they have suddenly gone bloodless.

At point of impact, the pavement width of the eastbound lane was 13 feet wide. The westbound lane was 27 feet wide.

One young man said, "My friends all think I'm crazy driving down here for this. They say, 'What do you think he's going to do, rise from the dead?'"

"But you know, today for me he will."

A group of Dada artists from Union City dressed as highway workers and painted a detailed portrait of Jimmy on the roadway in the early 1980s.

J

jacket

The red zippered jacket Jimmy Dean wore in *Rebel* became a symbol of the rebel to be produced and sold under authorized imprint by his estate. The original jackets for the film — there were reportedly three — were purchased at Mattson's, a Hollywood store. A year after his death, Mattson's was experiencing a run on them at $22.95.

But what happened to the original three jackets Dean wore in the film? Stories abound, so many that for all to be true, the three original jackets would have had to reproduce like rabbits over the years. But here are three reported stories: On the twenty-fifth anniversary of Dean's death, fan Art Bean recalled how Jimmy Dean offered him a ride when he was hitchhiking on Lake Avenue. It was the beginning of a friendship that would survive the actor's death. Bean claimed that Dean eventually gave him three bags of clothing, one of which contained the red jacket.

An article on movie cults in a 1982 *American Film* magazine reported that when Henri Langlois opened his Musée du Cinéma in 1972 at the Palais de Chaillot in Paris, the most prominent item on display was James Dean's red jacket from *Rebel Without a Cause*. Some months later, because of an inadequate surveillance system guarding the sixty-room museum, this singular relic was stolen.

Dean collector David Loehr believed that one original jacket remained in the hands of the widow of Sammy Davis, Jr.

Jade Productions

A largely mail-order source of Dean-related items in the 1980s. The name is a compaction of James Dean's first and last names. James Dean Gallery founder David Loehr and life partner Lenny Prussack originated Jade, selling Dean collectibles and souvenirs from their home in New York prior to moving to Fairmount, Indiana, and establishing the James Dean Gallery in Jimmy's hometown.

James Dean/A Dress Rehearsal

This was the title of a play produced in Denver, Colorado, in June of 1985. It was written and directed by Patricia Leone, who played Dean's director. The premise is that the audience is watching a dress rehearsal of a play, *The Eddie Branigan Story*, at the Helen Hayes Theatre in New York during the summer of 1955. As part of a charity benefit, James Dean is starring. Originally, the idea was for Dean to be rehearsing *A Hatful of Rain*, but when it was pointed out to the author-director that she did not have the requisite permissions, she changed the title of the play-within-the-play to *The Eddie Branigan Story*.

Rocky Mountain News staff writer Jackie Campbell reviewed the opening night: "Leone is a director undaunted by theatrical convention. Her script plunges into a morass of problems created by her 'dress rehearsal' premise." Reviewers agreed that the audacious idea didn't come off.

A year later the play was revived, to better reviews, after tightening and a change of casting. The production also secured rights to excerpt *A Hatful of Rain*.

James Dean, American Legend

This 1997 documentary produced and directed by Alan Hauge was never sold or released commercially. It was the result of the series of fiascos that surrounded the James Dean Murders (*see* Emr, Jon, and Hauge, Alan). Hauge did not have extensive experience as either producer or director, but he became enchanted by James Dean and the story and purchased the rights to make an authorized documentary.

The picture that emerged from all of Hauge's expense and travail was incoherent and disjointed. The thrust was a revisionist history of Dean that portrayed his iconic image often against the American flag, and much of the film was concerned with refuting allegations of Dean's homosexuality.

The film drew on some writings of Dean's that had recently been discovered in Winton Dean's basement — the so-called James Dean diary.

Read in voice-over, they were disappointing, self-important and sopho-moric ramblings on the thespian's art and told nothing of his personal life. A more interesting element was some animated short film Dean made in his spare time.

With Hauge's resources, it is remarkable that the film was such a fail-ure on all scores. But it never strays far from its defensive agenda of recast-ing Dean as a heterosexual patriot and nice guy.

Hauge's real goal was to acquire financing to make a dramatic biog-raphy of Dean, and the documentary contains several uncomfortable dramatized sections with bucolic depictions of Dean's Fairmount, Indi-ana, days. They are seriously out of place in the documentary, which is muddled by having too many narrative voices, including actor Anthony Michael Hall. Hauge himself appears in critiques of books that assault Dean's legend, showing their covers and giving inadvertent publicity to the very works he would discredit.

The picture premiered at Sony Theaters in a private screening for participants, but the film was never picked up or shown commercially. It was too confused and amateurish. The special footage Hauge had been given by Dean's family was later used in an AMC documentary.

"James Dean: An American Original"

This is a tribute episode of the 1983 television series *Hollywood Close-up*. Interviews included Ursula Andress and Bill Bast.

James Dean and Me

This television documentary won several prizes, including a Telly Award. First airing on the Learning Channel in 1996, it was nominated for an Emmy in the category of Entertainment Specials. Produced by Nineteenth Star LLC.

The James Dean Athletic Hall of Fame

In Canada, Chatham-Kent Secondary School features the James Dean Ath-letic Hall of Fame, which inducts new members at an annual Student Ath-letic Association banquet. The 1998 inductees were Lindsey Anderson, Jen Ball and Corrine Ronson.

James Dean, Beyond the Grave

This privately published and indispensable book is from the pen of Texas Dean writer, expert and archivist Bob Rees. He writes:

For the first time, ever, this definitive, well-illustrated factual overview explores the afterlife phenomenon associated with James Dean, his influence beyond the grave. Of all the haunted Hollywood personalities, James Dean reigns supreme in the realm of the paranormal. Shortly after his tragic, premature death in a car accident in 1955, strange ghostly communications from Dean commenced. This book reveals some of these spectral events as the exploitive hoaxes they were, while other occurrences are left up to you to decide.

A fine part of this thin book is the introduction, where the author describes the genesis of his book in an encounter with his son:

"Brandon," I offered, "just when you're ready to say the Loch Ness Monster is a complete and utter impossibility ... don't forget the coelacanth." "The what?," he said as he scrunched up his face quizzically. "Look it up in the dictionary," I retorted. My son read back to me what "American Heritage" had to say on the subject. "'Coelacanth,'" he began, his eyes filling with wonder as he progressed, "'Any of a variety of fishes known only in fossil form until a living species of African marine waters was identified in 1938.'"

He was astounded. I interjected at this juncture, "You see! Just because everyone *thought* this fish had been extinct for thousands of years didn't necessarily make it so. Rare, unusual, unexplainable things can really happen sometimes. Just because you hear the sound of hooves on a bridge — don't assume horses are coming. Sometimes, in life, it can be zebras you hear on the bridge! Let's keep an open mind about things we don't fully understand."

Rees continues:

Do you yourself a favor, suspend your disbelief. Relax — allow yourself to be enlightened and entertained at the same time. And just when you're about to say it's all foolishness ... join the coelacanth and go with the flow — "Don't look now, but isn't the laughing helmsman of our boat a fellow that looks an awful lot like ... James Dean?"

James Dean Death Club

Mentioned in a homely James Dean newsletter of the 1980s, whose correspondent writes:

More disturbing is the history of the bizarre James Dean Death Club. These fifties throwaways with their pathological fixation on the image of Dean found in him a savage and suicidal God of highway destruction. In their souped-up rods painted eerily in fluorescent silver, they account for many of the strange highway deaths, which occurred from 1957 to the early sixties on the 90 mile stretch of Highway 466. Convinced that Dean was alive but disfigured on an isolated ranch off a dirt road in San Miguel, they believed that true identification with their idol could be achieved only by a constant replaying of his final scene. They perhaps account for some of the more bizarre of the strange encounters and experiences of motorists on this fabled stretch of California Highway. Even the briefest interview with one of the original members of this club is enough to send chills up the most resolute spine. Their ritualistic runs commenced near midnight, and ended with a caravan of headlights at the intersection where Dean had died.

James Dean Died Here: The Locations of America's Pop Culture Landmarks

This book by Chris Epting has the famous Dean crash intersection on its cover and uses it as a jumping-off point for presenting a host of quirky factoids about America's cultural hotspots.

James Dean, He Never Said Goodbye

Rod Wimmer and Caprice Records jumped on the Dean bandwagon with this tribute album. The tracks include "I'm Just the Singer of this Song," "He Never Said Goodbye," "The Gift," "Momma's Hope, Momma's Dream," "Because of My Dreams," "Lord, I Believed Your Lie," "That Tree Upon the Hill," and "I'd Like to Be Alone with You."

James Dean ... Just Once More

This unusual book, by Di Elman, purports to take the reader on a personal journey into the soul of James Dean. Elman writes, "I always liked being alone. I knew I was a misfit.... Thick glasses and an inward awkwardness around other people confirmed my 'aloneness,' when I would decline to speak.... Then one day ... a young man seemed to grab my heart and soul, and every part of me that was missing ... to be with him on the screen. His name was—James Dean."

The sepia-toned, motorcycle-babe-inspired cover shows the author in a three-quarter view from the back — long, permed hair, black leather jacket, oversized shades— her picture superimposed in the foreground and facing a faded full-body portrait of Jimmy leaning against a tree. The author is looking at Jimmy, but he is looking away. The haunting image reflects the yearning quality of the author's musings.

The James Dean Memorial Fund

Arthur Loew, Jr., was a film producer and friend of James Dean. The cousin of Stewart Stern, who scripted *Rebel Without a Cause*, Loew established the James Dean Memorial Fund at the Actors Studio in New York. Al Pacino, an Actors Studio alumnus, said, "If you were a poor actor — and most actors I knew were poor — there were funds like the James Dean Memorial Fund, which could give you money for basics."

The James Dean Memorial Rally

Established by Carmel native Roger Cannon in 1979, for several years this free-form Zen rally offered Dean fans a chance to relive their idol's last hours at thirty dollars a pop, for which the entrant received a map for the self-guided tour. Cannon's flyer read:

> The James Dean Memorial Rally is a great adventure. Starting in Los Angeles you leave your day to day routine behind and discover the route that James Dean followed. The Rally Map and Route Guide to the annual James Dean Memorial Rally points the way to fresh perspectives, new points of view. We all have the power to transform our lives. The James Dean Memorial Rally is an experience where verbal descriptions do not really capture the experience. Time is the only thing we really have. Life is a precious gift to be appreciated at all costs. The James Dean Memorial Rally is a celebration of life, through it we come to terms with death. Through it one may realize true potential for producing new aliveness and satisfaction in life.

The James Dean Memorial Run

Founded by Will O'Neil of the National Woodie Club, this run was held each year through 1983 during the last weekend of September. Street rodders and enthusiasts in and around Southern California participated in the retracing of Dean's last day. Six checkpoints were established to make sure each car went the whole way and did not cheat by taking the Interstate 5 direct route.

The James Dean Memorial Scholarship Trust

This scholarship was established by Dean's old drama teacher, Adeline Nall, to reward exceptional speech and drama students. It was established at the Citizen's Exchange Bank in Fairmount, Indiana.

The James Dean Memory Club

Founded by the late Therese Brandes in the New York City area in 1956, this gathering of fans met monthly to view Brandes' extraordinary Dean Memorabilia collection and to take walking tours of Dean's Manhattan haunts. According to Dean archivist Brian Lewis, the club was still active in the 1990s.

James Dean: Portrait of a Friend

The friend is Bill Bast, portrayed in this teleplay, which was broadcast by NBC on February 19, 1976. The major deviation from Bast's book is the revelation of the homoerotic undertones in his relationship with Dean. This was the first public pronouncement of Dean's sexual ambiguity. Stephen McHattie played Dean, while Michael Brandon portrayed the Bast character. In this dramatization, the character is in analysis for his guilt over the death of James Dean. At the end, he realizes his major regret is that he never told Jimmy he loved him.

James Dean: Race with Destiny

The gruesome car crash at the end of this 1997 biopic left some of the Dean fans depressed when they attended the premier. Release of this picture, which starred Casper Van Dien as James Dean, and a "Custom Spyder Race Car" by George Barris, became mired in lawsuits between the producers. The film costarred Van Dien's offscreen wife, Carrie Mitchum, and the big casting coup was landing her grandpa, Robert Mitchum, to play George Stevens. Sadly, it was one of the last pictures Mitchum made. Also featured were Mike Connors, Diane Ladd, Connie Stevens, Joseph Campanella, and the ever-annoying Casey Kasem. The washed-up casting gave the whole project an aura more like a rerun from the TV series *Love Boat* than a biography of James Dean.

The James Dean Revival Club

The Australian magazine *Pix* reported on October 7, 1961, the formation of the Australian "James Dean Revival Club." The club was devoted to keeping Jimmy's memory alive. Members kept candles burning before his photograph and set up little flower-decked altars before which they listened to Dean tribute songs such as "He Walks the Future" and "We'll Never Forget You."

James Dean: Soundtrack Excerpts, Dialogue and Music from James Dean's Three Greatest Performances

This Warner Bros. compilation includes snatches of dialogue from Dean's three films mixed with music from the soundtracks.

The James Dean Story

Dean's studio explored several angles to cash in on the posthumous popularity of their dead star, entertaining briefly the idea of a biopic that would possibly star Elvis Presley. Ultimately, they decided on a documentary featuring distant figures impersonating Dean. The result, 1957's *The James Dean Story*, was helmed by director Robert Altman. Tommy Sands' lachrymose crooning of *Let Me Be Loved* sets the tone for the film. Dean's relatives look discomfited, his friends are self-conscious, and every one else interviewed seems bewildered by the postmortem hoopla in this stilted black-and-white film, which suffers—remarkably, since it was released by Warner Bros.—from an absence of clips of Dean from his films.

There are a few gems, such as an improvised and decidedly homoerotic *Eden* scene featuring Dick Davalos and Jimmy on his recorder (his only musical performance on film). Jimmy's friend Lew Bracker was enlisted to drive a later-edition Porsche Spyder in the early section when Dean's final drive is retraced. Filmed at the actual locations, it shows the intersection as it existed at the time of Dean's fatal crash, replete with a 1950 Ford Tudor crossing the frame to simulate the crash.

A soundtrack album was also released.

The James Dean Story (Steve Allen recording)

This 1956 release was another attempt to cash in on Dean's death. It was the studio creation of Steve Allen and Bill Randle and did not include any actual movie soundtracks but rather a chorus and orchestra recreating the film music. With narration by Allen and Randle, it featured Dick Jacobs, George Cates, Gigi Perreau and Jimmy Wakely.

James Dean: The First American Teenager

This 1975 TV documentary on Dean's life and times was narrated by Stacy Keach and included screen footage, film clips and interviews. Friends and co-workers Elizabeth Taylor, Rock Hudson, and Natalie Wood shared stories and insights about Dean. The documentary also featured original songs by David Bowie, Mike Oldfield, Lou Reed and Neil Sedaka.

"James Dean, the Legend and the Facts"

The cover story that appeared in the October 16, 1956, issue of *Look* magazine, coinciding with the premiere of *Giant*.

James Dean: The Night Before

A 1994 stage production written by Dan Sefton, who would later script the movie *James Dean: Race with Destiny*.

James Dean—The Untold Story of a Passion for Speed

A cartoon book—Jimmy Dean meets Speed Racer. By Philippe Defechereux (Los Angeles: Mediavisions Publications, Inc., 1996).

The James Dean walking tour of New York

David Loehr conducted this tour for years. It lasted six hours and included over twenty-five points of interest associated with James Dean's life in New York in the early 1950s. Starting on the Upper West Side and continuing downtown through Times Square and into Greenwich Village, the tour visited places Dean lived, theaters in which he performed and coffee shops where he had coffee, in addition to assorted bars and restaurants.

Participants were encouraged to wear comfortable shoes.

Japan

Yujiro Ishihara was known as the "The Japanese James Dean," a title that was bestowed on him by no less than *Time* magazine in 1963. The motion was soon seconded by *Life* magazine. The actor died in 1987 of liver cancer.

jazz *see* Baker, Chet

"Jimmy Dean Live Onstage!"

Within two years of Dean's death, enterprising dirt racing track promoters, their revenues suffering from the competition of television and their radar picking up the current Dean craze, availed themselves of an entrepreneur who provided as half-time entertainment the materialization of James Dean live at their shows. In ghoulish advertisements ("Direct from Hollywood in House of the LIVING DEAD!") garnished with renderings of a hollow-eyed Jimmy, they promised to produce his sports car and ghost as a diversion between races. What they did produce, with the help of a burst of smoke and an elevator hidden beneath the platform, was a distant figure with sunglasses and zippered jacket, standing and smoking a cigarette next to an MG. The promotions drew the ire of reverent Dean disciples, who wrote letters of protest to their favorite fan mags.

"Jimmy Dean Returns" *see* dreams of death

"Jimmy Dean: The Assignment I'll Never Forget"

Photographer Sanford Roth, who along with actor Bill Hickman had been following James Dean's Porsche on the day of Dean's fatal collision, had died of a heart attack in Rome before this article was published under his byline in the July 1961 issue of *Popular Photography*. "Jimmy Dean: The Assignment I'll Never Forget" featured a photo of the wrecked car, with the injured Rolf Wuetherich visible by the side of the Porsche. Many readers assumed that Dean was still in the car at the time the photo was taken, but he had actually already been placed in the ambulance.

The photo was pored over by readers and the Dean fans who snatched up the magazine and collected it over the ensuing years. More than a few claimed to see portions of Dean's head, or an arm, in the blurry pixels.

The article was a cornerstone in the legend of the Sanford and Beulah Roth friendship with James Dean. By the eighties, Roth's widow had expanded it into a cottage industry and would exclaim, "Thank you, Jimmy," when his popularity brought her a new windfall, like the sale of her husband's negatives of the dead actor to Japanese businessman Seita Ohnishi for a reputed quarter-of-a-million dollars.

See also Roth, Beulah.

"Jimmy-Without-End-Amen"

This perceptive article was written by contributing editor Kathryn Marshall and published in the September 15, 1990, edition of *American Way* magazine. It is the first article to focus on the fan phenomenon by an objective journalist investigating the annual pilgrimages to Cholame, which bring Deaners to the crash site between 5 and 8 P.M. on the Friday closest to September 30. Marshall describes hooking up with a young fan named Amy:

> Amy has made the trip from L.A. to the memorial at Cholame ... seven times. But this is the first time she's come on an anniversary weekend. What prompted today's trip was a curious book called *The Death of James Dean*. Amy has read it twice. "That book," she says emphatically, "zapped me into reality: *I'm not alone in this.*"
>
> "These aren't your generic fans," Amy explains.... The ones we'll meet tonight are just like me. They're the world-without-end-amen fans—the ones who have a true personal relationship with Jimmy."

The Junkman

This is the title of a low-budget bang-'em-up car picture shot on location at Dean's death site and environs by eccentric millionaire and film auteur H.B. Halicki. It was boasted that 150 cars would be destroyed during the course of the filming. Locals thought all the carnage was bad luck, but their apprehensions were lost on Halicki.

Apparently enthralled with the Dean legend, Halicki filmed bizarre homage to his hero. His picture features the monument, inquest photos, and even Highway Patrolman Ernie Tripke brought out of retirement to make his screen debut as himself. An exact replica of Dean's tombstone was also brought to the location site. Halicki starred in the film, which featured Hoyt Axton and Peter Lawford. The poster featured a sexy young woman posing by Dean's tombstone.

The Dean Curse (*see* curses) kicked in on a subsequent Halicki picture, when he was killed in a car while filming one of the stunt sequences he loved.

jurors

The jurors in the James Dean inquest were drawn from a jury panel given to the coroner by the county clerk. It was the same panel used by the justice court and the superior court. All jurors were from the Paso Robles–Shandon area of the county. The jurors were Dorothy Schwartz, Enid Eddy, Mrs. Alan Dale, Kenneth Harris, Charles Ashton, Ray Samp, Cliff Bickell, J. G. Hanson, Mac Mazorini, J.P. Brush, L.C. Dauth, and foreman D. H. Orcutt.

juvenile delinquent movies

In the vernacular of the film buff, a JD movie is a juvenile delinquent movie. But conveniently, and perhaps not coincidentally, JD is often taken to stand for James Dean in the same context. The success of *Rebel Without a Cause* gave rise to a new genre that attempted to emulate that movie's success, though the attempt was usually hampered by an abysmally low budget. Here is a chronological list of some of the *Rebel* imitators and their taglines:

Running Wild, 1955
The Stark Brutal Truth About Today's Lost Generation!

Teenage Crime Wave, 1955
The screen-scorching story of today's immoral youth!

The Violent Years, 1956
Untamed thrill-girls of the highway!

Teenage Rebel, 1956
You wanted to get rid of me ... so you could be alone with that woman!

Hot Rod Girl, 1956
Teenage terrorists tearing up the streets!

Untamed Youth, 1957
Youth Turned 'Rock-N-Roll' Wild and the 'Punishment' Farm That Makes Them Wilder!

Hot Rod Rumble, 1957
The slick chicks who fire up the big wheels!

Teenage Daughter, 1957
Born good with a desire to be bad!

Dragstrip Girl, 1957
Car Crazy! ... Speed Crazy! ... Boy Crazy!

Juvenile Jungle, 1958
A jet-propelled gang out for fast kicks!

High School Hellcats, 1958
...what must a good girl say to "belong"?

The Cool and the Crazy, 1958
Seven savage punks on a weekend binge of violence!

Teenage Thunder, 1958
Revved-up youth on a thrill rampage!

Hot Rod gang, 1958
Crazy kids ... living to a wild rock 'n' roll beat!

K

Kardell, Lilli

In a colorful Hollywood career that included a lawsuit against Troy Donahue for roughing her up, this Swedish-born actress (who died in 1987) was reputed to have been a call-girl for the big studios who specialized in entertaining out-of-town dignitaries. She was also a girlfriend of James Dean and kept a diary of her affair. She noted of the day Jimmy died:

> Jimmy Dean my only love died on his way to Salinas for the races. Auto crash. Please take care of him, God, and let him be happier now than before. I can only hope I will find my Jimmy in some other person. My thoughts will always be with you, Jimmy. Goodbye, forever. I love you and will never forget our memories.

Hollywood Dean artist Kenneth Kendall owns the diary.

Kardell's "film career" consisted largely of brief appearances on TV shows like *Wagon Train* and *Route 66.*

"Ken" doll

The advertisements read, "This handsome, Ken-sized 11½ inch JAMES DEAN doll will make your heart swoon. He is such a great likeness to the actor from TV and movies. He has very detailed face sculpting and features, piercing eyes, and great hair. He also has a very well defined and muscular body and is fully jointed at the arms, elbows, waist, and knees, making him perfect for posing. This exquisite Mattel doll is a fabulous and affordable way to add some fun to your Barbie displays and is BRAND NEW." It retailed for around $20.

Kendall, Kenneth

For the past forty years, sculptor and painter Kenneth Kendall has devoted most of his time to work depicting James Dean. His studio is jammed with paintings and sculptures depicting Dean in myriad moods and poses, and frequently enlivened by the scores of fans who come from all over the world to bask in his images of Dean. Dean actually came to Kendall's Melrose Avenue studio to offer himself as a subject in 1955, but Kendall was unimpressed. Soon after the actor's death, however, Kendall commenced work on a bust of Dean. Since that time, he has become the preeminent Dean artist.

Born in Los Angeles in 1921, Kendall was the son of a vaudevillian father who toured the world before becoming a theatrical agent. His aunt was Marguerite Armstrong, a silent film actress who called herself Miss Du Pont and appeared in Eric Von Stroheim's 1922 classic *Foolish Wives.* Kenneth Kendall himself eventually augmented his income by appearing as a bit player in such films as *Juarez* and *Julius Caesar,* and he was even a stand-in for Yves Montand in the Marilyn Monroe epic *Let's Make Love.* He was close to bodybuilder Steve Reeves and considered the stone lithographs he produced of Reeves his breakthrough in celebrity portraiture.

The large head of Dean he produced was presented to the Fairmount (Indiana) High School in 1956, and a replica was installed in 1957 at Park Cemetery, where it resided for less than a year before it was stolen. The original bust can be viewed at the Fairmount Historical Museum. In 1988 another bronze copy of this bust was placed on a plinth at California's Griffith Park with an inscription celebrating both Dean and the observatory.

Witty and urbane, the erudite Kendall is generally tolerant of the generations of Dean fans who come to lionize him. He is a regular at the Dean

Days festivities held annually in Fairmount, and a portion of David Loehr's James Dean Gallery is devoted to Kendall's paintings. He has portrayed Dean in all his roles and even inserted the actor into some famous paintings. His house has for many years been host to an annual James Dean birthday party; guests have included Adeline Nall and Maila Nurmi.

Kinnaman, Mark

Although he was raised only 20 miles from the Dean farm in Indiana, Mark Kinnaman traces his fascination with the star from a viewing of *East of Eden* on TV when he was only 13. Since then, Mark has traveled around the world and has witnessed the international devotion — Dean postcards in Istanbul, a Jimmy lookalike selling cigarettes in Berlin and a showing of *Rebel* in Cypress.

Mark is a talented artist and writer and has a website where he sells art and other merchandise and communicates with Dean fans from all over the World.

See also ghosts and hauntings; disfigurement.

The Knickerbocker

Known as "the Suicide Hotel" because so many celebrities have chosen it as the stage for their final scene, the Knickerbocker hotel is at 1714 Ivar in Hollywood. James Dean was a frequent guest, perhaps drawn by the Hollywood landmark's peculiar history and its reputation for being haunted.

Frances Farmer ran naked through the bar while being chased by sanitarium workers who wanted to give her a lobotomy — the incident is depicted in the film *Frances*. The famed dress designer Irene jumped to her death from the roof in 1962. It was several days before her body was discovered because she landed on the awning over the front door, rather than the sidewalk (presumably her intended target).

It was at the Knickerbocker in 1948 that movie pioneer D.W. Griffith died of a cerebral hemorrhage, reportedly under the chandelier in the lobby. William Frawley, of television's *I Love Lucy*, was a frequent drinker at the Knickerbocker; he walked out of the bar one night, turned left and promptly dropped dead at the corner of Hollywood and Ivar. Houdini's widow, Beatrice, held rooftop séances here for ten years as she tried to contact her husband. Elvis Presley lived here when he came to Hollywood to make his first film, the 1956 *Love Me Tender*. Jerry Lee Lewis, Frank Sinatra and Bette Davis were also residents. William Faulkner wrote *Absalom, Absalom!* in his room here.

Kuehl Funeral Home

The gothic red brick Kuehl Funeral Home still stands on Spring Street in Paso Robles, California, nearly identical to the way it looked in 1955 when Paul Moreno's ambulance delivered the body of James Dean. Martin Kuehl was proprietor of the family business, and John Stander was his assistant. Stander claimed to have encountered Dean on the road earlier in the evening when he was en route to Bakersfield for a football game, and he knew something was up when he returned late at night to find all the lights ablaze at the mortuary and the phone ringing off the hook with calls which included hysterical inquiries from South America. Mercedes McCambridge recalled in her memoirs driving by the mortuary that evening to find it surrounded by cruising cars full of the curious.

John Stander recalled that Dean's friend Bill Hickman stayed with Dean's body after it was cleaned up, and that Winton Dean arrived the

Death certificate of James Bryon Dean, Setember 30, 1955, showing Kuehl Funeral Home as the funeral director.

next day. Deputized as a coroner for the convenience of the county, Stander prepared a brief report on the body and signed the death certificate. He also attempted to conduct a blood alcohol test for the highway patrol, but noted there was not enough blood in the body. On Tuesday, Stander loaded Dean into the hearse and headed for Los Angeles International Airport via the coastal route to ship the actor back home.

A picture of the funeral home appeared in the magazine photo essay "Jimmy Dean's Last Miles." It became one of the stops for the faithful who wanted to feel close to Jimmy.

Even into the 1990s, when the original employees were long retired, boldly inquisitive Dean fans approached the proprietors wanting to know if they could take a peek at the room where Jimmy Dean had been embalmed.

L

La Scala

This legendary Hollywood restaurant, opened in 1956 by ex-waiter turned vintner Jean Leon, was in its heyday in the late 1950s and the 1960s, enjoying the patronage of big-name directors and stars. The likes of Marilyn Monroe, Warren Beatty, Paul Newman, Joanne Woodward and Elizabeth Taylor were said to dine there nightly.

Jean Leon claims Jimmy Dean was his business and creative partner from the beginning and would have reaped the rewards of the restaurant's remarkable success if not for his untimely passing. In an article entitled "The Showbiz Wines of Jean Leon," published in *Valencia Life*, an English-language Internet magazine published in Spain, the author writes of Jean Leon:

> As a young man he was able to hang out with others who were trying to make their way in Hollywood and he became a particular friend of the enigmatic movie icon James Dean. The Dean Team of James and Jean conceived, created and ultimately launched Hollywood's most famous restaurant, La Scala. The restaurant was an instant success but the tragic death of James Dean left Jean Leon the sole owner. However he recovered from the loss of his friend and business partner and went on to create three more restaurants through whose portals passed the mega-famous, from Presidents (e.g., Kennedy and Reagan), to all the top Movie Stars of the day. Jean Leon had truly arrived!

Larrabee House *see* ghosts and hauntings

"The Last Autograph"

This is the title of a country and western song about James Dean getting a traffic ticket shortly before his death. Bakersfield, California, songwriter Scott Sturtevant, who penned the song and who records under the name Slim the Drifter, says it was the result of years of hearing stories about Dean's ticketing near his hometown. "It's a Bakersfield story. A lot of people in this town have heard little bits and pieces over the years. Everybody has a little take on the story."

last phone call

Marvin "Monty" Roberts, of "Horse Whisperer" fame, claims that James Dean's last telephone call was to him at his ranch in Salinas. Roberts claims to have been put in charge of rusticating Jimmy when *East of Eden* was in preproduction, and that Jimmy spent a month with him at the family ranch in Salinas. As a result, Jimmy not only bought a horse, but (according to Roberts) had Roberts negotiating on a farm up in *East of Eden* country at the time of his death.

Roberts told Dean biographer Joe Hyams that Jimmy called him the day before his fatal crash, asking if he and Rolf Wuetherich could stay in the guest house on the ranch. Roberts says that Jimmy also called him from Blackwell's Corner, within a half hour before the accident. He told him that he would be arriving in the early evening and that Roberts should have a pot of chili on the stove. When he heard of Jimmy's death on the radio that evening, Roberts started to bawl like a baby, feeling like he had lost a brother.

See also *The Man Who Listens to Horses*.

last story

Shortly before James Dean's death on September 30, 1955, the *Los Angeles Herald-Examiner* published perhaps the last story the actor ever was to read about himself. The ironic headline was "James Dean Planning to Go on a Racing Kick When Giant Ends," and it appeared on September 16, 1955.

lawsuit

Attorneys for Rolf Wuetherich charged in the complaint of their lawsuit against Donald Turnupseed, filed March 25, 1958, that on or about the 30th day of September, 1955, at or about the hour of 5:30 P.M. on said date, plaintiff was riding as a passenger in a vehicle being driven by James B. Dean, now deceased, in a general northerly direction on and along the said Highway Number 41; that at or about the said time, the said 1950 Ford Sedan Automobile, drive [sic], operated and controlled by the defendants, Donald Gene Turnupseed and/or Doe II, was being operated in a generally southerly direction on and along the said California Highway No. 41; that at or about the said time, both vehicles were being operated on and along the said California Highway No. 41 at or near the intersection thereof with the said U. S. Highway No. 466 within the County of San Louis [sic] Obispo, State of California.

That at or about the said time and place, the defendants, and each of them, so negligently, carelessly, recklessly and unlawfully drove, operated, controlled and maintained said 1950 Ford Sedan Automobile so as to cause the said vehicle to come into violent collision with the vehicle in which plaintiff was riding as a passenger, thereby causing severe injuries and damages to the plaintiff as hereinafter set forth.

lawsuit chronology

August 20, 1956	Attorneys for Rolf Wuetherich, working on 30 percent contingency, file complaint for personal injuries against estate of James Dean.
September 28, 1956	Complaint amended to include Donald Turnupseed as defendant.
December 4, 1956	Attorney for auto insurance carrier for James Dean files suit against Donald Turnupseed for $6,049.30 — the damage sustained due to total loss of Dean's Porsche Type 550 Spyder
July 3, 1957	Attorneys for Turnupseed file answer denying charges to complaint of Dean's auto insurance carrier and declaring that Dean was responsible for the accident.
July 19, 1957	Pretrial conference in the suit by Dean's auto insurance carrier set for Friday, March 18, 1958. Trial date set for Tuesday, August 19, 1958.
March 8, 1958	Attorney for Dean's insurance carrier takes deposition from Turnupseed in Fresno, California. Turnupseed claims that he never saw Dean's Spyder until impact and that he tried to swerve and miss him when he heard the scream of Dean's engine.
March 25, 1958	In the case of *Wuetherich vs. Turnupseed*, attorneys for Turnupseed file motion to quash service of

summons and dismiss action on grounds that court has no jurisdiction because no summons was issued within a year of the commencement of the action.

May 1, 1958	Dean's insurance carrier files waiver of jury trial.
May 6, 1958	In *Wuetherich vs. Turnupseed*, motion to quash is denied by Judge J.E. Rose.
May 8, 1958	Turnupseed files request for trial by jury in action brought by Dean's insurance carrier.
May 9, 1958	Attorneys for Turnupseed file new motion to dismiss case of *Wuetherich vs. Turnupseed* on grounds that Los Angeles Superior Court is not proper court because defendant resides in Tulare County and accident occurred in San Luis Obispo County.
May 23, 1958	In *Wuetherich vs. Turnupseed*, Turnupseed enters request for change of venue to Tulare County. His attorneys also file demurrer that "complaint does not state facts sufficient to constitute a cause of action."
May 29, 1958	Attorneys for Wuetherich request that if change of venue be granted, it be to San Luis Obispo County rather than Tulare County.
June 2, 1958	Turnupseed's request for change of venue to Tulare granted by Judge E. O'Brien.
July 14, 1958	Court records in that action are transferred to Tulare County and action is filed there.
July 30, 1958	Dean's insurance carrier files for request of dismissal "with prejudice."
July 31, 1958	Judgment of dismissal in that case is entered. In *Wuetherich vs. Turnupseed*, attorneys for Turnupseed file affidavit alleging accident was Dean's fault and ask for dismissal on grounds that service of summons by plaintiff was unreasonably delayed.
August 7, 1958	Attorneys for plaintiff file affidavit stating that delay was due to their good faith efforts to effect settlement with insurance carriers for Turnupseed. It is stated that it was not until October 14 that they received letter from Turnupseed's counsel withdrawing insurance company's willingness to settle should Wuetherich's damages be determined when his condition stabilized. Letter also requested a jury trial to determine liability.

August 11, 1958	Wuetherich's attorneys file against Turnupseed's motion to dismiss.
August 25, 1958	Motion to dismiss denied. Motion of default filed against Turnupseed.
September 2, 1958	Defense enters answer alleging the accident was caused solely by negligence of James Dean and asks that default be set aside and case be heard. Default is set aside. Defense also offers that Wuetherich and Dean were involved in a joint venture at time of crash and plaintiff had consented to Dean's negligence.
November 3, 1958	Pretrial conference held in Tulare with attorneys in attendance.
November 26, 1958	Trial set for Tuesday, February 17, 1958.
January 9, 1959	Competition Motors' industrial indemnity carrier, which paid for Wuetherich's medical treatment and disability compensation, joins in action against Turnupseed because of its lien against compensation received by Wuetherich.
Jan 20, 1959	Turnupseed files answer to charges denying responsibility for accident. He claims James Dean as the proximate cause due to his negligence of which Wuetherich had full knowledge.
February 3, 1959	Attorneys for Turnupseed summon Wuetherich to appear for deposition on Monday February 16, 1959, at Bakersfield, California.
February 18, 1959	Attorneys for Turnupseed request change of trial date to May 19, 1959.
March 26, 1959	Attorneys for Turnupseed assign Wuetherich a new deposition date and ask him to appear in Fresno on Friday, April 17, 1959.
April 28, 1959	Attorneys for Turnupseed request trial be dropped from calendar due to unavailability of Wuetherich for deposition, date to be reset upon motion by any party to the action.
August 20, 1959	Attorneys for Turnupseed request Wuetherich give deposition in Fresno on Friday, September 4, 1959. They also apply for setting of a new trial date.
August 31, 1959	Attorneys for Wuetherich make motion that plaintiff not give deposition on grounds he is out of the State of California.

September 22, 1959	New trial date set for Tuesday, October 27, 1959.
October 16, 1959	Wuetherich's attorneys are granted new trial date of Tuesday November 3, 1959.
October 22, 1959	Stipulation for recontinuance agreed to by both parties. Wuetherich is apparently out of the country.
October 2, 1961	Attorneys for Turnupseed file motion to dismiss for failure to bring to trial within 5 years.
October 16, 1961	Motion of dismissal granted by Judge Leonard Ginsburg. Only attorney for Turnupseed is present.
November 13, 1965	Attorneys for Wuetherich file for return of $60 deposit for jury fees.

Ledgerwood, Larry, Jr.

In December of 1986 eighteen-year-old Larry Ledgerwood, Jr., said, "There are two guys in Michigan who want to make a film about James Dean. I'd like to get that part." Ledgerwood, a graduate of Bloomington High School, had won two trophies and a plaque in Dean lookalike competitions.

In a 1986 interview with Warren Beath, Ledgerwood said, "A lot of the things that have happened to him have happened to me and there are a lot of similarities in our lives. He was a farm boy from Indiana, and so am I. He changed moods easily. One minute he'd be laughing and the next, he'd be mad as all get-out. That's just how I am. He liked fast cars and adventure and so do I. He never seemed to fit in with any certain crowd, kind of a loner. That's how I am."

Ledgerwood went to the 1985 Dean festival, but came a day late for the lookalike contest. For an entire year he prepared for the next contest by working on the look, facial expressions, clothing and hair. He won both the lookalike contest at Museum Days and the James Dean Rod Run — a first for anyone.

Lee, Toni

The *New York Herald Tribune* of January 30, 1954, featured a portrait of an attractive lady with the heading *Singer Sues for Loss of Leg*. The leg in question belonged to songstress Toni Lee — now Toni Lee Scott. Her relevance to the Dean saga is that she was a close friend of Dean's after her accident; according to her account, his sensitivity to her maiming helped her to recover her own sense of wholeness. The lawsuit was filed against three motorists involved in a collision with a motorcycle she was riding. It was that collision that eventually led to the amputation of her leg.

left barrel

By some accounts the left barrel — an evasive maneuver in racing — was employed by James Dean in a desperate attempt to avoid the accident that claimed his life. George Barris opined on Dean's tactic in a Steve Roeser interview which appeared in the June 1990 issue of *Sh-Baam* magazine:

> He did just what a professional race-car driver does when he finds a car ready to hit him in a front-end impact. Never applying the brakes, he geared down to get more power into his engine — getting compression — and then he put his foot back into it and tried to go around the guy. He pulled his wheel to the right, slid and went into a left barrel — what we call a wraparound. He would have been able to wrap right around that guy's front end and get away from him, but the guy kept going and just went right into him. Jimmy didn't have a chance then. If he had hit the brakes, he would have slid sideways, and he would've been in all different directions. His time was meant to be, no matter what he was going to do to save his life.

A dissenting opinion was offered in Jane Williams' article "Did Jimmy Dean's Spirit Haunt the Studio?" that appeared in *Movie Life*, September 1956. It is an account of the supernatural events supposedly attending the production and editing of Robert Altman's 1958 documentary *The James Dean Story*. Williams wrote, "In recreating the crash, by the way, the producers were able to prove that Jimmy would have been saved had his split-second driving decision been different. He apparently thought his best chance to avoid the other car was to circle to the right. If he had spun his car and circled off to the left and to the rear of the other car, he would be alive and at work in Hollywood today."

Probably not. There were several cars following the Turnupseed Ford, as Dean was perhaps aware in those final nanoseconds, and he would have been just as likely to collide with oncoming traffic in the other lane.

La Legende de Jimmy

This 1991 French rock opera, composed as homage to Dean, is set in the Fairmount, Indiana, cemetery where he is buried. The strange tale involves a chance meeting at the gravesite between two teenagers, a boy who is called "Jimmy" by his friends because he resembles Dean, and a girl who is a devout Dean groupie. There they encounter the ghostly apparitions of two people, a Reverend J.W. (probably James De Weerd) and a Hollywood diva named Angelica. The phantom duo reveals Jimmy's life to the teenagers who, after much singing and dancing, leave with a vow to forget Jimmy and find themselves. The musical includes original songs such as

"The Beauty of the Devil," "On the Empty Screen," "Conversations Around a Tomb 1," "Conversations Around a Tomb 2" and "To Die Like Him."

"Let Me Be Loved"

This is the name of the theme song to the 1957 film *The James Dean Story*. Sung by Tommy Sands, it was composed by Jay Livingston and Ray Evans, composers of schmaltzy standards such as "To Each His Own," "Mona Lisa" and the Christmas classic "Silver Bells." The sheet music for "Let Me Be Loved" is now a collectible.

Lewis, Brian

An ardent Dean collector and archivist, Brian M. Lewis has been on the Dean trail for decades. When Lewis was struck by Dean's charisma in the 1950s, a lifelong hobby was born which would ultimately include the acquisition of every type of Dean collectible released for four decades. Owner of the one of the largest collections of Dean-related memorabilia in the New England area, Lewis hooked up in the 1960s with the "James Dean Memory Club" which was headquartered in the New York home of its founder, the late Therese Brandes. He is frequently interviewed as a Dean authority in the New England area, and is the author of such articles as "James Dean: 50's Legend Lives on in the World of Collectibles."

In February of 1987, a large portion of his collection went on display at the Taunton, Massachusetts, Public Library to commemorate Dean's 56th birthday. The circulation supervisor deemed it the most popular exhibit the library ever had, nearly causing one female fan to swoon before the glass display case of "Deanabilia."

life mask

Soon after Dean's death, a caressable mask of fleshlike material was sold by mail to those who wanted to stroke his face. Hollywood artist Kenneth Kendall has sold a painted Dean mask for years, apparently made from a Warner Bros. life mask. In 1999, yet another copy of one of the Warner Bros. masks came up for sale in an Internet auction. The description read:

> Life Mask — This fabulous lifecast of James Dean was done during the filming of *Giant*, his last film. It is from the original life cast and perfect in every detail. Done in dental plaster, this unique collectable is truly one-of-a-kind. It is from a personal collection. This cast was done by the makeup artist on the film by putting plaster over Dean's face. Every detail

. is reproduced. The original is in the Warner Bros. Museum and the eyes have been sculpted open in that piece. The cast offered here is in the original closed-eye form!!

Bidding commenced at $225.

"Little Bastard: The Search for James Dean's Spyder"

This is the title of a Lee Raskin article that appeared in *Porsche Panorama* of July 1984. It chronicles the author's thorough tracing of parts taken from Jimmy Dean's missing Porsche Spyder. "The engine and gearbox have been found, but no one has seen the chassis of Dean's Spyder since five years after his death." Raskin hooks up with friend Bob Devlin:

> Together, we sensed that James Dean's chassis number could finally be uncovered. All we had to do was link the engine number to Dean's title. Competition Motors' records had been destroyed long ago, but Dr. Eschrich generously provided us with a copy of the original California Certificate of Ownership for Dean's Spyder, which he acquired after purchasing the wreck.

Devlin gave the engine number on the certificate, P90059, to Jurgen Barth, head of Porsche's Customer Racing Department. A search of factory records uncovered the desired information:

> The factory's records revealed that the Spyder in question was delivered from their doors on July 15, 1955, with an engine number of 90059, a transmission number of 10146 and a chassis number of 550–0055. Imagine that, 550–0055!

locations

Los Angeles is replete with places associated with James Dean and sacred to his most ardent devotees. Here is a short list:

WHERE JAMES DEAN WORKED: Warner Bros. Studios is located at 5000 Warner Blvd. in Burbank. It is now The Burbank Studios.

WHERE HE PLAYED WITH HIS MONKEY: The opening shot of *Rebel Without a Cause* was filmed before the mansion at the northeast corner of Franklin and Sierra Bonita in Hollywood.

WHERE SAL MINEO'S *REBEL* CHARACTER DIED: Griffith Park Observatory is the site of the filming of *Rebel Without a Cause*. Enter Griffith Park near Los Feliz from Western or Vermont Avenue. The road leads to the top of the mountain with the observatory.

WHERE SAL MINEO *REALLY* DIED: On February 12, 1976, he was stabbed to death in the driveway a few yards to the right of 8563 Holloway Drive in West Hollywood. He lived at 8565 Holloway Drive.

WHERE DEAN LIVED: Dean's last house was a rustic cottage that was located at 14611 Sutton Street in Sherman Oaks, California. While filming *Rebel*, he reportedly lived in an apartment above a garage at 1541 Sunset Plaza Drive; he called this residence a "wastebasket with walls." While filming *East of Eden*, he lived in apartment number 3 at 3908 W. Olive.

WHERE HE BOUGHT HIS CAR: Competition Motors, 1219 N. Vine Street.

WHERE NICK RAY PLAYED THE HARMONICA: Chateau Marmont, 8221 W. Sunset Blvd. The cast of *Rebel* met in a bungalow here. On one occasion Nick Ray weighed in on an impromptu jazz session with his hot harmonica.

WHERE HIS STAR SHINES: Dean's star on the Walk of Fame is located one-half block north of Hollywood Blvd on the west side of Vine Street.

WHERE HE STUDIED: James Dean and Bill Bast took an acting class from James Whitmore. It was held at 225 26th Street in Santa Monica.

WHERE HE PARKED CARS: Dean was a parking lot attendant for a time at the CBS offices, 6121 Sunset Blvd.

WHERE HE DIDN'T HAVE A DONUT: It is frequently reported that on his fatal day Dean and his party had a snack at Farmer's Market at 3d and Fairfax. More likely, he went to Hollywood Ranch Market, which was located close to Competition Motors.

WHERE HE DIDN'T LEAVE A TIP: Googies was located at 8100 Sunset. Schwabs was on the southeast corner of Sunset Blvd. and Crescent Heights.

WHERE HE WEPT: St. Timothy's Catholic Church at 10425 W. Pico Blvd in Los Angeles is the site of Pier Angeli's wedding to Vic Damone. Legend has Dean crying outside during the service, then gunning his motorcycle and roaring off.

WHERE HE BORROWED MONEY: Dean's management team was headquartered at Famous Artists Agency at 9441 Wilshire Blvd. in Los Angeles.

WHERE HE PUNCHED A BROTHER: Dean was kicked out of the Sigma Nu House after punching a frat brother. It was at 601 Gayley Avenue in Westwood.

WHERE JIM WALKED JUDY TO SCHOOL: The house used in *Rebel Without a Cause* is at 6122 Citrus in Baldwin Hills. The alley behind it was used extensively in the filming, notably when Jim Stark (Dean) walked Judy (Natalie Wood) to school.

WHERE *EAST OF EDEN* PREMIERED: The Egyptian Theater is at 6708 Hollywood Blvd.

Loehr, David

Known as the "Dean of Deanabilia," David Loehr is probably the most avid Dean collector in the world and the collaborator with David Dalton on books about Dean. A New York clothing designer, he didn't get into Dean until the seventies, but then he quickly amassed the premier collection of Dean memorabilia — Deanabilia — and began pilgrimages to Dean's hometown of Fairmount, Indiana, where he dreamed of opening a gallery devoted to Jimmy.

The February 1996 edition of *Chicago* magazine describes his "soul-searching drive through the country. That night, he stopped by a cornfield and looked to the sky. 'I thought, Man, Jimmy, should I be doing this or not? And the second I said it, a shooting star went across plain as day, the whole horizon. And I thought, well, that's the answer.'"

In September of 1988, David and close friend Lenny Prussack bought a Victorian house on Main Street in Fairmount and opened Loehr's collection as the James Dean Gallery, charging admission.

the lost highway

A stretch of original road surface upon which James Dean drove is forgotten except by the jackrabbits and tumbleweeds that have taken it over. In 1959 Highway 46 was widened and straightened in its descent from Polonio Pass to one mile east of the intersection where James Dean died. Known as the Cholame Lateral, the bypassed stretch of highway — visible from some parts of the new road — fell into disrepair and collapse. Silent, bereft of cars and with faded highway markers at angles askew, it is occasionally walked by the die-hard Dean death devotee, who may take home a crumbled highway reflector as a souvenir. But it is an eerie place at night.

The story is told locally of a traveling salesman who is heading inland from his route on the coast. Tired and unfamiliar with the area, and sometimes confused by the coastal fog, he pulls to the side of the road to rest for a few moments. When he awakes and resumes his drive, he accidentally gets on an entrance to the old highway. Thinking he's lost, he becomes more and more anxious and is at last relieved to see lights ahead. Upon approach, they turn out to be highway safety flares. He sees a wrecked sports car and a smashed Ford and hears moaning and crying — but there are no people or policemen present. Frightened, he backs up the road and eventually gets back on the main highway.

Daylight comes and he inquires at the local diner about any car wrecks the previous night. The helpful proprietor presses him for more information, then smiles and tells him the story of Jimmy Dean and the Lost Highway.

Lost, Lonely and Vicious

This 1958 film starring Ken Clayton, Barbara Wilson and Richard Gilden was a thinly fictionalized tabloid-style James Dean knockoff about a rising young actor whose moodiness is matched only by his obsession with fast women and fast cars. He dies in a sports car accident. "Boys and Girls Clawing Their Way to Success in Hollywood" reads the tagline. Directed by Frank Myers and written by Norman Graham.

Lotus

There has been a persistent story that James Dean intended to acquire a Lotus Mark 9 racing car at the time of his death. Perhaps he had the car on order. In 1987 New York auction house Christie's sold a Lotus that they claimed had been delivered to James Dean. The car, reportedly valued at $25,000, sold for $46,750 to a California man.

love child

Both Joe Hyams and John Gilmore write in their Dean biographies that Jimmy Dean fathered a "love child" before his death. Joe Hyams wrote in *Mislaid in Hollywood,*

> On the preceding Wednesday night (before his death) I drove by his house to wish him well. As I pulled into the driveway, Pier passed me, coming out in her car. I waved and honked but she only nodded to me, and her face looked tear-stained.
>
> Jimmy, too, looked distraught when I went in. For the second time since I had known him I felt it was best to leave him alone. Before going out I asked if there was anything I could do.
>
> He looked down at his hands; he was balling his fingers into fists, over and over.
>
> "It's already done," he said in a choked voice. He looked at me, and what I saw in his face shocked me.
>
> "Pier's going to have a baby," he blurted out, finally.
>
> I was stunned by the news. I knew he had seen her from time to time since the wedding, and I had been hoping that somehow they might get back together again. I stood there silently, not knowing what to say.
>
> Then Jimmy started to cry and for the first and only time in my life

I took a man in my arms and I rocked him the way he had rocked Pier's picture.

"Did Jimmy Dean Leave a Son" was the cover story of the August 1957 edition of *On the QT* magazine. Writer Larry Ashenden claimed, "The rumor that Mary B.'s mysterious child could be none other than Dean's began making the rounds about three months after the sensitive, moody young actor died in the flaming crash of his Porsche sports car." The mother was a carhop at a Sunset Boulevard drive-in. Dean enjoyed "rolling full blast into a drive-in restaurant for a chance to meet pretty car-hops who made themselves extra-available when Jimmy was on the lot." The love child supposedly was born in the summer of 1955 and put up for adoption.

John Gilmore, in his *Live Fast— Die Young: My Life with James Dean*, writes of "Karen," who visits the site of Jimmy's death with Gilmore. She is pregnant with Dean's child and says, "I'd given thought to having a miscarriage before he was killed. Maybe it was the only we could have been together — Jimmy and myself. We'd have to have done it without my being pregnant." Gilmore says a studio rep had visited Dean on the Marfa set of *Giant* to advise him on the Karen problem, invoking Charlie Chaplin's paternity court case. Dean reportedly responded, "I can't be bothered with this sort of bullshit. If it isn't my kid, then why are you even talking to me about it? I don't know that I even fucked her, man. This is the chick that gave me a blowjob. How the hell's she supposed to get pregnant from giving me a blowjob?" But he had confessed to Gilmore that he had intercourse with her. "She was tight, he said, really tight. He'd had to push hard to get all the way in her."

Lurie, Rod

Los Angeles host of KMPG-Radio talk show and film critic for *Los Angeles Magazine*. He is author of the 1995 true crime book *Once Upon a Time in Hollywood*, which recounts the murders and con games surrounding the making of a proposed James Dean film biography.

M

magazine articles

It's estimated that 198 articles appeared in the United States during the two years following the death of James Dean. Articles appeared in *Collier's*,

Commentary, Coronet, Cosmopolitan, Esquire, Evergreen Review, Life, Look, Modern Screen, Motion Picture, Movieland, Movie Life, Movie Mirror, Movie Stars Parade, The New Republic, Newsweek, Photoplay, Popular Photography, Redbook, The Reporter, Saturday Review, Sight and Sound, Seventeen, Screen Stars, Screen Stories, Time, Theater Arts and Vogue.

Dean biographer John Howlett lists some titles:

"Is Natalie Wood Betraying Jimmy Dean?" "Jimmy Dean Suicide Rumors." "Did Jimmy Dean Leave a Son?" "Did Jimmy Dean Really Die?" "Jimmy Dean's Hidden Heartbreak." "Death Drive." "I Almost Married Jimmy Dean." "The Ghost Who Wrecked Pier Angeli's Marriage." "The Strange Lovemaking of Jimmy Dean." "You Haven't Heard the Half About Jimmy Dean!" "James Dean's Black Madonna." "Jimmy Dean: Why Parents Fear Him." "James Dean's Last Ride—A Great Actor on the Road to Becoming a Greater Driver, When Death Released His Heavy Foot from the Throttle."

See also posthumous articles.

Malecfarum Coven

Ron Smith wrote a fascinating article, "The Car, the Star—and the Curse That Linked Them," which was featured in the August 1990 *Robb Report.* He details his own investigations into Jimmy's involvement in a witches' coven that met in the Hollywood hills.

Smith wrote that the studio had been nervous about Dean's "acknowledgment of Satan" and "would have been apoplectic" had they known that he dabbled in witchcraft. Nevertheless, Jimmy apparently pursued his interest through visits to the Malecfarum Coven, one of the oldest such groups in Hollywood.

Although he had considerable trouble tracking down any Malecfarum members to interview for his article, Smith finally made contact through a television producer. This resulted in a meeting—in a seedy diner frequented by junkies—with a man who identified himself as "Wet Willie."

Willie led Smith to a 30-room mansion high above Mulholland Drive, where he was introduced to a warlock, known for the purposes of Smith's article as "Sir Patrick Nigel." In dim light, surrounded by Dean artifacts arranged in what could only be called a shrine to the deceased, Sir Patrick spoke reverently of his association with Jimmy:

> "He (Dean) was one with the spirits," recalled Sir Patrick. "The first night he came to a celebration, he had an aura about him. We all felt it."
> "Was he a member of your group?"
> "Do not use the past tense. He is still with us."

Sir Patrick said that he had instructed Jimmy in several important arts:

I had taught him astrology, and how to read tarot, and he was progressing with *The Book of the Dead*. He often talked of death — *his* death — and he said that he was ready to come back in yet another life.

The Man Who Listens to Horses

This is the title of the autobiography of real life "horse-whisperer" Marvin "Monty" Roberts, who claimed to have taken James Dean under his wing for four months in Salinas to rusticate the former farm boy for the role of Cal Trask in the upcoming *East of Eden*. *The Horse Whisperer* was a novel by Nicholas Evans, made into a movie starring Robert Redford. Roberts was popularly recognized as the model of the equine-empathetic horse trainer of the novel, largely due to his own self-promotion.

Time Magazine, in a December 14, 1998, review of Roberts and his book, subtitled *We know that Monty Roberts talks to animals. Question is whether what he says to people is true*, said, "Call it horse puckey for the soul, if charges by Monty's younger brother Larry and others close to the author's life are to be credited. By these accounts, backed up by *Time's* reporting, the stirring tale with more than 800,000 copies in print — out this month in paperback — contains an embarrassing number of seeming untruths, some harmless, others outrageous."

Among the fibs the scathing book section article, by John Skow and James Willwerth, claimed to uncover are Monty's depiction of his own father as a brutalizing murderer and his claim that he was a young Elizabeth Taylor's stunt double for *National Velvet*.

And James Dean's farm pal was actually a man named Tony Vargas, and his relationship with James Dean was a fiction concocted out of the convenient circumstance that *Eden* was shot in Monty's hometown of Salinas.

Monty's publisher, Random House, said that the accusations were merely a family squabble. He was also quoted as emotionally telling an audience, "Don't take this wrong, but if everything I said was 100 percent false, look at the good it's doing"— presumably, for horses' rights.

Roberts' aunt, Joyce Renebome, and her daughter were reportedly at work on a book of refutation called *Horse Whispers and Lies*.

Mansfield, Jayne

The nuclear-chested fifties flagship of female sexuality auditioned for the part of Judy in *Rebel Without a Cause*. Losing out to Natalie Wood, she was given the part of a waitress as a consolation prize, only to wind up on the cutting room floor. Her career in decline by the 1960s, she died when her Cadillac slammed into a mosquito abatement truck on a foggy road. Rumors abounded that she had been decapitated, but it was only her detached blonde wig in the accident photos. Her chihuahua also died in the wreck, in addition to her boyfriend. She was buried in Pennsylvania, but her fans established a cenotaph — a marker for someone buried elsewhere — near the lagoon at Hollywood Forever Cemetery. The graveyard was formerly Hollywood Memorial Park. Since going bankrupt, it has been revived under new management.

Marfa Lights

The Marfa Ghost Lights are eerie luminescent globes seen crossing the hills outside of this small Texas town that was headquarters to the cast and crew of *Giant* during filming. Some say the lights look like lanterns twin-

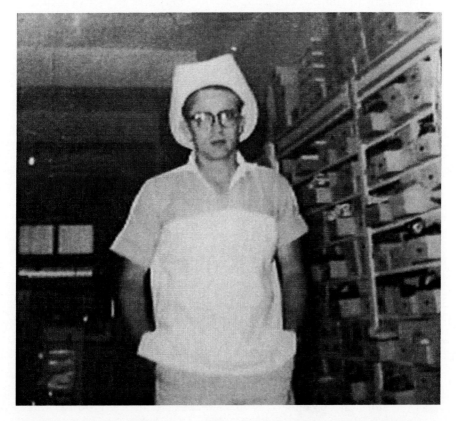

People in the small town of Marfa, Texas, still tell stories about when James Dean and crew came to town for the filming of *Giant*. This photograph shows James Dean in a Marfa shoe store (courtesy Marfa Public Library, Marfa, Texas).

kling in the foothills, while others report brighter lights that flare up and cast shadows before fading. Frank Kendal tells this story in a 1984 article in *National Examiner:*

> Not long ago, Samuel Whatley was driving home just before dawn when he saw what he thought were car lights speeding toward him. The next thing he knew, a cantaloupe-sized globe of orange-red light appeared and hovered a few feet outside the window of his pickup. Whatley slammed the gas pedal to the floor, but the globe stayed with him for two miles before disappearing.

The lights have been chased from the air and ground, photographed and televised. One theory is that the lights come from phosphorescent minerals. Some say they are produced by swamp gas. Some Marfa residents think the lights could be produced by jack rabbits with glow-worms clinging to their fur. Kendal reports that Gabriel Green, president of the Amalgamated Flying Saucer Clubs of America, believes the lights are due to atmospheric ionization around spacecraft piloted by extraterrestrials: "They zigzag around to get our attention and expand our awareness." Green believed that aliens had set up bases under nearby mountains.

marriage

The May 1957 issue of *Lowdown* magazine carried a story by editor Joel Raleigh in which he claimed to have discovered that at the time of his death, James Dean was engaged. Assuring his readers that personal investigation of each issue's "most important story" was his "custom," Raleigh relates how he made five separate trips to Fairmount, Indiana, "to settle once and for all the question of his death" — whatever that may have been. "Obliged," he says, to make frequent visits to the cemetery, he discovered there "one of the most disturbing stories ever to come to light" — he "met the girl James Dean was going to marry!"

The story continues:

> He planned to marry her within a week of the date on which he lost his life.
> It happened this way. Often, I stood hard by his grave at the Fairmount burial grounds and observed the girls and women who came to weep, to pray. Many had come from thousands of miles away.
> But always, promptly at noon, I noticed a proud-faced girl arrive with a sprig of flowers. Tenderly she would kneel and place the sprig — simple daisies, the wild variety. Then she would catch her breath, rise and walk rapidly away.

Her name was Betty Lou Simmons and she lived on a farm outside of Baton Rouge, Louisiana. According to Raleigh, she had met Jimmy Dean on November 2, 1954, when he was on a short vacation in his sports car. "He preferred the simpler entertainment spots where a man could enjoy a beer in shirtsleeves." Taking a clay road, he stopped beneath a weeping willow drinking in the sylvan beauty.

"Try this," a melodious voice said. And there stood a girl, holding out a sheaf of rice leaves. Jimmy was startled. Then he smiled and looked at her again. She was wearing shorts and a halter. She was dark and lovely and his heart pounded within him.

Staying three days at her father Ab's farmhouse, and insisting on paying for his room and board, Jimmy proposed, and a wedding date was set for a week after the shooting of *Giant* closed. The plan was apparently to take Betty Lou on a sports car tour of America and then move her family to the Santa Clara Valley to raise prunes. On March 6, 1955, he sent a Western Union telegram:

BOUGHT YOU A DIAMOND RING AND HAVE PLACED ORDER FOR TEN COUNT THEM TEN CHILDREN STOP MISS YOU TERRIBLY AND PRAY FOR YOU EVERY NIGHT STOP PRAY FOR ME AND LOVE ME JIMMY.

But Jimmy was killed. Betty Lou sold the jewels he had bought her and purchased a ticket to Fairmount to place flowers on his grave.

McHenry, Troy

Troy McHenry has the unfortunate distinction of being the only bona fide victim of the curse of Jimmy Dean's car. On Sunday, October 21, 1956, he was racing at the Los Angeles County fairgrounds before a crowd of 30,000 in an hour-long semi-main race for modified sports cars under 1,500 cc when his sleek Porsche Spyder spun out of control and hit a tree. The fatal car had been equipped with the back swing arms that had been in Dean's car when he died. McHenry had received the parts from his friend and colleague Dr. William F. Eschrich. He also had Dean's transmission, but it was not installed in McHenry's car at the time of the crash.

Dr. McHenry had come to the United States from Australia at age fifteen and had a brilliant career in medicine, attaining the position of Chief of Staff at Doctors Hospital in Los Angeles. In 1956 he was forty-five years old and a successful Beverly Hills orthopedic surgeon. An avid sportsman, he had participated in Trans-Pacific Yacht races and had married Dr. Amanda Marshall. Had he lived, he would have in one week ascended to the presidency of the American College of Osteopathic Surgeons at the Detroit convention.

Meatloaf

The 1970s rockster, real name Marvin Lee Aday, visited Dean's grave in 1990 along with songwriter Tommy Sands.

medallion

Beginning in 1988, Keepsake Medallions, out of Hartford City, Indiana, offered annual issues of "The James Dean Silver Medallion Collection." The 1995 medallion, priced at $20.00, featured his tombstone in relief.

Memento Mori

Mementoes such as bones or garments have often been preserved with honor and religious awe by the credulous faithful. Relics provide a connection to the revered dead and may even become amulets. The ghosts are flattered and therefore friendly. The ancient Celts collected the heads of heroes, while some cannibals felt that by eating the dead hero they absorbed his qualities. The disciples of St. Polycarp wrote in 156, "We took up his bones, more precious than jewels and finer than gold, and laid them in a suitable place where the Lord will permit us to gather ourselves together, and celebrate his martyrdom." This is essentially what goes on at dealer tables at fan conventions, and though none of his disciples so far claims to have the bones of James Dean, his relics are avidly sought for adoration.

His underwear is sold at auction, and fans as early as the fifties pleaded for a scrap of wallpaper from a room he had been in. A fleck of paint from the Spyder is kept in a Lucite reliquary by one man, while another treasured a supposed lock of Jimmy's hair. A soil sample from Jimmy's schoolboy science project is venerated like dirt from the Holy Land. With the decline in the number of bona fide souvenirs of Jimmy, fans in subsequent decades have been reduced to scrabbling for items with ever more tenuous connection to the icon. Dirt and stones from the crash site and grave are picked up as treasures. When the Baldwin Hills location of *Rebel Without a Cause* was remodeled, parts of the fence were saved. Bricks from a wall of Jimmy's high school, accompanied by a letter of certification, were sold for $5 to $15 plus shipping and handling. Splinters from the "Reata Ranch" set of *Giant* are requested by mail of the landowners.

A cottage industry sprang up which manufactured relics unconsciously and cheerfully linking Jimmy to his death. He poses by the fatal Spyder on collectible coffee mugs and collector's edition plates.

Merc

From *Classic & Custom Magazine*, July 1989: "Harrah's Automobile Collection of Reno, Nevada is the present owner of the Merc Jimmy Dean drove in *Rebel Without a Cause*. According to Ray Borges of Harrah's, the Merc is in its original state and only required minor detailing to bring it up to its present display status. The black paint is flawless and so is the chrome. Harrah's has a copy of the California title that shows the registered owner from 1955 to 1970 to be Warner Bros./Seven Arts Studios—Hollywood, California. Harrah's purchased the Merc from Movie World Cars of the Stars who had shown it previously. The current display at Harrah's has the Merc set atop a ramp made to look like a drive-in movie, with a speaker pole and a large screen showing a giant image of James Dean."

The black 49 Merc has the serial number 9CMI70063.

Merrick, Paul

The deputy coroner of San Luis Obispo County at the time of the death of James Dean. Merrick, who assumed office on January 3, 1955, signed the California death certificate for Dean. He died in 1973 at the age of 72.

Michaels, Scott

Do you want to know where Jimmy lived and dined in Hollywood? Scott Michaels is the former Director of Undertakings for the infamous Grave Line Tours of Hollywood. Scandal monger and death hag Scott created *www.findadeath.com* for likeminded enthusiasts of the underbelly of Tinseltown. His site features a unique and informative section on James Dean that runs refreshingly counter to much of the sniffy fan-based sites on the web. Scott has been published in several magazines and featured in tabloids, and he is co-author of cult film books. Scott's newest venture, Dearly Departed—The Tragical History Tour of Hollywood, is enjoying tremendous success. The tour includes many Dean-related sites.

Mineo, Sal

Salvatore Mineo was the son of a Sicilian coffin maker. He joined a Bronx gang at age eight and was kicked out of Catholic school. He headed for

State of California

County of __San Luis Obispo__ } ss.

In the matter of the Inquisition upon the Body of

__James DEAN__

Deceased.

Before

__Paul E. Merrick__

Coroner.

We, the undersigned, jurors summoned to appear before __Paul E. Merrick__ _____ Coroner of the County of __San Luis Obispo__, at __The Civic Center, 10th__ and __Park Streets, Paso Robles,__

on the __11th__ day of __October__ 19__55__, to inquire into the cause of the death of __James DEAN__

having been sworn and charged according to law, and having made such inquisition, after

hearing the testimony adduced, upon our oaths, each and all do say:

That we find the deceased was named __James DEAN__

and that __he came to __his__ death on the __30th__ day of __September__, 19__55__, at __Cholame__

in the County of __San Luis Obispo__, State of California, by injuries received in an accident at the intersection of Highway 41 and 466, according to evidence presented, in a two car collision. We find no indiciation that James Dean met death through any criminal act of another, and that he died of a fractured neck and other injuries received.

All of which we certify by this inquisition, in writing, by us signed, this __11th__ day of __October__, 19__55__.

/s/ D. H. Orcutt _____ Foreman

/s/ Dorothy Schwartz

/s/ Enid S. Eddy

/s/ Mrs. Alan A. Dale

/s/ Kenneth G. Harris

/s/ Charles H. Ashton

/s/ Ray J. Samp

/s/ Cliff O. Bickell

/s/ J. G. Hanson

/s/ Mac Mazorini

/s/ J. P. Brush

/s/ L. C. Dauth

Coroner's Form No. 614 INQUISITION BY JURY, CORONER'S. (Gov. C. Sec. 27504.)

Report from the inquisition on Dean's death.

Hollywood in the fifties after being bitten by the acting bug. Mineo appeared with Dean in both *Rebel Without a Cause* (as John "Plato" Crawford) and *Giant* (as Angel Obregón II).

"At moments of doubt or insecurity, he's a source of tremendous strength to me," said Mineo at one point, according to an article by Brian O'Dowd in *Hollywood Studio Magazine*. "After he died, I became obsessed with him, trying to make contact with him. I feel his presence and I hear his voice in my own reality. I know it's him, because he called me Plato, the same name as in the film."

Sal Mineo was in rehearsal for a play when he was stabbed to death on February 12, 1976, in the driveway a few yards to the right of 8563 Holloway Drive in West Hollywood. He lived at 8565 Holloway Drive. He was thirty-seven years old. After the stabbing, Mineo's knife wound was excised and preserved. Kept in forensic storage by the Los Angeles Police Department, it was held for the day when it might be matched to the weapon of his unknown assailant.

See also Who Killed Sal Mineo?

Minkoff, Brad

Warren Beath met Brad Minkoff at Todd Bello's house off Melrose in January of 1990. John Gilmore was also there. Brad was a smallish sycophantic presence in the shadow of actor Damian Chapa, who had made an impressive screen test and been signed to play Jimmy Dean in a biopic in development. The flick was never made. But Damian eventually played one of the Menendez brothers in a TV movie and married Natasha Henstridge. And eighteen-year-old Brad Minkoff got his name in lights. No one knew that January evening that while Brad did his sullen and spooky Dean impression, his brother lay dead of a gunshot wound.

Actually, Brad was more of a Jack Simmons, Dean's hanger-on roommate, to Damian's Jimmy Dean that evening. He had told everyone over the last two weeks that he had shot his brother on New Year's Eve while his parents were on vacation in Mexico. No one believed him because, as the *Los Angeles Times* would say (Jan. 17, 1990), "he appeared to be mimicking his idol, brooding 1950s actor James Dean, and reciting melodramatic bits of movie dialogue." It got to be a running gag.

Apparently, there had been a sibling rivalry to rival that of Jimmy and Dick Davalos in *East of Eden*. The body of Michael Minkoff, an engineering major, was found December 31 on the kitchen floor of the family's Agoura Hills home after deputies responded to a 911 call apparently made by the victim. He had been shot three times, in the head, back and chest.

His body was lying in a pool of blood with the fallen phone receiver two inches from his hand.

Initially, sheriff's homicide investigators said they only wanted to question Bradley and had not ruled out that he was also the victim of a crime. But Bradley was missing, hiding out with young actor friends who had no idea they were harboring a fugitive. They knew Brad by the name Johnny Boy, which he had borrowed from the Robert De Niro character in the movie *Mean Streets*.

Bradley was taken into custody by Los Angeles police at a friend's home in North Hollywood, three days after deputies obtained a warrant charging him with the murder of his brother. He was on $1.5 million bail.

Minter Field

On Highway 99 twelve miles north of Bakersfield, turn west on the Lerdo Highway Exit. One mile beyond is the Shafter Airport. Continue on Lerdo Highway and to your right is the barren and weed-shot tarmac that was used as an airport racecourse demarked with bales of hay by sports car aficionados in the 1950s. This is the tarmac over which a speed-loving James Dean raced to third place on May 1, 1955, during a weekend off from the filming of *Rebel Without a Cause*. It was windy and rainy that day, and Arizona driver Jack Drummond was killed when he flipped on Turn 3.

The Minter Field Air Museum next to the runway features a section devoted to James Dean and the day he raced there.

See Drummond, Jack.

Minton, John

An acclaimed neo-romantic artist living and painting in London in the 1940s and 1950s. Known for his landscapes, town scenes, and figure subjects in oil and watercolor, he was also an illustrator. Minton's homosexuality greatly influenced his art, and his attraction to the manly ideal of the era led him to portray handsome working class lovers and other archetypes of masculinity such as guardsmen and matadors.

While Minton had many friends and loved witty banter and parties, his inner life tended toward melancholy and depression. He also had a fascination with death. He was particularly moved by James Dean's accident. The loss of the young, brooding star inspired Minton to create what would be his last painting, depicting the fatal crash. The unfinished work was called *Composition: The Death of James Dean in September 1955*.

Although he experienced success as an artist and illustrator, his depression finally overtook him and Minton committed suicide in 1957.

Miracleflesh

The death of James Dean resulted in the development of Miracleflesh, a simulated flesh of plaster and plastic. It was used in the reproduction of lifelike effigies of the actor's head, which could be fondled. A studio in California produced about 300 of them a day in 1956. Each was painstakingly hand painted. They reportedly went for merely five dollars, according to Ezra Goodman in the *Life* magazine article "Delirium Over a Dead Star" (September 24, 1956).

missing tapes *see* **tape recordings**

"Mister Marion"

Marion, Indiana, booster Glen Allen. An indefatigable champion of James Dean fans, in 1980 he succeeded in placing an honorary star in Marion to mark the site of the demolished Seven Gables House, Dean's birthplace. Three years later, he died at age 59.

model car

Exoticar Model Company of Framingham, Massachusetts, offered a ¹⁄₂₄ scale model of the car in which Dean died. It went for $129.00 in 1998.

Modern Screen Magazine

In the years following the actor's death, they published many stories remarkable for their ghoulish titles, such as:

1955	*The Secret Love that Haunts Jimmy Dean*
	The Last Story about Jimmy
	Appointment with Death
1956	*A Tenderness Lost*
	Jim Dean's Funeral
	Goodbye, Jimmy
	It's Me, Jimmy
1957	*Jimmy Dean's Last Message*
	His Love Destroyed Him
	Was Jimmy Dean's Sports Car Jinxed?
	Death Drive
	The Last Story About Jimmy

Mondo James Dean

This 1996 book by Lucinda Ebersole and Richard Peabody was published by St. Martin's Press as part of a series on pop icons including Elvis, Marilyn and even Barbie.

"This bittersweet book resurrects James Dean," says the introduction. "It is a guidebook for disciples, for new initiates, for romantics, for wannabes—for everyone who has ever wanted to live fast, die young, and leave behind a good-looking corpse."

monkey

The toy monkey that Dean fondled so memorably in the opening scene of *Rebel Without a Cause* (filmed at the intersection of Franklin and Sierra Bonita in Hollywood) changed hands at auction for $7,000 in the 1980s. The monkey also figured in a supernatural occurrence, according to the story "Did Jimmy Dean's Spirit Haunt the Studio?" that appeared in *Movie Life* magazine in October 1986 under Jane Williams' byline. According to the article:

> A group of young Hollywoodites had gathered at the apartment of Dennis Hopper. There were numerous Dean pals, among them Natalie Wood. On the wall was an inscription about how to become a man, which Jimmy had always admired. As the story goes, someone at the party remembered how Jimmy had liked it and those in the room saw the inscription move. Or thought they did.
>
> Later in the evening, a guest examined the little toy monkey on the fireplace mantle. It was the same one shown with Jimmy beneath the opening titles of *Rebel Without a Cause*. As the group discussed Jimmy, the little toy monkey started to clap his hands. It must have been the wind from the open window that caused it, but all the young people were so startled — and even a little frightened — that they ran out of the room.

monuments

Seita Ohnishi was a fifty-year-old Tokyo businessman in 1977 when he erected a $15,000 stylized sculpture in the tiny town of Cholame, California, to commemorate the death of James Dean. The memorial is wrapped around the trunk of a tree of heaven. Though he spoke no English, he made three trips from Japan to oversee his project. The sculpture was cast in Japan and transported to Cholame. The memorial has Dean's name, the date of his birth, the time and day of his death, and a figure of infinity. The stainless steel shaft mirrors the bend in the road where Dean died.

The polished stones at the foot of the monument were also from Japan. Fans took so many that they had to be regularly replaced.

The monument faces 17 degrees north of true east.

"There's always somebody out there," the current owner said in 1985. "They stop, look, have lunch and steal the rocks."

In 1988 a bust of Dean was installed in Griffith Park among statues of Copernicus and Isaac Newton. The bronze bust was donated by Kenneth Kendall, who fashioned the work 33 years earlier. Tourists spilling out of buses unloading at the site have been heard asking some strange questions.

"Will his eyes light up?"

"Is this where he went over the cliff?"

"Was he Jewish?" (In reference to the star on the monument.)

By 1993 a movement was afoot to have a replica of the Griffith Park bust of Dean installed in his hometown of Fairmount, Indiana. A bank president offered a Main Street lot, but it was next to a filling station and the vibe was not right. Another site was considered nearer to the business center, but the owner was a guy Dean had punched out in high school, and he was asking forty thousand dollars. Applications to Curtis Management, the state of Indiana, and Dean's family were to no avail.

Moreno, Paul

The Cholame ambulance driver at the scene of the accident, rumored to have photos of Dean in the crumpled car, died in 1980 at age 65. His obituary listed him as a former deputy of the San Luis Obispo County Coroner's Office as well as the owner and operator of a restaurant. He was buried in Greenlawn Cemetery. There is no marker on his grave.

Morrissey

Eccentric singer who won his fame as front man for the Smiths. He wrote a book about Dean entitled *James Dean Is Not Dead*, which was published by Babylon Books of Great Britain in 1983. The video for his "Suedehead" was filmed around Jimmy's houses in Fairmount, Indiana. The song is featured on Morrissey's solo album, *Viva Hate*.

"The Movie Star"

In 1962, the Dupont Show of the Week presented a drama inspired by the death of James Dean, entitled "The Movie Star." The title was played by Dane Clark, a tough Brooklyn native who was a staple in World War II movies including *Destination Tokyo* and *God Is My Co-Pilot* and film noir classics such as *Whiplash*.

mug

One of the first products licensed by Curtis Management upon sewing up their deal with Dean's family was a set of "four sturdy stoneware mugs based on the film career of James Dean." Suggested retail for a set of four was eighteen dollars. There was the "Rebel" Mug, "Loner" Mug, "Wrangler" Mug and "Jimmy" Mug.

Murnau, Friedrich Wilhelm

Director of *Nosferatu* (1922), the single film production of Prana-Film, a company founded by ardent spiritualist Albin Grau. Grau had never made a film before, and all the potential projects under his company's consideration displayed, according to David Skal in *Hollywood Gothic*, "a distinct predilection for the occult, the Romantic, and the bizarre." But the single production would be *Nosferatu,* and Grau's art direction "almost explicitly evokes film itself as demonic magic." In 1921 Grau and his partner engaged as director thirty-two-year-old F. W. Murnau.

The result is a highly stylized retelling of Bram Stoker's *Dracula.* Stripped to its mythical elements and consisting of a series of strong and carefully composed visuals, the story became an interpretation of the Parsifal legend. The Grail Castle has become the vampire's home, and Parsifal is the young estate agent Hutter who ventures out of the safety of Germany and into the mythical Wild Wood to encounter the sexually maimed Fisher King. The land has fallen under the distinctly foreign sway of the exotic and erotic Graf Orlock, who is visually an embodiment of the sexual threat and dysfunction that underlay the fear of racial pollution that permeated pre–World War II Germany. He is the walking lance of the Grail legend, storied to have pierced the side of Christ. His contamination has distinctly to do with blood and bodily fluids. The director's well-known homosexuality gave a strong subtext to the nature of the wound.

Over thirty years later and across the ocean, the closest thing Hollywood had to an auteur was the maverick director Nicholas Ray. For Warner Bros. he would produce another retelling of the Grail Legend, which had more in common with the German expressionist vision than the medieval romances.

Rebel Without a Cause replaced the ominous Grail Castle with Griffith Observatory. The winding roads and careful visuals portray it as a cosmic way station high above Hollywood. Young Parsifal is Jim Stark, who assays the perilous journey to this Art Deco repository of mystery and confrontation with the eternal. The conundrum he encounters is again sexual, embodied in the peculiar choice he faces between winsome and nubile

Natalie Wood and the equally nubile Sal Mineo as the provocatively Greek-named Plato. As in *Nosferatu,* the story is resolved with the crack of dawn.

In Murnau's film, the vampire was held past his bedtime to evaporate in the sunlight. In Ray's version, it is half of the sexual psyche that is destroyed when Dean unintentionally causes the death of Plato. Director Ray is revealed just before the credits in a signature walk-out. It reminds you of when the curtain was pulled back and you finally got to see the Wizard behind Oz.

A few years after *Nosferatu,* F. W. Murnau went to Hollywood. There in 1931 he died in his roadster under mysterious circumstances. By that time German expressionist occultism had already jumped the ocean and been nestled in the bosom of Hollywood for some years.

Music James Dean Lived By

A Dean tribute album compiled and performed by artist Bob Graybo and others for Unique Records. The tunes Dean lived by include "Dream Lover," "Masquerade," "Love Story," "We Could Make Such Beautiful Music Together" and of course, snatches of signature music from Dean films.

N

namesakes

Biographer John Howlett reported that of the forty-eight boys born in Dean's hometown of Fairmount, Indiana, in 1956, twenty-seven were named after Jimmy.

necrophilia

In 2002 Dean fans were shocked when two respected icons in the pantheon of fandom earned sound bytes in the increasingly competitive field of Dean documentary by alleging that the recently-deceased Jack Simmons had had sex with Jimmy's corpse in the funeral home in Fairmount, Indiana.

Bill Bast reported in the video *Hollywood: The Rebels: James Dean* that he had heard something about the coffin being broken into the night before the funeral so that someone could steal a last kiss. He gave no further

.details— until the AMC documentary *The Final Day*. Both Bast and Maila "Vampira" Nurmi claimed that Dean sycophant Jack Simmons—who was also accused by rumor during his life of robbing Jimmy's home after his death—sneaked into the Hunt Funeral Home and satisfied himself sexually in some way with Dean's body.

The allegation is so controversial it is worth looking at in its entirety. The documentary's narrator asked Bast if indeed anyone had broken into the coffin and tampered with the body. Bast responded that there had been a young fan hanging around during the filming of *Rebel* who had seemed very infatuated with Dean and had been telling people he wanted at least a kiss from him. Nurmi named the fan—Jack Simmons—and said he had been her chauffeur because she didn't drive. "He had this old car, an old hearse, and he made himself very handy." She explained that Simmons was gay and that he was totally in love with Dean, always "touching Jimmy with his vulture-like claws." Nurmi said that Dean and Simmons never had sex: "That goes without saying."

Bast confirmed that someone broke into the casket the night before the funeral. He said that rumors pointed to "a young man who'd come along with the group from Hollywood." It was left to the imagination, he said, to figure it all out—but here the documentary helpfully flashed a picture of Simmons on the screen, perhaps for viewers lacking imagination.

Nelson, Ron

This CHP officer, who was on the scene, told interviewer Warren Beath in 1981: "There was never in our minds any evidence that the Porsche was traveling at any speed. If Dean had lived, I would have cited Turnupseed for violating the other lane. There's a lot of damage to the Porsche, but if he'd been going that fast, I think it would have looked different. I think he slowed down, either by changing gears, or braking."

Nichols, Terry *see* Bazooka, Nicky

Nicholson, Jack

Did Jack Nicholson and James Dean ever meet? The answer is yes, according to Nicholson biographer Donald Shepard in *Jack Nicholson: An Unauthorized Biography*.

Shepard holds that Dean met—and snubbed—Jack Nicholson at the home of Samson DeBrier in the spring of 1955. Dean had come to the house with John Gilmore, who introduced Dean and Nicholson. According to Shepard, "Dean was not friendly; he mumbled something to Jack and turned his back to resume his conversation with DeBrier." Supposedly Nicholson never mentioned Dean again, at least not directly. Shepard writes, "He would always raise the subject obliquely, Gilmore said, usually by discussing Dennis Hopper and the possibility of Dean's influence on him, thereby steering the conversation around to Dean without seeming to do so."

Nigel, Sir Patrick

Hollywood warlock uncovered by writer Ron Smith for his article "The Car, the Star — and the Curse that Linked Them" which appeared in the *Robb Report* of August 1990. Nigel, a member of the Malecfarum Witch Coven, claimed to have given Dean his occult instruction: "He [Dean] was one with the spirits. The first night he came to a celebration, he had an aura about him. We all felt it." Nigel told Smith that he schooled Jimmy in astrology, tarot, and *The Book of the Dead*.

noose

Dean seemed to have a premonition he would die of a broken neck. His most bizarre foreshadowing was when he had Sanford Roth photograph him with a noose around his neck on the set of *Giant*, his head at an odd angle. He also kept nooses hanging from the ceilings of some of his Hollywood digs. Many of those who later claimed to have foreseen his death in the Spyder made reference to broken necks in their warnings to him.

Maila Nurmi told Warren Beath, "When I met Jimmy, he had no car — only a cycle. We sometimes all rode about in Jack (Simmons') antique Cadillac hearse. Once Jimmy strung up a noose in the spacious back seat then said, 'That's how I'm going to die.' Death by broken neck in back of an ambulance is so very like death by broken neck in back of a hearse. The accuracy of the precogniscence [sic] is so stunning as to leave me gasping!"

North by Northwest

When Cary Grant died the television coverage of his death invariably featured what was inarguably the most famous scene from his films: the crop duster sequence from the 1959 Alfred Hitchcock classic *North by Northwest*. The scene was considered remarkable for its use of the empty spaces and the length of camera time spent on the passing cars through the sere and empty landscape. The desolate geography and the flat topography becomes itself a character in the scene. The scene was filmed in August of 1958 on Corcoran Road in the vicinity of the James Dean crash site.

Hitchcock received his inspiration for the scene while driving along Highway 99 en route to his coastal home in northern California.

Nurmi, Maila

Maila Nurmi had brief fame in the 1950s as the host of a late-night horror show on KABC-TV in Los Angeles. The character she created, Vampira, was loosely based on the ghoulish woman in Charles Addams' famous *New Yorker* cartoons. An import from Finland, Nurmi started her show business career as a model and show girl before landing her stint as Vampira. It was in that role that she caught the eye of Bela Lugosi, leading to her being cast in Ed Wood's infamous B-horror classic *Plan 9 from Outer Space*, which today regularly shows up on lists of the worst movies of all times.

Nurmi was one of several strange characters who hung out with James Dean and his cronies at familiar Dean haunts such as Barney's Beanery in Hollywood. In an interview with Hedda Hopper, Dean said that he had become friendly with Nurmi because he hoped she might know something about the occult, a subject that interested him. Disappointed in that hope, he told Hopper that Nurmi was a phony. I don't go out with witches, and I dig dating cartoons even less.... I have a fairly adequate knowledge of satanic forces, and I was interested to find out if such a source obsessed her. She was a subject about which I wanted to learn. I met her and engaged her in conversation. She knew absolutely nothing! She uses her inane characterization as an excuse for the most infantile expression you can imagine."

Whisper magazine wrote that she was a witch who had placed a fatal curse on Dean because she was angry about his remarks to Hedda Hopper. After that article appeared, fans at personal appearances would call out to her: "Did you kill James Dean?"

Perhaps sensing an opportunity, Nurmi clung tenaciously to Jimmy's coattails after death, apparently hoping to ride them to celebrity. In tabloid magazines she was portrayed sitting before an open grave in Santa Monica's Woodlawn Cemetery, offering Jimmy an invitation to join her. On her living room wall she kept a photo of Dean with a dagger piercing his eyes and ears. She gave interviews to occult magazines saying she was so terrified of Dean's ghost that she returned home only to feed her cats. She held séances. She received phone calls from the dead Dean, who also sent her songs on the radio.

"Finland, where I was born," Nurmi told Warren Beath, "has the highest psychic ability per capita in the civilized world—according to Duke University's researchers. We were taught, for example, to run out into the first snow and take snapshots as the bodies of departed ones manifested themselves in the shadows of the snowdrifts—we were told. Each family album proudly exhibited first snowfall pictures of the dearly departed grandpas, grandmas, aunts, uncles, et cetera. So—little wonder I accept these things that were bred into me."

Nurmi currently lives in Los Angeles and paints self-portraits of Vampira, which are much sought after as collector's items.

O

Oates, Warren

Quirky leading man and character actor of the 1970s who got his first big break testing stunts on the TV show *Beat the Clock* when James Dean quit the job to assume a role on stage. Oates, who died young, was notable for his starring roles in *Dillinger*, *Two-Lane Black Top* and *Bring Me the Head of Alfredo Garcia*.

observatory curse *see under* **ghosts and hauntings**

The Official James Dean Anniversary Book

The Official James Dean Anniversary Book was a one-shot magazine put out by Dell in 1956. It sold for 25 cents; collectors now pay as much as $100 for copies in good condition. The one-shot phenomenon was covered by *Time* magazine, which called Jimmy "Dean of the One-Shotters."

A plaintive letter in this magazine sets the tone and identifies the constituency at which these magazines were aimed:

Dear Editor:
I was president of a James Dean fan club and I and my members would like a *special favor* from you. You can imagine how we felt when Jimmy met his painful death recently. You see we felt very close to Jimmy because we used to see him a lot when he was in N.Y. before *East of Eden*. I would like to tell you he was sweet, kind and good and that is the honest truth.

In the December issue of *MODERN SCREEN* you printed such beautiful photos of him, some of the best ever taken of him. Could you *please* send us a copy of one — we haven't any pictures of him because he never let us take any. If you only knew how we felt about him you would understand us wanting these pictures. We haven't any pictures at all to remember him by and we never, never want to forget him. Oh, Mr. Saxon, we are counting on you — *Please, Please* don't let us down!

Respectfully,
Patti & members.

O'Hara, Frank

Minor New York poet of the 1950s and 1960s who was fascinated by a variety of contemporary phenomena — Hollywood, jazz, abstract expressionism, and James Dean. The product of strict Irish Catholic parents, he grew up in Maryland and was educated at Harvard. His move to New York, where he finally had the opportunity to live openly as a homosexual, freed him to pursue his love of art and words. Perhaps the struggle to escape his past gave him the feeling that he shared Jimmy's pain. His poem "On Thinking of James Dean" was written upon hearing of his death.

O'Hara himself had a short life, hit by a vehicle while vacationing on the beach at Fire Island. He was only 40.

Ohnishi, Seita

Tokyo businessman who erected the James Dean monument at Cholame, California. From the widow of photographer Sanford Roth, he bought 1,500 negatives of Dean photos for a reported $250,000. He also reportedly bought land near the crash site, perhaps with a mind to establishing another memorial. He commissioned a giant sculpture 36 feet high to be executed by renowned sculptor Yasuo Mizui for $30,000. The 120-ton masterpiece in limestone was to be called "Wall of Hope." It would depict Dean's head on one side and an opening curtain on the opposite side. Ohnishi's intention was to have the monument created in sections so that it could be dismantled and shipped to California. The hollow bust was designed to break if anyone tried to remove it. Replacement heads could be easily reinserted, thwarting vandals, but perhaps swelling private collections.

Had it been installed, the monument would have cost $200,000. But the Hearst Corporation, which owned the surrounding land, and state regulatory agencies seemed to find the project a bit grandiose. Ohnishi had to settle for a smaller, stylized sculpture wrapped around a tree at the site (*see* **monuments**).

Beulah Roth told Warren Beath in an interview:

I had an antique Venetian chair, Fifteenth century chair, very rare, that Jimmy used to sit in — he loved that chair. But it was Fifteenth Century, so he'd sit in it like this, and I would die, and I would hear it creak. And Jimmy would fall asleep in it, and I don't know how. I would say, "Jimmy, I hear it creaking!" So Mr. Ohnishi came here. He said, "I'd like that chair that Jimmy used to sit in."

In some of the photographs, you'll see that wood mannequin. He bought that from me. That belonged to Degas, the painter. I bought that in Paris many years ago. And because Mr. Ohnishi loved it so, I let him have it, because Jimmy posed with it and Jimmy touched it.

Then, I had a Greek marble head that was in some of the photographs—just a head of antique Greek marble that we bought in Rome. And Mr. Ohnishi wanted that. "Whatever the price is, I want that for my Jimmy Dean Museum." It's a museum piece of golden glint marble.

At the unveiling of the smaller monument that was actually installed, Ohnishi distributed cards with a message of praise for Jimmy Dean superimposed over the faces of John Kennedy and George Washington. "This monument stands as a small token of my appreciation for the people of America, from whom I have learned so much. It celebrates a people who have over the years courageously followed the path of truth and justice, while expanding the limits of mankind with their boundless pioneering spirit."

Once Upon a Time in Hollywood

Subtitled *Moviemaking, Con Games, and Murder in Glitter City*, author Rod Lurie's 1995 hardback from Pantheon is an account of what the police called "The James Dean Murders"— the events surrounding the con games of scam artist Jon Emr and the making of a proposed authorized biography of James Dean, which culminated in Emr's murder in broad daylight. It's a fascinating inside look at Curtis Management and its relation to the Dean family, and also a parable about the seduction of glamour and gullible investors.

See also Emr, John; Hauge, Alan.

The Onion Field

On the day of his death, James Dean received a speeding ticket on Highway 99 just south of Mettler Station. The spot became a minor shrine known as the Ticketing Site. A homely plaque was placed on a phone pole at the approximate spot, and car magazines featured photos in their annual coverage of the car runs and tributes. The place was rife with the odor of onions from the surrounding fields.

Five years after Dean's death, a crime was committed on the other side of the road. Gregory Powell and Jimmy Lee Smith forced Los Angeles Police Department officers Ian Campbell and Karl Hettinger to drive from Hollywood to this onion field in Kern County. Campbell was shot to death. Hettinger escaped into the darkness, running over the plowed fields until he reached a farmhouse. Smith and Powell were soon arrested. Smith was released from prison in 1982 but returned for five years in 1984 on a new conviction of possessing and selling heroin. Gregory Powell, the leader, was sentenced to the state prison at Vacaville. He had been scheduled for parole in 1982, but that was blocked by public outrage.

Karl Hettinger moved to nearby Bakersfield after his well-publicized travails and even served on the board of supervisors there until his death.

This crime was eventually the subject of Joseph Wambaugh's bestselling book *The Onion Field* and the ensuing motion picture.

Oscar

The French awarded James Dean a Crystal Star citation, and the British gave him an Academy Award. But he never received an Oscar in his own country. However, Maila Nurmi claimed that she and Jack Simmons had presented him an Oscar that had been stolen from Frank Sinatra. It was reportedly inscribed, "To James Dean for the best performance in Googies 1955," and it held pride of place atop his television at the time of his death.

Ouija board

Writer and Dean archivist Bob Rees of Texas has written in *James Dean, Beyond the Grave* of attending Ouija board séances, replete with candles and theme music from Dean films, that attempted to contact Jimmy in the beyond. In these séances, Dean supposedly reported the number of his death car — "1-3-0" — before issuing the warning, "Seek me no more lest you find yourselves beside me. If I materialize, you must follow my footfall into darkness ... there you meet your mentor." A drinking glass was tossed across the room by an unseen hand. A wall painting twitched. A bottle of spray starch fell off an ironing board.... At this point the intrepid psychic voyagers ran out into the street.

P

Palais de Chaillot

J. Hoberman and Jonathan Rosenbaum report in their fascinating book *Midnight Movies:*

> In 1972, Henri Langlois's long-awaited Cinema Museum opened its doors at the Palais de Chaillot in Paris with an exhibition that included such priceless movie totems as the robot Maria from *Metropolis* and two of the Dior originals worn by Delphine Seyrig in *Last Year at Marienbad.* The most prominent item on display was James Dean's red-zippered jacket, encased in glass, its sleeves eerily cradling the script of *Rebel Without a Cause.* Some months later, due to an inadequate surveillance system guarding the sixty-room museum, the singular relic was stolen....

See also jacket.

pallbearers

The local boys who carried James Dean's casket to the grave were Bob Pulley, Bob Middletown, Rex Bright, James Fulkerson, Whitey Rust and Paul Smith.

Pardini, Laura

Laura Pardini is significant for being the first female author of a James Dean biography — even if she had to publish it herself. *Buscando al Ángel* (*Looking for the Angel*) is largely in Spanish. Laura is Uruguayan but lives in Indiana. The blurb for her book, which appeared in one of the fan club cyberzines, lets you know it cost her $28 to publish each copy. "Laura has met her first goal, to give birth to the book. Now it is up to us to buy it."

Peachey, I., M.D.

The Paso Robles surgeon who, along with Dr. Robert Bossert, treated Rolf Wuetherich for the injuries sustained in the collision that killed James Dean.

phallus

A persistent story circulated in the gay Hollywood of the 1960s concerning a most sought-after conversation piece. It was said that a bronze casting of Jimmy Dean's privates had been made when he was a student of Melrose sculptress Pegot Waring. The casting was reportedly done in plaster and originally used to make wax candles, which Dean gave to lovers of both sexes as intimate keepsakes. After his death, the cast was stolen from his Sherman Oaks cottage and eventually transferred to a stronger medium to make bronze castings.

These attractive souvenirs were apparently seen occupying pride of place on the mantles of Hollywood homosexual cognoscenti, often displayed on velvet or sable and with a key light that brought out Jimmy's etched signature across the shaft. They proliferated until the original mold was broken, or stolen, in the late 1960s. Castings were made of some of the existing dildos and inferior castings made of a variety of materials.

Hollywood legend traces the ownership of one of the original castings to a grisly murder. In 1968 sixty-nine-year-old silent screen star Ramon Novarro, whose star had waned since he had played Ben Hur, picked up two young brothers and took them to his secluded Hollywood Hills home for a private party. The two young hustlers had just blown in from Chicago, and once alone with Novarro they proceeded to ransack his home and beat the aged actor to death. Thrust down his throat was one of the James Dean dildos.

Variations of this story describe the dildo as actually a memento of Rudolph Valentino, another parallel in the legends of the two idols. Oddly, some accounts say that Novarro had in the 1950s been up for consideration of the part of Old Polo in *Giant*. It would have been his return to the big screen and possibly revived his dead career.

phantom hitchhiker *see under* **ghosts and hauntings**

The Picture of Dorian Gray

James Thompson wrote in *Cavalier* magazine (November 1956):

> *Giant* though. Wow! What a way to go out! What an epitaph! *Giant* was some heavy dues. But then he couldn't have known he was going. Or could he? I remember a sort of fantasy I had once about Dean down there in Texas making the movie. He comes back to his trailer after shooting his last scene, the drunk scene in the wine cellar. Tired, hot, disgusted, he bends over the sink to wash off the greasepaint wrinkles and the gray spray on his hair ... and he discovers that they won't come off, that the face he sees in the mirror before him has really and suddenly aged thirty years. Hollywood has made him Dorian Gray in reverse. And it was then that he got into his Porsche and drove off into the sunset, heading out into the desert....

Pike, Loren

Palm Springs native who in 1987 approached the Dean family for cooperation in making a movie about the actor's life, paying $50,000 for a one-year option on the rights. The project that followed was a fiasco of epic proportions, the fallout continuing to this day. The scripts Pike submitted to the family were objected to on various grounds. Then a woman named Audrey Gillette, from Tucson, Arizona, emerged with accusations that she had answered a newspaper ad for investors, and met a woman who claimed to be in Pike's employ. Gillette invested $70,000, which was to be repaid in three months.

It never happened. The FBI reportedly raided Pike's office, but found no evidence to support charges. Pike claims to have also been victimized by an employee using his name. Unable to repay the loan for the money he had borrowed to purchase the rights from Dean's family, Pike essentially lost the project.

pilgrimages

A feature of the religious life of all people in all parts of the world, a pilgrimage is when one abandons the normal world and its pursuits to seek spiritual benefits obtainable in a particular holy place. In most religious history, our world and the supernatural are believed to exist in parallel, but they meet at certain special points of intersection — places that are consecrated by the presence of deity. There are sites at which a deity is believed to have revealed himself, and these spots serve to mediate the power of the deity with ordinary people.

There are pilgrimages to James Dean's hometown of Fairmount, Indiana, and surrounding environs, with stops at the sites that were connected to him. These include the Winslow Farm, the Back Creek Church, the various homes where his parents lived, his birthplace in Marion, Carter's motorcycle shop, the spots where he was photographed, his mother's grave, and his own grave.

There is a James Dean walking tour of New York, which was for years conducted by Dean of Deanabilia David Loehr.

There are treks to his deathsite that retrace the route he took on his final day, his Via Dolorosa. The stops along the way — the site of Competition Motors, Tip's, the Ticketing Site, Blackwell's Corner, The Fatal Intersection, the monument at Cholame, and Kuehl Funeral Home, are the Stations of the Cross.

The newsletters distribute lists of hallowed Dean sites in the Los Angeles area, including the addresses of the Santa Monica Home where his father lived, Griffith Observatory, and the Baldwin Street house used as the Stark home in *Rebel Without a Cause.*

Plant, Bobby Joe

Bobby Joe Plant was a young highway accident victim who was forever linked to Dean's demise by the headline of the Paso Robles newspaper on October 3, 1955: "Weekend Crashes Kill 2, Hurt 14." The two fatalities were Dean and Plant. The article reporting Dean's death led off with, "Disaster rode the highways of San Luis Obispo County over the weekend, taking the lives of two speed-loving young men, one of them James Dean, 24, stage and screen star, and the other a 19-year-old Camp Roberts soldier, Bobby Joe Plant of San Bernadino."

Plant's accident happened at 10:30 on Saturday, .7 mile south of the Monterey County line on Highway 101. He hit a utility pole after losing control.

poison

Was Jimmy Dean poisoned? Not on the day he died, but as a child? Biographer Donald Spoto theorizes that the young Jimmy Dean suffered from lead poisoning, and that the culprit was his beloved mother. Much has been made of Mildred Dean's artistic proclivities, but the painting to which she seemed to devote herself with almost obsessive intensity was the repainting of each of the several houses in which they lived. Lethal fumes were a result, and tasty paint chips, which were attractive to the toddler.

Jimmy apparently was about to enter kindergarten when he came down with a low-grade fever and chronic fatigue accompanied by a rash that covered most of his body. He vomited and produced tarry stools. Tests revealed anemia, and blood transfusions and vitamins were prescribed.

Spoto's theory about lead poisoning is, however, hard to reconcile with his statement that the diagnosis of Jimmy's illness was Erythema infectiosum. This infectious disease, a fairly common childhood malady (also known as fifth disease), has nothing to do with lead poisoning.

Poland

The Polish actor Zbigniew Cybulski won international recognition for his role as Maciek Chelmicki in the film *Ashes and Diamonds* by director Andrzej Wajda. The role he created led to his being dubbed "The Polish James Dean." Although he created some other memorable screen characters and was often copied in his homeland, he never reached the level of fame to which he aspired. He met a sudden and violent end at 40, in Wroclaw, Poland, when he fell under the wheels of a moving train.

Polonio Pass

A rugged pass east of the James Dean crash site. According to author Sam Schaeffer, it is haunted by the ghost of James Dean speeding in his spectral Death Car. In a *Whisper* magazine story from 1957, Schaeffer recounted the stories of locals who reported being driven off the road by ghostly Porsche, or hearing the screaming siren of an invisible ambulance or the sounds of a terrible collision. One old timer-explains that perhaps there are "things outside the range of humans, maybe there are some humans who are able to see and hear things beyond the ability of other humans."

> There are some noises, the Mexicans say, like the scream of a young girl dying, or a mother being torn from her young, that are so piercingly intense with emotional energy that they leave their imprint on every tree, rock and grain of sand around them, to echo back for a long time to come.

See also ghosts and hauntings.

poltergeists *see under* ghosts and hauntings

posthumous articles

The following magazine and newspaper articles all appeared in 1956: *Movie Stars Parade*: "The End ... or the Beginning." *Motion Picture*: "Jimmy Dean Is Not Dead." *Rave*: "Did Jimmy Dean Really Die?" *New York World-Telegram and Sun*: "Jimmy Dean Still Gets Mail." *Movie Secrets*: "The Truth Behind the James Dean Stories." *Movie Life*: "Jimmy Dean Fights Back from the Grave." *Newsweek*: "Star That Won't Dim." *American Weekly*: "The Strange Revival of James Dean." *Chicago American*: "Macabre Build Up of James Dean." *New York Post*: "The Legend of James Dean." *Florida Times Union*:"Dean's Still Alive in Death to Fans." *Movie Show*: "The Man They Won't Let Die." *New York Daily News*: "They Won't Let Him Rest in Peace." *Motion Picture*: "You Can Make Jimmy Live Forever."

premonitions of death

- George Barris said, "Ever since I started having anything to do with the car I had felt bad vibes coming from it. It was bizarre."
- Dean made a public-service announcement promoting Highway Safety just two weeks before he died, ad-libbing the lines, "And remember: drive safely — because the life you save may be... mine."

- His final scene in *Giant* was the "Last Supper" scene.
- Alec Guinness reported telling him, upon seeing the new Spyder, "Look... please do not get into that car because if you do (and I looked at my watch), it's now Thursday (whatever the date was) 10 o'clock at night, and by 10 o'clock at night next Thursday you'll be dead if you get into that car." He was.
- Patsy D'Amore, owner of Dean's favorite restaurant, said to Dean the night before he left, "I tell him he *die* in that car."
- Ursula Andress said, "I told him that the car gave me a bad feeling... I knew that I would never see him again."
- He gave away his Siamese cat, Marcus, the day before he died. A gift from Liz Taylor, it was left with actress Jeanette Mille along with detailed feeding instructions and the cryptic comment, "Who knows, I might not be back."
- He received a speeding ticket two hours before he died speeding. The nickname of the officer issuing the ticket was "Buzz," the same name as Jim Stark's racing nemesis in *Rebel Without a Cause*.

See also noose.

psychiatrist

In an interview with Warren Beath, *Eden* and *Rebel* composer Leonard Rosenmann says that Jimmy "was in analysis when he died. What's his name, he's dead now, a very kind of Freudian strict guy. He (Jimmy) went to the wrong guy. Very unwarm, the kind of guy you say What time is it? And he says, 'What time do you think it is?' Or, you are fine, how am I? That kind of thing. Vandenheimer, that was his name. He was a well-known analyst in the area because he played cello. He was a bad cellist. But, ah, I don't know why he went to Vandenheimer. I pushed him to go to an analyst. He's a very disturbed guy. He was unfocused, you know he was narcissistic, unfocused. Sexually, he may have had problems."

Psycho

Who could forget Anthony Perkins as the quirky and hopelessly Oedipal killer in the Alfred Hitchcock classic *Psycho*? But some avid Dean fans, fixated on Jimmy's last day, study the film for different reasons. The movie, filmed in 1959, features footage obtained by second-unit crews of the James Dean Death Route much as it appeared to Jimmy before modernization and improvement.

Slowing down the film frame by frame, they follow Hitchcock's embezzling heroine Marion Crane, portrayed by Janet Leigh, along the stretch of State Highway 99 from Gorman — where Marion is startled by a highway patrolman when she pulls off the road and falls asleep — onto Bakersfield's Union Avenue, which is today a mere business route through town.

For these fans— who call themselves students of Jimmy Dean's last day — Hitchcock's picture affords them one of the best contemporary records of the route Jimmy Dean took to his crash site at Cholame, featuring as it does sporadic footage of some sixty miles of the death route. While the inattentive are absorbed in Janet Leigh's progress to her fatal rendezvous with Norman, the Dean fan is participating vicariously in Jimmy Dean's last drive.

Pulley, Bob

He was one of Jimmy Dean's pallbearers, and, eventually, president of the Fairmount Historical Museum. A favorite of Dean fans, he is consistent in affirming Jimmy Dean's heterosexuality, which he says Jimmy demonstrated on return trips to his hometown.

R

Raskin, Leon

Leon (Lee) Raskin was born in 1945 and has been a racecar aficionado since the late 1950s. The Maryland native is a superb Porsche historian and the author of two invaluable articles, "Little Bastard: The Search for James Dean's Spyder," which appeared in *Porsche Panorama* in July 1984, and "Through James Dean's Rearview Mirror," printed in *Excellence* in December 1995.

Lee also co-produced and consulted for two videos about Dean's racing experiences, *James Dean at High Speed* (1997) and the *Behind the Headlight* series on James Dean for SPEED TV (2004). In addition, Lee co-authored *The Porsche Speedster TYP 540: Quintessential Sports Car* (2004), in which he wrote about celebrities who owned or were involved with the 356 Porsche Speedster.

ratings war

The grudge match occurred in 1956, and the contestants were Steve "Schmok! Schmok!" Allen and Ed "Really Big Shew" Sullivan. A grudge

Lee Raskin and his Porsche Spdyer (courtesy Lee Raskin).

match, because the two had already clashed, each trying to be the first to feature teen sensation Elvis on his variety television show. To capitalize on the posthumous Dean craze, five months later they vied for the privilege of presenting the first tribute show on the late James Dean. Allen, who had won the tussle over Presley by signing him for NBC's *The Steve Allen Show*, scheduled a Dean tribute for October 21, 1956. Sullivan countered by scheduling his own Dean tribute for October 14.

There was a fight over Jimmy's Fairmount relatives, which must have been confusing to them. Allen desperately rescheduled his show for October 14, opposite Sullivan's rival tribute. Sullivan might be declared a winner, offering a preview of *Giant* and featuring Jimmy's aunt and uncle. Allen eventually recorded a James Dean album called *The James Dean Story* on Coral Records.

Raul

According to Bob Rees' indispensable book on Dean and the supernatural, *James Dean Beyond the Grave*, a young man named Raul appeared on the Houston, Texas, radio show of DJ Paul Barsky near the anniversary of Dean's death. His mission was to be the subject of psychic Sharon Capehart in an attempt to meet James Dean. A true Dean fan, the nineteen-year-old Raul was in his trance within twenty minutes. Another Dean fan had brought along a sweater supposedly owned by Dean to heighten the connection.

"Breathe deeply, Raul...," began the psychic. Raul reportedly responded with a Deanish giggle and a few lines from *Rebel*. The psychic greeted Jimmy with, "We miss you. We love you." A moment later Raul said, "Someone's got my car!" The alarmed psychic woke an anxious Raul from the trance. She said, "Other things were said by James Dean through Raul personally to me, but I can't repeat these things. James wasn't upset, but there were other messages he wanted me to work on.... Dean was a spiritual individual and thought this was all very funny!"

Ray, Nick

Nicholas Ray, born Raymond Nicholas Kienzle in 1911, developed his unique film style from such desperate resources as Frank Lloyd Wright, at whose Taliesin art colony he studied briefly, and Elia Kazan, who invited Ray to shadow him during the entire shoot of *A Tree Grows in Brooklyn*. He was to credit Kazan with teaching him how to make films.

Ray's protagonists were always tragic, and his films infused both male-female and male-male pairings with erotic and romantic dynamics arguably born of his own bisexual proclivities. Even though he was still working under the old studio system, he was able to affix his heterodoxal stamp to films such as *They Live by Night, Knock on Any Door, Johnny Guitar* and of course, *Rebel Without a Cause*.

In *Rebel: The Life and Legend of James Dean*, Donald Spoto writes:

> For decades, rumors circulated of an erotic relationship between Dean and Ray (especially during their time in New York earlier in the year, when Ray often stayed the night in Jimmy's tiny garret). The suggestion, however unverifiable, is not outlandish: it is easy, for example, to imagine Ray making love to the image of himself (whom he saw in Jimmy Dean as in Jim Stark)—an image that was then taking concrete shape. It is equally understandable if Jimmy had tried to please another respected mentor-father (like Rogers Brackett, for example). What might have happened between them sexually is less important than the fact that the bond between Dean and Ray was, according to Stewart Stern, "an odd version of acolyte and master, because Jimmy was torn between fear of Nick and a desperate need to trust him."

Said film composer Leonard Rosenmann in an interview with Warren Beath, "He was a really sweet guy in many ways. He was, of course, a very strange guy.... A great story about Nick Ray which really defines Nick Ray which was actually told by Bogart, who said, 'You know, to define Nick's personality, you ask Nick, What time is it, Nick? Nick kind of slowly shakes his head and looks off into the wild blue yonder—and you think he's kind of forming some kind of proverb about time. And about three minutes later you'll say, Nick, What time is it? And he'll say, 'Oh — around three o'clock.' Basically, there's nothing going on in his head at all."

The Real *James Dean Story*

A one-shot magazine from Fawcett Publications which sold for 25 cents in 1956, featuring articles including "James Dean's Life Story in His Own Words," "The Man Behind the Legend," "My Friend Jimmy" by Bob Hinkle, "The Jimmy Dean I Dated" by Lori Nelson, and "The Dean I Knew" by Sal Mineo.

Risking his neck — whenever, however, whichever way he pleased — was one of Jimmy Dean's inalienable rights. He loved life as well as the next guy, but it was a gift exclusively his own, belonging to no one else. And he could never feel the pulse of life as strongly as when he threw it on the scale. Life and death were opposites, and Jimmy could not conceive of one without the other. Only in facing death could he fully taste life itself.

The Rebel Gift Pack

An attractive assortment of James Dean Cologne, merchandised by Salle International in Gurnee, Illinois. This unlikely film tie-in sold for $14.95.

Rebel: The Life Story of a Film

Nick Ray was working on this uncompleted manuscript on the making of *Rebel Without a Cause* at the time of his death, according to biographer John Francis Kreidl. No trace of this book has surfaced.

Rebel Without a Cause deaths

Like James Dean, the other stars of this watershed movie all met untimely fates. Sal Mineo was stabbed to death behind his apartment on February 12, 1976, at the age of 37. Natalie Wood died on November 29, 1981, at age 43. In 1968 Nick Adams was discovered dead at age 38, victim of an apparent drug overdose.

Rebels United

This unusual 1983 book by Indiana native Elbert Jones, who writes under the pen name Joel Dickenson Brean, is a self-published dialogue with Jimmy in the afterlife. Subtitled *The Enduring Reality of James Dean*, it offers six "conversation transcripts" with a "temporarily materialized" Jimmy, who expounds upon varied topics such as "love, human sexual behavior, religious faiths, philosophical beliefs, the arts, scientific knowledge, a hereafter, reincarnation, the possible development of psychic powers, and rebelling against wars by living ways of peace." These dialogues were promised to "inform, entertain, or motivate concerns in the minds of both the young and the not so young." The book was published by Infinity Press.

Brean claims to have attended Dean's funeral and "caressed" the casket. Shortly afterwards he wrote these thoughts:

> Tragic as was his being separated from his earthly body, there is this thought on which to rejoice: Jimmy, though free from that body, is able yet to "communicate" — as he would put it — to inform and inspire those persons who will listen to this enduring reality.

Reddick, Ben

Ben Reddick was the delightfully curmudgeonly editor of *The Daily Press* of Paso Robles, and a perennial naysayer when he was inevitably interviewed about the James Dean hoopla on the anniversary of the actor's death.

"Anybody driving that fast was committing suicide," he told *San Jose Mercury* reporter Timothy Larimer in an interview (September 26, 1985) when he was seventy years old. "We had two very good boys just killed. They were good athletes, good students. They weren't drinking. Then you have this dunce. I have never been a fan of his, and it's a miracle he didn't kill a whole bunch of local high school kids.

"He had it made. And here he was racing 85 miles an hour down this dark country road where there are a lot of kit foxes, coyote and deer. My God."

reenactment

The *Los Angeles Times* of Monday, October 30, 1989, helped generate hype for a proposed motion picture on Dean to be directed by Lorann Pike. Writer David Ferrell focused on the participation of car customizer George Barris and the spectacular finale to the film. "Now Barris," the article said, "is changing gears, devoting his time to a more personal project: creating a high-speed re-enactment of the rural highway crash in 1955 that killed his good friend, actor James Dean."

The film was expected to dwell for several minutes on the violent crash, and Barris was in charge of coordinating the 85 mph stunt. It was to be filmed the following year and employ two helicopters and five ground-based cameras trained on the exact place of Dean's death.

"It's going to be very, very dangerous, believe me," independent director Pike told the *Times*. "But I know it's going to be done right because George Barris is involved."

It was reported:

> Work on the film is already under way. On Sept. 30 at nearly 6 P.M., the anniversary of the crash, cameramen shot the deserted intersection of California 41 and 46, capturing the angle of the sun as it was setting on the collision scene 34 years ago. Barris has begun building six replicas of Dean's two-seat Spyder, and in coming weeks he expects to meet with his two top industry stunt men — Jerry Summers and Jack Gill — to work out the complex calculations and precautions necessary for the stunt.
>
> Those details, known in the stunt trade as "rigging," are 90% of the success of any high-speed stunt, Summers said. In this case, the stunt must be rigged so that the two cars collide and the Porsche Spyder spins as it slides off the road — a tricky chain of events, Barris said.

The article noted that Barris's stunt experience was limited. The film eventually foundered and the spectacular crash was never recreated.

Rees, Robert

Texas writer and Dean archivist Robert Rees is distinguished by having published more articles on James Dean than any other author. He has written several books including *James Dean, Beyond the Grave* and contributed to numerous documentaries in addition to being a helpful source of rare video for Dean fans and collectors. He has interviewed many celebrities connected with Dean's life, and his body of work comprises a major contribution to any serious Dean scholarship.

The Reincarnation of James Dean

The "reincarnation of James Dean" wasn't even a man, but a New York Hollywood hopeful named Linda Manze, who surfaced in the 1970s. She promoted herself by authoring a script about a girl who discovers she is ... *The Reincarnation of James Dean*! Manze had a role in Dennis Hopper's 1982 movie *Out of the Blue*.

religion

Fandom is one of the many modern expressions of the ancient impulse to cheerfully celebrate the death of a god. If the forms are many and their expressions exhausting, it points to the confusion of the religious impulse operating outside of a formal structure. The death cult doesn't want to call itself that, but publicly proclaims the life-affirming elements of a consuming preoccupation, which an observer would call *morbid*—an ugly word, ugliest to the cultist, or rather, *fan*.

In the proliferation of shrines, pilgrimages, icons, relics, conventions and a hierarchical priesthood, the posthumous adoration of James Dean confirms to every criterion of a religion. If the average cultist seems not so much touched by fire, as wandering in a James Dean haze, it is perhaps not the fault of the god, but the failure of his apostle to follow the hero's journey to its ultimate conclusion—enlightenment. Through celebrity death, we confront our own fears of the Grim Reaper at a safe remove, antisepticized through cultural filters.

In an article called "God of a Morbid Cult" (*New Republic*, 1957), journalist Herbert Mitgang quoted a Dean fan club's letter from the 1950s: "Everyone who joins the club is so happy. They write the club to tell how good it makes them feel inside, how it brings inner peace. We can't accomplish anything by it but his faith is spreading. It is just wonderful meeting people who love Jimmy so much and want to keep him alive in their hearts always."

See also cults; religious symbolism.

religious symbolism

In the middle of the twentieth century a boy died on a lonely highway in California. The boy was movie actor James Byron Dean, and the site of his death was at a confluence of two roads which formed the peculiar occult aspect known as the finger of God. The boy was found with his head over the passenger door in a pose reminiscent of the tarot card called the Hanging Man. He is the man whose feet are planted in the heavens prior to his transformation as Way Shower and Light to Men.

Far from Hollywood, the clearing dust revealed the aftermath of the collision of the actor's brand new Porsche Spyder with a Ford Crestliner driven by a twenty-three-year-old college student. The time was approximately 5:45 P.M. and the date was September 30, 1955. Though the event was unheralded at the time, a cultural juggernaut was immediately set in motion with the rolling away of the stone nearly three days later—the release of Dean's primary gospel, *Rebel Without a Cause*. The resonances of that highway accident continue to this day to ripple through our cultural universe like the wrinkles in time which evidence an early and primordial Big Bang.

Dean, an avid racing buff, had just purchased a new sports car and was en route to an airport race when another car made a left turn across his bow and collided with him. It is not known for sure whether he was dead at the scene. What is beyond dispute is that the ambulance carrying him to hospital made a stop on the road, and that the actor was dead upon arrival at the hospital. From there he was taken immediately to the local funeral home. What is also a matter of record is that upon arrival the body was so evacuated of blood that there was not even enough to perform tests to check the alcohol level.

In a death like Dean's the vehicle of death becomes a religious object in its own right, like the Cross. It is an object of mystical revelation and assumes its own life and history of superstition and supernatural anecdote.

DESIGNER GOD

James Dean was a cultural creation, guided and molded from an early age into perfect conformity with the hero cycle. His eruption into public consciousness was a deftly orchestrated campaign that cynically identified him with a larger timeless heroic cycle expressed in twentieth century terms. If Christ had slipped into irrelevance, there was a vacancy of unfulfilled religious aspiration. The target was the newly emerged phenomenon of the youth market. The hero would define and express his constituency.

He was the agent of an occult group, which was an offshoot of Aleister Crowley's Golden Dawn (there were many) and which wanted to nurture a select group of wunderkinds for movie stardom. Perhaps inspired by Joseph Fraser's *The Golden Bough*, and the heroic cycle as defined by Joseph Campbell, this group wanted to raise up a designer god in the middle of the twentieth century and harness the force of the collective unconscious which would be released at his death.

GODHOOD

In June of 1956 *Photoplay* printed a letter sent in by a fan:

> What were you that you could be so much more
> Than flesh and blood? A spirit and a force
> That reached beyond the thoughts of other men
> Up past the planets to infinity.

The godhood of James Dean may be in its final stages, with his transformation into commodity. He is licensed and packaged, marketed tirelessly by a management group that is quick to slap injunctions on sellers of unauthorized products. The fifty-year-old cottage industries of fans most responsible for keeping his flame burning bright since his death live in paranoia and fear of crossing the phalanx of aggressive lawyers protecting their property.

Reventlow, Lance

Both Lance Reventlow and his mother, Woolworth heiress Barbara Hutton, have a bizarre connection to James Dean. David Heymann, in his controversial biography *Poor Little Rich Girl,* claimed that Barbara had once encountered Dean at Googie's in Hollywood and jumped on the back of his motorcycle. They spent that night together. If true, would it have been an awkward encounter for Jimmy when he ran into her 21-year-old race driver son at Blackwell's Corner a half hour before his death? Reventlow was en route to the races in his own gull wing 300 SL Mercedes. Reportedly, they chatted and Dean told him he had got the Spyder up to 130 miles per hour on the straightaways. Other accounts say they planned a dinner rendezvous at Paso Robles up the road.

Lance Reventlow himself died a premature and violent death, killed in a plane crash in 1972. His mother died in 1979.

Rey, Del

Del Rey is an artist and college professor who traces his interest in Dean to a TV movie portrayal:

> It was in the 1980s that Dean really got a foothold in my worldview. On TV I had one glimpse of the Stephen McHattie portrayal of Dean, based on Bill Bast's 1956 biography. That did it. Those images and the Dean mystique sank into me like seeds taking root. Entering manhood I needed a model, for style as well as conduct. Dean's life and acting roles were shining examples of what to be. (A story common to most fans.) When I saw those re-created scenes of Jimmy driving his Porsche, I knew I had to acquire a sports car. Later when I bought a 50s American car, it had to be one that was made while Jimmy was alive — a 1955 Buick Super. It became my time machine, in which I've driven many times to the town that time forgot: Fairmount, Indiana.

Rey, who is also a Dean lookalike and has ended up in many finals of the lookalike contest held in Fairmount, Indiana, manages to work a few clips of Jimmy into his college art classes. He writes eloquently about the legend:

> James Dean was an artist of unsurpassed integrity. He had the magic touch — the ability to turn every thing in life into art — his art — his acting performances on stage and screen. His focus, that amazing power he had to center his energy, transformed the events in his career into a three-part epic about himself as the quintessential American myth of heroic individuation. He commandeered the spotlight, changing everybody else

into supporting cast or mere extras in his own story. His gravitas captivated all those around him. He became the sun, and all of the planets revolved around HIM. His directors couldn't prevent it, and never got over it. How many times did Kazan or Stevens grow weary when every interview would turn to the topic that audiences really wanted to know: what was it really like, to work with James Dean?

Riddle, Rose Marie

The little girl was found face down in a fog-shrouded bleak area, less than half a mile north of Highway 466, and a mile east of Blackwell's Corner. It was the culmination of a grisly search that had galvanized the area and garnered national headlines.

Little six-year-old Rose Marie Riddle had been kidnapped from the labor camp of a town 35 miles away on Friday, January 13, 1961. She had a congenital heart condition, and her frantic and impoverished parents appealed for her return, after her mother had given her permission to accept a dollar and clean house for a man and woman. The mother had assumed the couple were neighbors. Unfortunately, they were two transients, Richard Arlen Lindsey — an ex-convict and former mental patient — and his pregnant wife, Dixie.

When her raped and battered body was discovered on January 17, her forehead was gashed by a heavy blow, and there were 18 other distinguishable wounds about her head. She had been strangled.

Arlen was sentenced to death, and his wife to life imprisonment.

Riding with James Dean

This film takes place in Dean's hometown a year after his death. A young girl, who was raised with Jimmy and visits his grave every day, becomes involved with a mysterious stranger who is in town to participate in a car race. The movie tagline reads: "She was in love with a legend ... until a hot-rodding stranger shattered her world." The movie stars Tina Corsini and Robert Mitchum's grandson Bentley. The film was made in 1998, which indicates the staying power of Dean's legend and the interest in him. Although little known and not widely distributed, this modest film did garner an independent film award for its haunting score by Kirsten Vogelsang.

ring

In a scene rife with homoeroticism, Rolf Wuetherich, the reputed source in his 1957 ghostwritten account "Death Drive," describes "a gift of friendship from Jimmy."

"I want to give you something," he said. "To show we're friends, Rolf."
I was touched. The ring just fitted on my small finger. My hand was much
bigger than Jimmy's.

The article ends with the statement,

> The ring Jimmy gave Rolf at Ridge Route was torn from Rolf's finger
> when he was thrown out of the car. He still has a scar where the ring was.
> This ring — Jimmy's gift of friendship to him — lies buried somewhere in
> the desert where Jimmy died...

The magazine was *Modern Screen* and the story appeared in October
of 1957. The story rewritten into second person by John Lindahl reappeared in *Pix Annual* in the fall of 1958. Though the story was shortened,
the ring episode was embellished.

> It wasn't an expensive ring, just a cheap little thing with the seal of
> Pan American Airways on it. But Rolf accepted it in the spirit in which it
> was given, and slipped it on his little finger.

Scores of fans who visit the crash site continue to look for the ring,
believing not only in its existence but — if found — its inestimable value.

In fact, the James Dean Ring trilogy rivals that of Wagner. In the first
movement, Dean places an inexpensive Pan Am flight ring on Rolf's finger
some two hours prior to the crash. In the second movement, Rolf reports
the ring missing after the crash, and this poignant episode is incorporated
into legend in the subsequent fan magazine accounts of Jimmy's death.
The third movement unfurls over forty years as legions of fans scour the
vicinity of the crash for the ring, which is now regarded as a priceless relic.

"It's out here somewhere, and I'm going to find it," says a Pasadena
postman in his late forties as he explores the area with a metal detector.
The detector picks up fragments of license plates, nails, spikes, and the
detritus of forty years of highway collisions.

Other fans, aligned in clubs, have mounted grid-like searches, sift-
ing through the weeds and cow droppings. They reconstruct trajectories,
place inquest photos of the crash site beneath acetate overlays of photos
of the present intersection, trying to identify the point of impact despite
the subsequent rechannelizations and reroutings. They examine the photos of Rolf next to the wreck with magnifying glasses and do amateur
reconstructions. Physics, telemetry, intuition — all are brought into play
by the rabid treasure hunters.

Psychics have been enlisted into service. "We've come from Santa
Barbara," said one fan, face flushed and sunburned as she pulled the burrs

from her socks after thirty minutes of examining the field north of the crash site. "I have the strongest feeling ... and I'm not often wrong ... the vibrations are really intense right here." She closed her eyes and began to "channel" direction from her spirit guide. "Here...," she said as her acolytes began to dig with garden trowels. Then, "Here...."

An older man with a dowsing rod had a try at it on the anniversary of Dean's death in 1995. "Nonsense, really, that's what I think. But my kids are really into this, and I told them I'd give it a try. Here goes nothing."

One confident fan was so sure she would find the ring that she made its eventual resting place the centerpiece of the Dean altar installed in her bedroom at home. Candles and photos surround a small jewelry box lined in sable. Despite her several forays to the crash site over the last three years, the display sits vacant.

Roberts, Marvin "Monty"

"Monty" to his friends, author of the book *The Man Who Listens to Horses*, model for the "horse whisperer" of Robert Redford movie fame, emerged as a player in the James Dean saga with the publication of Joe Hyams' 1992 James Dean biography *Little Boy Lost*. In 1954 Roberts was a horse trainer and Roddy McDowall's double in *My Friend Flicka*—and Liz Taylor's in *National Velvet*, though that is more difficult to visualize.

Roberts' story is that Elia Kazan sent a pale and skinny Jimmy Dean to him prior to the shooting of *East of Eden*, to acclimate the boy to a farming community (though he had grown up in one). As a Warners rep told Roberts, "He's going to star in *Eden*, but we want him to learn ... what vegetable growing is all about." Roberts was to be paid two thousand dollars a month.

Jimmy reported, the story goes, to the Roberts family's two-hundred-acre spread near Salinas. He followed Monty around, even wearing his clothes. He learned rope tricks, including the Drunken Butterfly. Despite encouragement, Jimmy showed no interest in girls, and got mad when Monty tried to get his protégé to go out with one of them. Later, Roberts joined Jimmy on the set of *Giant*.

Roberts told Hyams that Jimmy called him Thursday afternoon, September 29, 1955, regarding his trip to the Salinas race on Friday. He asked if he and Rolf Wuetherich could stay in the guesthouse on the ranch, which would give them a chance to look at the ranch Roberts was buying on Jimmy's behalf. Roberts says that Jimmy also called him from Blackwell's Corner, within a half hour before the accident.

Author Val Holley, though, wrote in a preface to his Dean biography about a tale that "materialized in a September 1992 *Entertainment Tonight* segment and was then elaborated in the 1992 book *James Dean: Little Boy Lost*, by Joe Hyams: that Dean spent a whopping four months in 1954 on a Salinas, California, ranch to prepare for his role in *East of Eden*. Although it is possible that Dean spent a few days at the ranch, he did not arrive in California until April 8, 1954, then spent a few days in Borrego Springs and San Francisco, and was back in Hollywood no later than May 4, the day Julie Harris arrived in California and was taken for a ride in Dean's new MG."

See also The Man Who Listens to Horses.

"Rock Hudson Murdered James Dean"

Rock Hudson was responsible for the murder of James Dean. That was the result of an "in-depth investigation" by *Examiner* magazine. Robert Slatzer, who uncovered a lot of dope surrounding the mysterious death of Marilyn Monroe, did a lot of the digging.

James Dean and Rock Hudson playing cards (courtesy Marfa Public Library, Marfa, Texas).

In this scenario, Rock Hudson ordered the murder of James Dean in a drunken moment of reckless jealousy against his screen rival. The article claims the rumors have been circulating in Hollywood for three decades. The motive was a fleeting physical attraction that turned to intense mutual contempt. Hudson supposedly was afraid Dean was going to "out" him. Slatzer said, "I've been told that some of Hudson's friends got to the car and tampered with its brake system. They claim it was cold-blooded murder — as if Rock pulled the trigger himself."

Ex-wife Phyllis Gates reported Hudson's bizarre behavior the day of Dean's fatal accident. "His big frame was convulsing in sobs. I asked him why the news had shattered him." Rock replied, "Because I wanted him to die. I've been jealous of him ... I've been wishing him dead." She says Rock was overcome by guilt and shame.

Why was Dean's Los Angeles home burgled shortly after the accident? And was there anything significant about the tape recorder and 16 mm movie camera that were stolen? Did Rolf Wuetherich carry the story of what really happened that fateful day to his grave? Was Rolf killed because he had signed a contract with an American book publisher to finally tell his story?

This story appeared in the October 1989 *Examiner* under the byline of Linda Decker.

Rosenmann, Leonard

Leonard Rosenmann is a notable Hollywood composer who won Oscars for his memorable scores of *Barry Lyndon* and *Bound for Glory*. His earliest scores were for *Rebel Without a Cause* and *East of Eden*. In these, his moody and sometimes sweeping compositions seem to echo and reinforce the James Dean persona on the screen. It was through Rosenmann that Jimmy met his car friend and insurance agent Lew Bracker, a cousin of Rosenmann's. Rosenmann eventually had a falling out with Dean. For years, he said the reason for the rift was that he refused to play basketball with Dean and to be a surrogate father. Joe Hyams reported that the real reason was Dean's interference in the affair the composer was conducting with actress Lois Smith during the making of *Eden*. Dean was also a friend of Rosenmann's current wife.

After Dean's death, Rosenmann found himself the recipient of unwanted communications from Dean fans. For example, he told Warren Beath about one late-night phone call:

> After Jimmy died, two to three months, I got a call in the morning from this lady from Erie, Pennsylvania. She dropped about a million coins

into the phone. I hear Bing. Bing. Bing. Bong. Bong-bong. Nickels, quarters, dimes, you know. And she kept saying, "Don't hang up, this is a very old lady." I said, "Well, madam, it's a pleasure to talk to you, but I'm still sleeping." And she said, "Ah, I just wanted to call you and tell you that I just spoke to Jimmy. He's been dead for about four months, you know. And he sends you his regards. And he's just very happy there and hopes to see you soon." I said, "Well, I hope I don't see him soon."

Rosenmann also received thousands of strange letters:

> When Jimmy died, people didn't know anything about me and they assumed I was like Jimmy. So they started to write all the letters to me. And all of a sudden, in one week, I got five thousand letters. And they were the sickest things I've ever read in my entire life. A lot of them were gay. A lot of them were young girls and older women too, sending me pornographic pictures of themselves. I almost left the country. People just seemed so incredibly sick. People were into leather and weird stuff like that. It's just very, very strange.

Roth, Beulah

Beulah Roth was the widow of Dean biographer and photographer Sanford (Sandy) Roth. Warren Beath had a conversation with Beulah shortly before her death in 1990. She talked about Jimmy and the day he died.

> I know that Jimmy used to go out after hours, but he'd call sometimes at 2 o'clock in the morning, or three. He'd say, "If you make me a pizza, I'll bring everything." He liked English muffins. I would make them with Jewish salami and mozzarella cheese and tomato sauce.
> We had a wonderful relationship. Now, the day that he died. September 30th ... that morning Jimmy called at 8 o'clock to me. I answered the phone. "Come on, kid." He called me Squeaky for some reason — "You're coming. You're taking the cat and we're going to stop on the way. You go in the station wagon with Sandy." And I said, "Jimmy, I can't go...." "But Sandy will be there." Well, he said tell Sandy to meet me at the place on Vine Street, the garage. So Sandy did, and they merrily went on their way.
> At a quarter of six at night, my phone rang and it was Sandy, and he said, "I have terrible news. Jimmy was killed and I'm calling you from the hospital. I went to the hospital with him in the ambulance, and the ambulance had an accident on the way. I don't know whether Jimmy was dead or not."
> And Sandy was in shock. And he said to me, "You have to call Warner Bros. and tell them." Well, I got up my courage and I got the projection room and I got somebody. It was the director, and I told him. The phone just went dead. From that moment on, the calls never stopped coming in

from Jimmy's friends, and everybody came to my house. It was the house of mourning. Ursula Andress came, stayed and slept with me that night.

Beulah Roth was not pleased with the way Dean was both idolized and besmirched after his death. She said, "All sorts of characters are coming out of this ... greed, rumors. These fan clubs—nuts."

Roth, Sanford

Ezra Goodman reported in *Life* magazine in September of 1956: "Photographer Sanford Roth, an old friend of Dean's who was behind him in another car the day he died, has been offered large sums for the shots he got of the dead actor in the smashed Porsche. 'They will never be released,' says Roth. 'And nobody will ever see them. It was a ghoulish, horrible sight. I took them for one reason — if there was a question by the insurance companies or police as to who was driving.'"

Roth's widow, Beulah, would claim in a 1986 interview with Warren Beath, "Sandy *never* shot a picture of Jimmy in the wreck. Nor were any the existing pictures of the wreck even shot for gain or publicity — but for insurance proof. As a matter of fact those photographs of the aftermath of the collision were used for the first time years after Sandy's death." Disputing reports from Dean's friend Bill Hickman, who said that Sanford Roth took pictures of Jimmy in the wreck rather than trying to help him, Beulah Roth sniffed: "Bill Hickman's opinion of Sandy is his personal opinion of himself as the great hero of the day. His facts were slanted toward himself!"

Of course, Sandy published the first picture of the wreck during his lifetime in an article he prepared for *Popular Photography*, unless the decision to use it was his wife's.

But Roth was being taken to task for his behavior by magazines within a couple years of Jimmy's death. Alfred G. Roller singled him out for scorn in the June 1957 issue of *Fury* in an article entitled "How the Ghouls are Picking at Jimmy Dean."

"Ghouls Won't Let JAMES DEAN Stay Dead," Roller proclaimed. "'Want a photograph of Jimmy lying bleeding in his death car? Fifty dollars or no dealing.' That's the kind of stuff that makes up the Dean legend. They're all after the quick buck." He went on:

> But the key to the whole Dean legend can be found in what took place minutes after the collision. Dean's station wagon with his own photographer arrived soon after the crash. And while Dean was lying slumped, dying, in the wreck of his own gaudy sports car, the photographer went to work with his camera. And these last pictures of Dean are really some-

sanford h. roth 1153 HACIENDA PLACE, LOS ANGELES 46, CALIFORNIA

8   October   55

Mr. Harry Murphy   Attention
The District Attorneys Office
San Luis Obispo
California

I hereby testify that on the late afternoon of
Friday, September 30th, 1955 I witnessed the
results of an automobile crash which caused the
death of James Dean. This I saw about ten minutes
after the fatal crash. I saw the body placed in an
ambulance and rushed to The Paso Robles Memorial
Hospital. When the ambulance arrived at the hospital I heard the doctor in charge pronounce James
Dean, dead. Having known James Dean for some time
there is no question but that this was the body of
James Dean.

Signed: _Sanford H. Roth_

Witnessed:

Witness that on the _8_ day of _October_ 1955 did
personally appear _Sanford H. Roth_ before me
Lewis A. Brewer A Notary Public residing in
Los Angeles County, State of California and
swear to the above statement being true.

My commission expires
April 4, 1959

Sanford Roth signed this statement testifying that he witnessed Dean's death and identified the body.

thing. They're strictly for the more morbid of his idolaters. And they can be bought — "Fifty Dollars or no dealing." It was reported that these really were "hot items" in his home town of Fairmount, Ind.

And of such grisly facts is the Dean Legend made.

George Stevens perhaps had the last word, quoted in *Fury* in 1957:

"And you know what is really funny, is that these people who are cashing in on the dead Jimmy are doing it with an aura of righteousness by saying they're the true friends of Jimmy Dean. This is what makes me feel downright nauseated."

Undercutting the moral tenor of the article was the fact that it was illustrated with one of Sanford Roth's photos of Jimmy's smashed car in the garage.

In 1995, French writer Philippe Defechereux weighed into the fray set up by the book *The Death of James Dean* in his own *James Dean: The Untold Story of a Passion for Speed*. Defechereux contacted Japanese businessman Seita Ohnishi, who built the Dean memorial in Cholame and who purchased all Roth's negatives of the crash. After all, when Ohnishi obtained the negatives and copyrights it was not (he said) "to turn a future profit but to make sure those pictures would never be used in a less than honorable way." One of his concerns was to verify if the photographer Sandy Roth, after arriving at the accident site, had taken any picture of James Dean dying.

Ohnishi was apparently preoccupied at the time by the terrific earthquake in his hometown of Kobe, but quickly sent the pertinent contact prints when he satisfied himself about the intention of Defechereux's book. The author reproduced apparently intact frames 14 through 19 of Roth's negatives. Frame 14 shows Jimmy and Rolf in the Spyder, and the very next picture shows Paul Moreno ferrying Dean across the highway to the ambulance. Frame 16 shows him being loaded in, while 17–19 show the attendants back at the Porsche preparing to lift Rolf.

Royal Academy

Distinguished British painter, illustrator and theatrical designer John Minton's portrait of James Dean was displayed next to Annogoni's Duke of Edinburgh at a summer exhibition at the Royal Academy in London in 1957.

Minton, a central figure in the neo–Romantic movement of the 1940s, had committed suicide just a few months earlier. He was 40 years old.

"Rubble Without a Pause"

David Colman is the author of this superb article on the Dean crash and the computer simulation by Failure Analysis Associates. It is an important addition to Dean crash theory, and stimulated further debate. A concise and lucid description of a scientific examination of the physical investigation by scientists and engineers, it appeared in the November 1995 issue of *Excellence*.

See also simulation.

Rummel, Jack

This retired California Highway Patrol officer claimed until the end of his days to have given James Dean a speeding ticket on the day he died. Upon his death, Rummel's obituary celebrated him as "Officer Who Ticketed James Dean," causing distress to the distant relatives of officer O. V. Hunter, who is confirmed to have actually ticketed Dean on the day he died.

The *Bakersfield Californian* reported of an interview, "Retired CHP officer Jack Rummel says that in 1955 he ticketed actor James Dean for speeding on the hill two hours before Dean was killed on Highway 46 in a car crash.

"Rummel says he also cited singer Merle Haggard for speeding, and helped author William Saroyan whose car crashed into a ravine off the hill in the mid–1960s."

S

Saint Sebastian

Dean biographer Donald Spoto wrote, "For a culture short of any heroes except celebrities, James Dean is a new St. Sebastian, pierced (his faithful followers believe) by the arrows of society's misunderstanding." John Gilmore has written of Dean "smoking and staring" at a Spanish painting of Saint Sebastian tied to a tree and pierced by the arrows of the Roman soldiers. "One sticking in his lower abdomen must have pierced organs, Jimmy said, and he had to be bleeding inside. 'That'd kill him,' he said with certainty."

St. Pierre, Roger

St. Pierre is the writer behind *James Dean: A Story in Words and Pictures*, a 1985 one-shot magazine devoted to Dean (Anabus Books).

salt and pepper shakers

Dean's family were all Quakers and now Jimmy's a Shaker — a saltshaker, that is, and a pepper shaker too. The pepper is Jett Rink, the salt is Jimbo in *Rebel*. The reasoning is perhaps that Jett was sharp and biting, while

Jim Stark was the salt of the earth. The set is 4.25 inches tall and sells for $14.95.

Sams, Dean

Owner-operator of the landmark Blackwell's Corner at the time it was destroyed by fire in 1967. Sams claimed to have waited on Jimmy Dean the day he stopped there just before his highway death, and to have sold him an apple.

Sanofi Beauty Products

Makers of Kirzia Uomo, the "James Dean Men's Cologne" of Japan. Their slogan is "A touch of the maverick."

Satanism

"I have a fairly adequate knowledge of satanic forces," James Dean boasted to Hedda Hopper in a column dated November 18, 1954. He was responding to the allegations he was romantically involved with spooky television hostess Vampira (Maila Nurmi). In his conversation with Hopper, Dean said he dated Nurmi "to find out if such a force obsessed her."

Hopper did not pursue Dean with the obvious questions, such as what he knew and where he got his knowledge. Was he a satanist?

Ron Smith researched the Dean curse for an article in the August 1990 *Robb Report* and found evidence Jimmy learned his occult ABCs through his involvement in the Malecfarum Coven, the oldest Hollywood coven, which held its meetings in mansions in the hills. An old warlock reported teaching Jimmy astrology, tarot and *The Book of the Dead*. They still consider him a member in good standing in the afterlife.

The studio could only have trembled over this admission by their young star. Murder conspiracy buffs think this could be the motive behind a studio-engineered murder: The studio wanted to silence Dean before his satanic allegiance became a public scandal, possibly leading to boycotts that would jeopardize their investments.

Dean rebuffed Vampira by concluding that she was really more interested in her makeup than the black arts. *See* **Malecfarum Coven.**

"Sausage King"

When California Highway Patrolman O.V. Hunter heard that a star named Jimmy Dean had been killed, he could only think of the country music star whose name graces packages of Jimmy Dean sausage. This was the experience of most people in the vicinity through which Jimmy raced to death on his last day. In fact, the two entertainers do bear a certain resemblance. Some researchers say that they are actually distantly related. One author has had some fun with the confusion between the two.

"Sausage King" is the title of a little story by James Finney Boylen that was published in the 1996 St. Martin's Griffin book *Mondo James Dean*. In Boylen's fantasy the identities of the actor and country singer are melded. James Dean has survived his accident and started over in another line of work, mainly, the production of pork sausages. It's fun.

Scandalous Sites

Scandalous Sites was a 2001 documentary series written and produced by Emmy winner James Golway for the Travel Channel. Featured on its inaugural episode was a tour of the James Dean death route hosted by Dean biographer Warren Beath. It included a visit to Minter Field outside Bakersfield, the site of Dean's May 1, 1955, sports car competition; a segment filmed on the old stretch of abandoned 466 near the accident site; and a commentary on the actual circumstances of the accident at the intersection where the events took place.

Schulte, Joe

James Dean fan from Fairfield, Tennessee, who, in 1956, made an 8mm amateur color film that recreated *Rebel Without a Cause*. Schulte himself portrayed Dean in the film-within-a-film, and 42 years later, in 1998, he finally had the film transferred to videocassette and showed it at the James Dean Memorial Gallery. The film, which ran about 27 minutes, was described as "terrific" in the Dean club newsletter, and fans hoped it would be copied and offered for sale in future issues. Schulte also placed honorably in a round of "James Dean Jeopardy" at the Lions Club in Fairmount, Indiana, on July 4, 1998.

Seberg, Jean

Another doomed actress, this one born in Iowa. She rose meteorically to fame at 17 when Otto Preminger selected her out of thousands of candidates to star in his *Saint Joan*. Seberg's films include *Paint Your Wagon, Airport* and *Bonjour Tristesse*. In 1979, three months after her last marriage, she overdosed on barbiturates.

Her biographer says that when she was still in high school, Seberg sent money for flowers to Dean's uncle, and was thrilled to receive in return a photo of her bouquet against the headstone from Marcus Winslow.

Senate, Debbie

Wife of California ghost hunter and author Richard Senate. At the age of six Debbie Senate saw the apparition of her great aunt. She continued to develop her gifts and eventually came to assist law-enforcement authorities on occasions when they were stumped. Her psychic "solution" of the Lizzie Borden case resulted in a monograph and the determination to apply herself to unraveling other mysteries.

In January of 2004 Debbie went to Blackwell's Corner as she retraced some of the stops James Dean made on his final day. The occasion was the filming of a British documentary series on celebrity ghosts, which eventually saw light under the title *Dead Famous*. Husband Richard recounted some of the events in an *Our Psychic World* article that appeared on his website, "Richard Senate, Ghost Hunter."

Using psychometry, Debbie summoned images from the past. She eventually received impressions of Dean and reported that he had stopped at Blackwell's Corner to use the bathroom. She reported that he argued with Rolf Wuetherich because Rolf wanted to drive. He was apparently angry about the speeding ticket Dean received earlier, and was also dissatisfied with the way the car was running.

The other news was that Dean had a headache at the time of the stop. He bought cigarettes and apple juice.

"Sentence of Death"

This is the provocative title of a *Westinghouse Studio One* television production, thought lost for many years. Jimmy Dean played a young man who witnesses a robbery and is then accused of being a killer. Sal Mineo was his costar in this drama, which aired August 17, 1953.

September 30, 1955

Television production starring Richard Thomas ("John-Boy" of television's *The Waltons*) as a college student in Arkansas who idolizes James Dean. Devastated at the news of Dean's death, he spearheads a vigil, which degenerates into drinking and goes badly awry. The production also stars Tom Hulce (Mozart in the movie *Amadeus*) and Susan Tyrell, who subsequently lost both her legs from a rare blood disease.

A soundtrack was released, perhaps the only musical record with a death-date as a title. Composer Leonard Rosenmann conducts his music from the soundtrack of the James Bridges television production released on MCA.

sex in the Speedster

Not all of Jimmy's sports car conquests were on the racetrack. Joe Hyams and Lew Bracker tell of Jimmy boasting to them that he had had sex with Natalie Wood in his Speedster.

Shady Character Unlimited

Purveyors of designer sunglasses with the James Dean imprint. The Japanese Optical USA Company also sells Dean sunglasses.

"Shirley"

It's not her real name, but "Shirley" was a young Hollywood woman who became obsessed with Jimmy's death. She not only attended the inquest, but also made repeated trips to the crash site. She even commenced her own private investigation of the event, which dovetailed nicely with her fetish for men in uniform. Apparently, with varying degrees of success, she tried to barter herself in exchange for information on the accident with the hierarchy of the law enforcement communities from two counties in the vicinity where Jimmy met his death. For her troubles, she wound up with a paltry handful of documents, which were public record, anyway, but many stories to tell at the Hollywood bars where she was a habitué.

In a 1981 letter to Warren Beath, Maila Nurmi (who claims to know "Shirley's" identity) recalled:

> Shirley went up [to the vicinity of the accident] and was there a few days. Jimmy's body had already left but Rolf was still there when she first got there. It must have been Tuesday, October 4, or Wednesday, October 5 when she arrived. She stayed on a couple of more days studying police files because she thought something didn't quite gel. Shirley, an attractive young blonde of perhaps 25 or 26, had been a police recording secretary somewhere and always had a fetish for policemen as well as a fascination for police work. She told me the files were very intricate and that something was wrong. The mystery piqued her, but she was unable to solve it.
>
> ...I remember something that Shirley said, quoting Rolf. 'Jimmy was alive when they put him in the ambulance — I know that for certain. But after the accident ... I wanted to look below me — to check on Jimmy — I couldn't separate the curtains — but I felt he was dead.

Siegmond, Warren E.

This resident of Palmerton, Pennsylvania, struck it rich while rummaging in a little antique shop on 44th Street in New York City in 1972. In a box of old letters he came upon a movie contract dated April 2, 1955, in which James Dean agreed to appear in *Rebel Without a Cause* and *Giant* for the princely sum of $1,500 a week. The documents he bought that day for $50 are currently appraised in the $20-$30,000 range.

The Silver Ghost

The ghost in question is Jimmy Dean's Porsche Spyder in this 1979 novel by Chuck Kinder. "If James Dean were alive to read *The Silver Ghost*, I suspect he would stroke the raised collar of his red windbreaker, cock his grand eyebrow, and grin wildly across the movie screens of America," says a friendly review in "advance praise" of the picaresque novel of coming of age in the fifties. Dean and the highway on which he died are featured on the cover along with this promotional copy:

> Jimbo Stark, teenage soldier of fortune, loves, fights, drinks, mopes and steals his way through this brilliant novel of the late 1950s. His America glows with an almost romantic light — it is an electric, song-filled garden for teenage love, where fathers are wise and strong and everything is possible, even heroism. Imagining himself sometimes as James Dean's reincarnation, sometimes as a beatnik gangster poet straight out of Jack Kerouac, Jimbo lives a legend of his own construction...

Simmons, Betty Lou *see* marriage

Simmons, Jack

Jimmy's somehow malignant little acolyte and roommate was also known as "The Hawk" to those who remembered what he looked like before Jimmy subsidized his nose job. With Maila Nurmi, Jack palled around with Jimmy at Googie's. Jack drove Maila's hearse while Jimmy swiveled his hips above his motorcycle in the headlights on Sunset. Flagrantly homosexual, Jack enjoyed Jimmy's patronage; Jimmy lobbied hard to get Jack the part of Plato in *Rebel Without a Cause*. Instead, he wound up with a minor role. Fans didn't care for Jack much because he was so possessive and mysterious about his memories of Jimmy. In restaurants, he often claimed to see Jimmy's ghost sitting at another booth. Even Maila thought him a tad eerie those last few decades. He would cover his eyes in grief when passing a portrait of the friend whose death he continued to mourn.

When he eventually gave an interview as he was dying of cancer, he insisted that his friendship with his old roommate Jimmy was not physical, and that they had "never touched genitals."

Many people think it was Simmons who burgled Jimmy's apartment after this death.

See also necrophilia.

simulation

Failure Analysis Associates is a Menlo Park brain trust of engineers who recreate accidents and produce animated simulations via a computer-based modeling program developed by Engineering Dynamics Corporation. It's called Engineering Dynamics Simulation Model of Automobile Collisions. It was inevitable that they eventually tackle James Dean's accident, if only for the publicity value. Gary Korst — who drives a Porsche 911 Targa — was the senior managing engineer for the recreation of Dean's crash for the 1995 TV series *What Happened?*

They went to the intersection of Highways 41 and 46 and performed measurements using original investigation photos overlaid on the current site to determine the length and location of skid marks, prior to impact. The data they collected was fed into a computer. It included, time simulation, impact separation and trajectory time steps, impact positions and velocities, vehicle dimensions and inertial properties, cornering stiffness for each tire, rear axle steer angles, tire/road friction and inter-vehicle parameters. The relative weights of the cars, differences in torsional rigidity and cars' final resting positions were all taken into account.

The firm decided that Turnupseed left two separate sets of panic skids because he "didn't know whether to speed up or slow down at first, so he braked hard initially, then accelerated, and then tried to brake again just before the cars collided."

California Highway Patrol Officer O. V. Hunter estimated at the inquest that the Spyder must have been averaging 90–100 mph to make the rendezvous with death at 5:45. Witness Clifford Hord testified the Porsche was traveling at "well over a hundred miles per hour or better" three hundred yards from the crash scene.

But from the post-impact trajectory and the resting place of the Porsche, the Failure Analysis team deduced that the speed at impact was only 57 mph. Had it been traveling at 67 mph, they said, it would have landed another 50 feet farther away. At 77 mph, it would have come to rest 100 feet farther. "The facts of the matter clearly demonstrate that witness Clifford Hord's speed estimate of Dean's car was way off the mark, and that CHP Officer Hunter's average speed guesstimate for Dean's trip was also erroneous," wrote David Colman in his authoritative article "Rubble Without a Pause," which appeared in the November 1995 issue of *Excellence.*

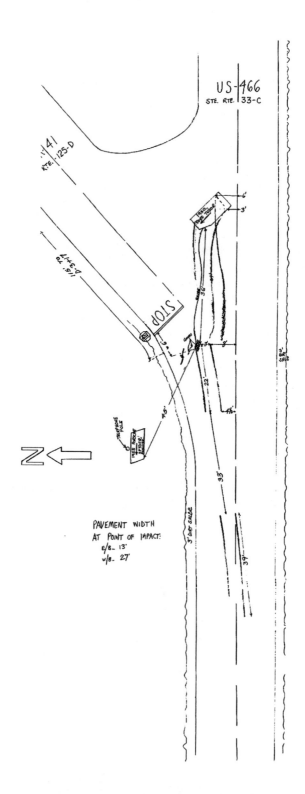

US-466
STE. RTE. 33-C

41
RTE. 125-D

STOP

1.53+?

36

22

4½

33

39

PAVEMENT WIDTH
AT POINT OF IMPACT:
E/B - 13'
W/B - 27'

N

3' DIRT SHLDE

3' DIRT SHLDE

The computer would seem to offer final scientific proof, and there the matter might rest — except that the computer possibly does not take into account the eyewitness testimony, especially that of Mr. and Mrs. John Robert White, who were traveling behind Dean and were deposed by insurance companies.

They testified that the Porsche became airborne after impact and rolled over before landing on its wheels. Failure Analysis depicts the Spyder spinning on the ground. But if the impact extended the Spyder's forward velocity vertically into the air, then the fact that it came to rest only 75 feet away would be less significant. This was the opinion of Porsche expert Lee Raskin, who took issue with the Failure Analysis verdict in a subsequent issue of *Excellence*.

Inquest witness Tom Frederick, who saw the crash from the opposite vantage point behind Turnupseed's Ford, also provides corroboration of this theory. When asked whether the Porsche spun or went straight after the impact, he said, "No, it looked like it just picked it up and set it over there, just straight."

skid marks

Though the inquest tried to discount the skid marks, California Highway patrol officer Ernie Tripke said flatly in 1982, "They were made by the Ford prior to impact."

```
                                                      00116



FACTS:

        Vehicle #1 was in W/bound lane of US 466 facing NW.

        Vehicle #2 was in ditch on N side of highway facing west.

        There were two sets of skids west of impact, one 22' and
one 30' with a 33' gap between, but the skids are in same arc.
There are 39' of broadslides and a 36' gouge E of impact mark to
Vehicle #1.



Dean/Turnupseed fatal TC
30 Sept 1955
```

Above: This page from the California Highway Patrol Vehicle Accident Report on . the wreck that killed James Dean. *Opposite:* California Highway Patrol diagram of the crash.

Tripke wrote in his report on the accident, "The Ford braked for the Porsche. The gap in the skids didn't give him time to accelerate. There has been (and no doubt will be) much conjecture on Mr. Turnupseed's statement about not seeing the Porsche. The skids indicate that he saw it only moments before impact and too late to take any evasive action."

See also Turnupseed, Donald.

Slauson Boulevard

It was on this Culver City boulevard near the Fox Hills Mall that would-be film producer and confirmed con man Jon Emr was gunned down, along with son Roger, in 1991, as he drove along with his mother and girlfriend in a white Lincoln town car. A disgruntled former employee, Robert Suggs, opened fire from another car. Emr had soaked investors on a would-be authorized James Dean biography. The case is described in author Rod Lurie's 1995 book *Once Upon a Time in Hollywood.*

See also Emr, John; Hauge, Alan.

Smith, Clark

He claims to have been on the road with James Dean the day he died, and in an interview with Timothy Larimer of the *San Jose Mercury* (September 26, 1985), he talked about his brush with greatness.

"We were going to the game. And my sister yelled, 'Lookit that car, lookit that car,' and whoosh, it was gone like a bat out of hell. Five minutes later he was killed. And we saw him right before, we did."

Smith, Paul

This unfortunate young man, whose picture appeared next to Jimmy Dean's in his high school yearbook, also died in a car accident in 1969.

"A Song for James Dean"

"A Song for James Dean" is the subtitle of a sort of American hymn by Larry Daehn entitled "As Summer Was Only Beginning." A complete orchestral version was reportedly performed to acclaim by the Topeka Symphony in 1998. The title is drawn from the Greek inscription on the shoulder of the Dean sculpture in Griffith Park. Daehn has been a Dean fan since his high school days, and selected for the melody of his tribute an old British air, "The Winter It Is Past, and the Summer's Here at Last," because Dean's Quaker heritage was rooted in England.

Larry Daehn was named Outstanding Wisconsin Bandmaster by Phi Beta Mu, the international bandmasters' fraternity, in 1988.

speeding ticket *see* ticket

spirit light *see under* ghosts and hauntings

Stander, John W.

A mortician for the Kuehl Funeral Home in Paso Robles, John Stander signed Jimmy Dean's death certificate. He went to a football game in Bakersfield that fatal Friday and encountered Dean's speeding Porsche on the road, a "mousy colored car" which he heard before it came into view. He lived next door to the mortuary, and when he returned from the game the lights were on and the phone was ringing off the hook with inquiries from New York, London and South America. It was customary to prepare a body immediately, and he worked on Dean for about three hours. He said Dean's friend Bill Hickman was in constant attendance. There was no autopsy because the cause of death was apparent. In an interview with Warren Beath, Stander said the body would have been viewed by a pathologist, an officer of the coroner's department, prior to embalming. "The body could have been viewed. Let's put it this way. They said it was to be closed casket. If it had been anybody but a movie star, it would have been open."

Stander said that Winton Dean came the next day with the chief of security from Warner Bros. He had his pick of effects, but the torn up clothes were probably destroyed. Stander later drove the body to Los Angeles, and had an uncomfortable experience when he stopped for gas in Santa Barbara and the kids saw the Paso Robles hearse. "Everyone knew the body had been with us. They wanted to do something, but they didn't know what." He removed the placards and continued the trip without incident. For years afterward, people would come by the funeral home wanting to see the room where Dean had been embalmed.

See also Kuehl Funeral Home.

Starkweather, Charlie

The violence that simmered beneath Jimmy Dean's cool veneer in *Rebel Without a Cause* was perhaps one of the elements that ignited one young Nebraska fan to a 1950s crime spree that swept across several states and left eleven dead. Charlie Starkweather was a runtish garbage man who emulated Jimmy's pompadour and the cigarette dangling insouciantly from his lips. Frustrated in his romance with fourteen-year-old Caril Ann Fugate by the objections of her parents, he stabbed and shot her family to death and embarked on a wave of terror, which ended when he was apprehended in the Badlands of South Dakota. He was sentenced to death, a sentence that was carried out. Caril Ann Fugate, whose involvement in the murders was never clearly determined, was sentenced to life in prison but was paroled in 1976.

The film *Badlands* was a barely fictionalized accounts of the events, which made headlines. Dean-admirer Martin Sheen starred as Starkweather in a portrayal which owed as much to Jimmy Dean as to the real-life counterpart.

Caril Fugate reportedly found God while in prison and is now said to be trying to live a normal life.

station wagon *see* **Ford station wagon**

statue *see* **vandalism**

Stevens, Leith

Wrote the music for the 1957 biopic *The James Dean Story*. Composer, arranger and conductor Stevens (1909–1970) died of a heart attack only minutes after being told that his wife had been killed in a car accident.

Other credits: *The Wild One, Destination Moon, The Gene Krupa Story,* and *Night of the Grizzly.*

stolen films

In August of 1983 the *Los Angeles Times* reported the seizure of stolen classic films from a Columbia Pictures film vault librarian. *East of Eden* was among them. The movies were believed to be original versions worth thousands of dollars each to collectors. Librarian Merle Ray Harlin told investigators that he found a majority of the film cans in trash bins outside the Burbank Studios, a storage facility for major studios including Warner Bros. But Warner Bros. told police that under no circumstances would they have thrown away the films in Harlin's possession. The films were later recovered following an anonymous tip when Harlin was seen loading film cans into a rental truck.

Suggs, Robert

In 1991 after an acrimonious breakup with his employer, Jon Emr, who was conning investors out of money for the making of a James Dean biography, this former private investigator—"Suggsy" to his friends—shot Emr, his son Roger, and Emr's father. He thought he would be Emr's partner and eventually a Hollywood player, but wound up instead as just another of Emr's con victims. He never received money for his services, and eventually depleted his girlfriend's money, causing her to break up with him. Suggs was, reportedly, a graduate of the G. Gordon Liddy Academy of Private Investigation, Corporate Security, and Executive Protection.

Suggs shot the Emr family on Slauson Boulevard. Next, Suggs killed his girlfriend and his dog, returning later to the same spot to kill himself — off Route 62 in the Mojave Desert.

See also Emr, John; Hauge, Alan.

suicide

The special edition British magazine *Fans' Star Library* in a special 1956 Dean edition said that Warner Bros. had received a letter from three hysterical teenagers which read, "Next September 30, the anniversary of his death, we're going to crash our car on the spot where he died. We don't want to live when Jimmy is dead...." The letter was supposedly turned over to the police.

The January 14, 1958, issue of the *San Jose Mercury* reported, "Girl Fan of James Dean Dies by Smashing Car into Tree." The pretty seventeen-year-old high school honor student crashed her car into a pepper tree south of town. Authorities were puzzled at her motives, but thought it could have resulted from "teenage group discussions of the death of actor James Dean in 1955 in an automobile crash. Friends said the girl was a member of a group which considered Dean's death as 'glamorous.'" She drove her car at an estimated 80 miles an hour against the tree.

A sixteen-year-old male classmate friend had died in a crash against the same tree the previous May — a death that was listed as accidental.

Biographer John Howlett wrote, "Two Hamburg girls killed themselves in 1959 saying that life without [Dean] was unbearable."

Suicide Hotel *see* **The Knickerbocker**

Superman

George Reeves, who won fame as television's *Superman,* was up for the part of Officer Ray in *Rebel Without a Cause.* He didn't get it. That might have been one of the events that led eventually to despondency and his suicide on June 16, 1959. An extension of the Dean curse? Some claim it was murder. That was what his mother believed, and she had Reeves' body shipped to Cincinnati for a second autopsy. Pictures of his body were taken and circulated for years at Superman conventions. They were called "the summer camp photos" due to the bark-like mottling of the flesh. The Benedict Canyon house in which he died is also said to be haunted.

·Swan, Billy

A singer whose big hit was "I Can Help." Apparently a big Dean fan, in 1998 he announced a CD which was a tribute to James Dean, featuring the songs *I Used to Be James Dean* and *James Dean: Gone but Not Forgotten.* He debuted the songs publicly at the 11th Annual Open House at the James Dean Memorial Gallery in Fairmount, Indiana.

sweater

In March 1982, newspapers reported that a sweater once owned by James Dean sold at auction for $475. It was purchased by Herman Darvick, a sixth-grade teacher in Coney Island, N.Y. Darvick also bought newspaper photos of Dean wearing the sweater.

T

tape recordings

Photographer Frank Worth claims that he went to Dean's house a few days before the actor died and was treated to some tapes Dean had made on his Webbcore tape recorder. "They gave me the creeps," he told *Modern Screen* in September 1962. "They were all about death and dying, poems and things he just made up! They were his ideas on what it might be like to die, how it would feel to be in the grave and all that."

These reputed tapes are said to be among the items taken from Dean's home when it was burgled shortly after his death.

teeth

Film composer Leonard Rosenmann told Warren Beath, "We had a very funny stunt we use to pull together at parties. [Jimmy] had broken his front teeth. Knocked out two or three of his front teeth in a motorcycle accident. And he had a bridge there, which he could dislodge with his tongue without anyone seeing it. Suddenly he wouldn't have any teeth in front. We do it kind of a face interview at these parties, and I say, 'Mr. Dean, do you do your own stunts? He says, 'I certainly do!' And he'd smile and he'd have no front teeth. It would be very funny."

Theme Music from The James Dean Story

Chet Baker was called "The James Dean of Jazz," and he was the artistic force behind this offering of the jazzed-up soundtrack from *The James Dean Story* (1957). Released by World Pacific Records, it also featured saxophone legend Bud Shank.

theme software

It's the James Dean Theme by Soft.seek, a desktop software bundle you can download featuring James Dean, "the original bad boy." You can install Jimmy on your hard drive and enjoy Dean-themed wallpaper, screen savers, icons, animated cursors and WAV sounds.

"Through James Dean's Rearview Mirror"

Article by Lee Raskin that appeared in the December 1995 issue of *Excellence*. The article was a response to Failure Analysis Associates' computerized reconstruction of Jimmy's crash, which was aired on the television show *What Happened?* Raskin's argument was to "counter Failure's conclusion that Dean's Spyder was only traveling 57 miles per hour at the time of impact." He cites the deposition of John Robert White, who was witness to the crash and saw the Porsche fly upward. The implication is that the velocity was expended vertically, and Dean could still have been speeding despite Failure's computer simulation.

    See also simulation.

ticket

Just a little more than two hours before his fatal accident, James Dean was cited for speeding by California Highway Patrol officer O. V. Hunter on Wheeler Ridge at the foot of the Grapevine Grade some 22 miles south of Bakersfield, California. Dean was ticketed for exceeding the 55-mile-per-hour speed limit, while Bill Hickman in Dean's wagon towing a trailer was cited for being twenty miles over the speed limit for vehicles towing an attachment. Hunter recalls Dean as being amiable and cooperative, offering as a defense, "She doesn't run right under eighty."

    Ironically, just two weeks earlier Dean had completed a highway safety spot on the set of *Giant*.

    Hunter had been traveling southbound on Highway 99, south of the settlement of Mettler Station, when he saw the obviously speeding Porsche approaching on the descent in the northbound lanes. After the ticketing he believed that Dean headed on into Bakersfield, though he acknowledged that he might have taken the Highway 166 cutoff and proceeded to Blackwell's Corner through Taft and Maricopa; that route was commonly known as the "racer's shortcut."

Hunter later was called to testify at the inquest, and was specifically asked about whether Dean was wearing his glasses. He did not recall, but suspected he was because he had a restricted license; had he not been wearing the glasses, Hunter would have cited him for that violation.

Officer Hunter misspelled Dean's middle name (Byron) on the ticket. When he heard that evening that he had ticketed a celebrity, he could only recall Jimmy Dean the country-western singer.

Dean's copy of the ticket was recovered from his body and submitted as Exhibit 10 at the inquest.

Speeding ticket received by James Dean just hours before his death.

time slips

Since the mid–1980s the stretch of route 46 upon which Jimmy Dean drove to his death has seen annual car rallies in addition to the lone pilgrimages of fans en route to his shrine at the settlement called Cholame. The forty-mile stretch between the death site and the eerily named Lost Hills is an empty vacuum of prairie that seems conducive to strange tricks of perception and imagination. Perhaps due to the heightened sensitivity of the fan hoping for an epiphany with the icon, many drivers report strange compressions or elongations of time. It is as if the arid waste where Dean raced to his death has become a sort of wound in the universe, a black hole in which time itself becomes distorted.

Drivers report leaving Lost Hills and arriving in Paso Robles only to discover that the one-hour drive has actually taken three, and they have missed dinner or their appointment. Others tell of going into a trancelike state upon leaving Lost Hills, and returning to awareness later only to find they've passed through the intersection — but have no memory of it. One man says he drove the route at night and watched in disbelief as his odometer rolled on and on for hours as if the highway was stretching and repeating itself under his wheels.

Some report electrical interference, the radio going dead and the engine faltering. The dashboard clock and any watch in the car freeze. Time seems to stand still, and then all systems resume normal functioning once the death site is passed.

Local news crews retracing the route in response to the stories have never succeeded in replicating the experiences.

See also ghosts and hauntings.

Tip's

It is ironic that James Dean, who reportedly never left a tip, stopped at a diner called Tip's on the last day of his life. He evidently had a milkshake and over the ice cream was moved to place upon Rolf Wuetherich's small finger a cheap Pan Am flight ring as a token of their friendship. Dean was

The former Tip's Restaurant as it appeared in the 1980s. (Now demolished.) It was here that Dean allegedly gave Wuetherich an inexpensive Pan Am flight ring as a gesture of friendship.

apparently eating light on his last day: a doughnut at the Ranch Market, a milkshake at Tip's, and an apple and Coke at Blackwell's Corner.

Tip's Diner was located at Castaic Junction until the early 1980s, when it was demolished in the hubbub of redevelopment involved with the development of Six Flags Magic Mountain. Before its demolition, the closed-up diner was a popular filming site for such notable television series as *Mannix*.

tire iron

"Did you ever feel anything so hard?" an amiable Jimmy joked to a female costar as he extended the tire iron that he wielded in the planetarium scene in *Rebel Without a Cause*. When the time came to play the scene moments later, he was all business, tossing the tire iron over the parapet in a plea for nonviolence that prefigured the peace movement of the 1960s. More than one fan-sociologist sees that moment as signaling a passive resistance movement that would transform the youth culture less than a decade later.

What ever happened to that tire iron? With the advent of VCRs and DVDs, avid Dean fans have stopped the frames of *Rebel* to identify the exact site from which James Dean cast the tool. They try to estimate where the thing would have landed in the scrub brush below. Most likely, it was recovered by a crewman after the scene. Nevertheless, hopeful fans, drawn by its panache as a relic of the film and a souvenir of Jimmy Dean, continue to scour the ground below the telescope and sift through the scrub with metal detectors.

Author Bentley Little examines the mythic implications of such a relic in a short story entitled "The Idol," which was published in the book *Mondo James Dean* (St. Martin's Griffin, 1996). In this story, the stone is discovered in an abandoned shed below the observatory.

> In the center of the room, embedded in a large square chunk of stone, was the tire iron. The tire iron Dean had thrown. The bottom half of the tool, with its curved chisel end, was sunk deep into the rock. The top half, with its rounded wrench end, stuck straight up. The metal was immaculately polished and showed not a hint of rust.

Pictures of generations of nude girls line the walls, and the reason soon becomes apparent to the young men who have discovered the sacred site, as some young women of their acquaintance approach. The phallic relic has been inserted in the stone to accommodate the rites of passage to womanhood. It has a sacramental function that recognizes Jimmy's deity and his efficacy as the soul guide of sexual transition. The site is the nexus of a modern mystery religion.

There was the sound of a belt being unfastened, the sound of a zipper. Something dropped onto the dirt, something soft, and it was followed by a low rustling noise. Someone walked into the middle of the shed.

Then there was silence again.

All of a sudden I heard a sharp gasp. A small moan of pain and an exhalation of air. Another gasp.

I had to know what was going on. Once again, I hazarded a peek over the rim of my box.

And immediately crouched back down.

One of the young girls, the prettiest one, was lowering herself onto the tire iron. She was squatting over the stone, completely naked, the rounded end of the lug wrench already inside her. Her face was contorted, physical pain coexisting with what looked like an underlying spiritual rapture.

tissue holder

What did Dean fans do before there was a licensed and trademarked James Dean Tissue Holder? Handcrafted decoupage that makes wiping your nose a homage to Jimmy, sells for $24.95.

Der Tod des James Dean see under *Der*

tombstone

James Dean's tombstone was stolen —for the *first* time —from the Fairmount (Indiana) Park Cemetery on April 14, 1983. Writing for the Marion, Indiana, *Chronicle-Times*, reporter J. Chilton Reed recounted its recovery on May 7. The stone was found resting on a tree stump at a highway junction in Grant County. Guy Ellis, a local resident, on his way home from work, had found the stone. The police reported that there didn't appear to be damages other than a few scratches and chips, which were likely the result of Dean fans wanting a memento of their hero. Reed wrote that the police didn't know how long the tombstone had been on the stump or who had put it there. The mother of the man who found the stone, Kathryn Ellis, said the stump was what was left after lightning struck a large tree on property belonging to James Leach. She said, "My husband was out walking the fields the other day, and he thought he might have seen it, the way you might see something sitting on a sign or a post in the distance." According to the article, Guy Ellis bundled the stone in a quilt to preserve any fingerprints that might be on it and delivered it to the Fairmount Police Department. The police report said eventually the tombstone was turned over to Marcus Winslow, Jr., Dean's cousin, to be stored until it could be put back in the cemetery, safely secured from further tampering.

Evidently, however, that security left something to be desired, for the stone disappeared again in May 1983. This time — according to a *Fort Wayne News-Sentinel* report four years later on the occasion of the stone's recovery — the thief was a ghoulish Good Samaritan who stole James Dean's gravestone to save it from what he saw as desecration. "You have heroes. How would you like to see their grave messed up? What would you think if you went to their grave and saw people had spray-painted their lovers' names all over and were snorting cocaine off the stone? We'd rather take it away entirely than have it die a terrible death." So he snatched the stone from the cemetery in broad daylight. In its ensuing four-year absence, it was buried, photographed by a documentary crew, and advertised for sale in a local paper for $10. Eventually, Fort Wayne, Indiana, firefighters found it next to a dumpster. The stone-snatcher had meantime moved to Southern California.

The man says that he went to the cemetery with accomplices and hefted the stone onto the front seat of a Cadillac at 7 A.M. on May 29, 1983. He said, "There were business cards from biker gangs stuffed under the stone. They said, 'If you can get this damn thing off here, you're a better man than me,' or 'If you can move this thing, I'll buy it.'"

The stone was driven to Elwood, Indiana, and put in the trunk of another car. The thief told a reporter by phone, "I've never bit off such a huge chunk of karma as that thing. From the very beginning, everything started to go wrong."

His car's transmission went out, and then that night it was vandalized with spray paint.

"I thought the devil himself had done it. I wiped off as much of the paint as I could and had it towed home." He buried the stone in his back yard for three months, then cleaned it up and put it in his garage when he thought "the heat had blown over."

The unidentified man's story was confirmed by a woman in Fort Wayne who found the headstone in the garage of a home she occupied after the twenty-seven-year-old man. "It gave me the creeps," she said. It gave her kids nightmares. So she tried to sell it for ten bucks through the paper. She gave it to her brother, who gave it to her father, who worked at the fire station in the event someone there might be interested in it. He was on vacation at the time, and perhaps it was his colleagues who deposited it by the dumpster.

The third theft of the stone occurred in July of 1998, when youths from a church camp were visiting Dean's grave. A Knight-Ridder newspaper account noted that there were severe pry marks around the base. Police chief Jim Grindle told the reporter, "They really worked at it." The stone was recovered shortly afterwards when it tore out the undercarriage of a police car that ran over it where it had been left on a road.

tow truck

Seita Ohnishi installed a $15,000 monument to Jimmy Dean at Cholame, and was soon approached by locals impressed with the foreigner's largesse and the intensity of his obsession. When a woman approached him offering to sell what she reported to be the tow truck that towed Jimmy's car from the crash site, he quickly peeled off three one-hundred dollar bills. It wasn't the truck. At last report, the truck was in a Paso Robles body shop awaiting restoration.

towing bill

Court documents indicate that Dean's estate was charged $174.37 by Paul Moreno to tow the smashed Spyder to his garage from the crash site. The bill presumably also includes a charge for temporary storage.

tribute songs

The death of James Dean gave rise to some of the worst music ever recorded, tributes by artists as diverse as Jimmy Wakely, Eydie Gorme, Mantovani, the Four Tunes, and Red River Dave. There were at least three different songs titled *Ballad of James Dean*. A number called *Jimmy, Jimmy* was recorded at least three times, and *Let Me Be Loved*, which was the theme song of 1957's *The James Dean Story* (itself an inept effort to cash in on the Dean craze by Jimmy's home studio), was recorded at least four. The worst tribute song—or at least the worst title—is probably *Deanie Boy*, performed to the tune of *Danny Boy*. Or maybe it's *James Dean's First Christmas in Heaven*. An artist named Red River Dave recorded no less than seven Dean tributes in his quest to get it right.

A Tribute to James Dean: Imperial Records

Imperial Records distinguishes itself in the Dean musical sweepstakes by offering a souvenir album featuring music from Dean's films conducted by Leonard Rosenmann—the composer of the *Eden* and *Rebel* scores.

A Tribute to James Dean: MGM Record

Art Mooney and MGM Records offer soundtrack music from *East of Eden* and *Rebel Without a Cause*.

A Tribute to James Dean: Warner Bros.

Warner Bros. musical stalwart Ray Heindorf serves up reheated music from Dean soundtracks on a platter released by Columbia Records. The Warner Bros. Orchestra lends the record that distinctive Warners brass sound. Heindorf was involved as a conductor or musical director in such prominent films as *Yankee Doodle Dandy*, *A Streetcar Named Desire*, *A Star is Born* and *The Music Man*. He died in 1980 at age 72.

Tripke, Ernie

California Highway Patrol officer who was at the scene of Dean's fatal crash. Tripke wrote Warren Beath:

> I joined the CHP in April 1948 at the ripe old age of 25 after putting in a hitch in the U.S. Navy. My first assignment was East L.A. I soon transferred to Paso Robles and remained there until February 1956, when I was promoted to sergeant and transferred to Eureka. From Eureka I transferred to CHP Headquarters in Sacramento, then to San Luis Obispo. In July 1960, I was promoted to lieutenant and transferred to King City as sub-station commander. In January 1969, I was promoted to captain and transferred to Yreka. A short time later I transferred to San Luis Obispo as area commander, where I remained until I retired in December 1976.

Tucker, Dave

In 1952 Dave Tucker saw an uncredited James Dean in *Has Anybody Seen My Gal*. He saw a smart aleck order a malt from Charles Coburn and then sat through the movie again just to see Jimmy order that shake. Whoever this young actor was, Tucker was a fan immediately.

When *East of Eden* came to Lubbock, Texas, Tucker missed it. He saw an ad in the paper for the film, but didn't connect the actor with the picture.

Before he had a chance to see any of Dean's landmark movies, he heard the news of Jimmy's accident the next morning. He then recognized Dean as the actor he had been drawn to in *Has Anybody Seen My Gal*. Tucker says the feeling that swept over him was one of depression and grief.

When *Rebel Without a Cause* played at a Lubbock theater Tucker thought it was a civil war picture. He went anyway, not knowing of Jimmy's critically acclaimed performance. He saw Dean's picture on the outside of the theater and inside, lobby cards showed different scenes in the movie. This was a different type of motion picture. He had admired Dean's work before, but now was a fan of Jimmy's forever. He saw the first movie start around 12:30 P.M. and watched it over and over until the last showing that night.

Dave Tucker and Vic Bent, another longtime Dean fan, have a memorial run planned to celebrate the fiftieth anniversary of James Dean's death. On September 30, 2005, Vic Bent will take his Porsche Spyder 550 from Sherman Oaks, California, to Cholame, California. Bent's perfect replica of James Dean's car will arrive at the intersection of California Highway 44 and 41 at 5:45 P.M., exactly fifty years after Jimmy's fateful trip. Dave Tucker will document the trip on video.

Turnupseed, Don

Driver of the 1950 Ford that collided with James Dean's Spyder in the fatal accident. For the rest of his life, Turnupseed was badgered by photographers, reporters, and Dean fans, but he consistently refused to have his picture taken, and he never granted an interview beyond the few unguarded remarks he had made to the local paper within twenty-four hours of the accident.

Turnupseed's 1950 Ford Tudor Custom Deluxe was license number 6A48142, and he had bought it on October 26, 1953.

He is quoted saying, at the crash site, "I didn't see him, by God, I really didn't see him." Author John Lindahl, among others, reports that he "cried when he was found guilty of causing the accident." This statement is incorrect in two respects: Turnupseed did not cry and was not found guilty.

Investigating officer Ron Nelson said later, "What he probably meant was, I didn't see him in time." Witness Tom Frederick testified at the inquest that he overheard Turnupseed talking to the cop and telling him that he didn't see the other car. "He said he looked up at the road sign just before that, and started to make his turn."

Ron Nelson testified about Turnupseed's statement at the scene:

> He stated he was going to turn, he had been traveling approximately 55 miles to 60 miles an hour, and as he approached this intersection where the signs point to Hanford and Fresno, he started to slow down, it was his intention to turn left. He said just before he made his turn, he looked straight down US 466 and for some unknown reason, he did not see the other car until he was already in his turn and he heard, he said he heard the squeal of tires and saw the car, and tried to turn to the right to avoid it, but was unable to.

Highway Patrol officer Ernie Tripke wrote later, "He did sustain minor injuries but was very rational and behaved normally."

He had to hitchhike home to be treated in Tulare, where his mother was a nurse.

Turnupseed was born in Porterville, California. An industrial arts student at Tulare Union High School, he was on the football squad in 1948 and 1949. He served two years in the navy during the Korean War, most of the time on a hospital ship. After the Dean mania overtook the country, Turnupseed reenlisted for four more years. He had married a local girl in 1950. She died of cancer in 1977, and he remarried in 1981. He had two sons and a daughter from his first marriage, and a stepson from his second. At the time of his death he had five grandchildren.

He had developed a fondness for cars while in high school. "He was car crazy," said friend and co-worker Wally Nelson. His first car was a Model A that he fixed up. "He turned it into a little race car," said boyhood friend Al Paggi.

Later in life, his interest in cars persisted. A former employee said he stopped by Don's house once and found Arnold Schwarzenegger there regarding their mutual interest in building dune buggies.

At the time of Turnupseed's death, his company, the 48-year-old Turnupseed Electric Service, employed 75 workers with several branch offices and annual sales of $15 million. Turnupseed handed over control of the company to Wally Nelson the year before his death as his lung cancer progressed, though he kept close ties to the business. On July 13, 1995, after being cared for at a Visalia hospice, he died at his home at age 63.

In Turnupseed's obituary in the *Visalia Times-Delta*, Wally Nelson said of the Dean accident, "It bothered him his whole life. That's not him. That's not Donald Turnupseed. He's been bothered by people constantly trying to write a story. There's always somebody calling up, or coming to the door. We had to push them out the door." Because 1995 was the 40th anniversary of the crash, requests had picked up again; a German journalist, Nelson said, was the last to call.

Said Al Paggi to the *Tulare Advance Register* upon Turnupseed's death, "It was hard to get close to Don." Because of the accident in 1955? Paggi said, "More than likely."

Of Turnupseed's company, Al Paggi (owner of Paggi Electric) said, "They were tough competitors. As a business person, he learned from his dad. His dad was a very, very tough-minded person. But they never shorted anybody on their work."

Turnupseed is buried, along with his mother, father, and first wife, in the Tulare Cemetery.

What happened to the fatal Ford? A fan contacted him via phone on a ruse and asked him. Don said, "No, I have no idea ... now ... where it's at." He said it was taken to a junkyard and never bought or restored, to his knowledge.

DEPOSITION

On August 20, 1956, attorneys for Rolf Wuetherich filed complaint for personal injuries against the estate of James Dean. On September 28, they amended the complaint to include Don Turnupseed as defendant. On December 4, an attorney for James Dean's auto insurance carrier also filed suit against Turnupseed. This attorney took Turnupseed's deposition on March 8, 1958. The text of the deposition follows.

SUPERIOR COURT OF THE STATE OF CALIFORNIA, COUNTY OF SAN LUIS OBISPO.

PACIFIC INDEMNITY COMPANY a corporation, Plaintiff

v.

DONALD GENE TURNUPSEED, defendant

No. 22350

DEPOSITION OF DONALD GENE TURNUPSEED

Fresno, California   **March 8, 1958**

Pursuant to the attached Stipulation, the deposition of Donald Gene Turnupseed, defendant in the above-entitled action, was taken by and on behalf of the plaintiff, before Ray E. Adams, Notary Public in and for the County of Fresno, State of California, at 505 Equitable Building, Fresno, California, on the morning of Saturday, the 8th day of March 1958, commencing at the hour of 11 o'clock.

A. H. Brazil, Esq., appeared as counsel for the plaintiff.

Hansen, McCormick, Barstow & Sheppard, by R. A. McCormick, Esq., appeared as counsel for the defendant.

The following proceedings were had, to wit:

DONALD GEME TURNUPSEED (defendant):

Called as to witness on behalf of the plaintiff, being first duly sworn by the Notary, testified as follows:

MR. BRAZIL:

Q   Will you state your name, please?

A   Donald Gene Turnupseed.

Q   And where do you reside?

A   At 627 North N Place.

MR. MCCORMICK: 627?

A   Yes.

MR. BRAZIL:

Q   In what city?

A   Tulare, California.

Q   Are you married or single?
A   I am married.
Q   And were you residing at that place in 1955 in September?
A   No.
Q   Where were you living at that time?
A   Well, my home address was

MRS. TURNUPSEED: 1001— At 1001 Academy, Tulare, California.

MR. BRAZIL:
Q   Where were you living in September 1955?
A   At 1001 Academy was my home address.
Q   In what city?
A   Tulare.
Q   Were you in the County of San Luis Obispo on that day?
A   Yes.
Q   And did you own an automobile?
A   Yes.
Q   And referring specifically to an area, which would be east of the City of Paso Robles, were you involved in an automobile accident —
A   Yes.
Q   On that day? And what kind of car were you driving?
A   1950 Ford.
Q   Where had you started from that day?
A   From San Luis Obispo; Cal Poly.
Q   Were you going to Poly at that time?
A   Yes.
Q   Was anyone driving with you at the time?
A   No sir.
Q   What time of day or night was it that you left San Luis Obispo?
A   Approximately 1 o'clock —
Q   And —
A   Between 12 and 1.
Q   Then where were you going, sir?
A   I was going to Tulare.
Q   Now bringing this case directly up to the accident, you were approaching the wye[Y] of Highway 466 and 41, is that true?
A   Yes.
Q   And your plan was to turn in a left — to the left in order to go on 41, is that right?
A   That is right.
Q   Up until that point we will say you were driving in a generally easterly direction?
A   Yes sir.
Q   Do you recall what your speed was immediately before you come to the intersection or junction?

Top: Turnupseed's view of US 466, looking east as he approached the Y intersection with State Highway 41 on the left. Note the dark skidmarks in the middleground along the center line of the highway, possibly from the Dean accident. *Bottom:* The late Charles Adams, a passionate investigator of the Dean accident, standing at left near the fence in 1956. Adams drew Turnupseed's Ford Tudor on the photograph to show where it came to rest.

A   Oh, approximately 45 or 50.

Q   And what was the condition of the day as to being dry or wet?

A   It was a dry day.

Q   Was clear?

A   Yes.

Q   Were you in a hurry to get any place?

A   No.

Q   Will you tell me in your own words what happened as you approached that junction with 41?

A   Well, I approached the junction and had a collision.

Q   Tell us what happened as you remember.

A   Well, as I was coming up, I was driving along and then I heard this screaming of an engine or saw it first, I am not sure which, in other words. It both happened and I had — it was right under me then, or there was a collision.

Q   Taking it from that point back, had you started to make a turn on to 41?

A   Yes, I had just started to turn.

Q   And had you been looking in the direction of 466, which runs straight east?

A   Yes.

Q   And was there any traffic on the road at that time as you observed before you started to make your turn?

A   No, not that would even call my attention to it.

Q   But you were looking directly up that highway?

A   Yes.

Q   Did you see any vehicle coming in the opposite direction?

A   No, I sure did not.

Q   You did not at all?

A   No sir.

Q   Now do you have any present knowledge of how far west of the point of impact it was that you started to turn toward the left?

A   That would just be a guess.

Q   Your best estimate only is all you can possibly give at this time?

A   Uh huh.

Q   Let us put it to you this way: Would it be more or less than 100 feet.

A   It would be less.

Q   It would be less?

Opposite top: This 1956 photograph shows Dean's view of the intersection of US 466 and State Highway 41, looking west. The man standing on the berm, near center, is Dean fan and self-styled accident investigator Charles Adams. The Spyder came to rest next to the first telephone pole on the right. *Bottom:* A closer shot of the same area shows a painted circle with an X in it; this mark indicates the point of impact. Adams is pointing to where he originally and incorrectly believed the car came to rest. Later he drew in the Spyder at its actual point of rest at the base of the telephone pole.

A   Yes.

Q   In other words you started to turn at a point less than 100 feet from the point of impact?

A   Yes, I believe it would be.

Q   Now just so we know — I guess — what are these blocks, do you know offhand.

MR. McCORMICK: I think they are 400 feet.

MR. BRAZIL: Now Mr. McCormick states that a block is about 400 feet, in other words the distance would be four times—

A   Uh huh.

Q   one hundred? You still feel that it was about 100 feet or less that you started to make the turn before the collision?

A   Yes, it would be.

Q   Now prior to the time you started to make the turn did you do anything in regard to the turn as to signal?

A   No sir, because there was no interference that I had seen.

Q   You saw nothing in front of you?

A   That is right.

Q   Now when would you say it was that you first saw the Dean car, if you did see the car?

A   The car I seen after the impact.

Q   In other words you did not see the Dean car until after the impact?

A   No. All I seen in the impact was an arm.

Q   What do you mean by that?

A   Well, I heard the car and I looked right down into it and into the seat after the impact, but at the time of impact I seen an arm come up over my hood.

MR. BRAZIL: The witness has indicated an arm raised with the hand and fist over the temple, forehead, is that right?

A   Yes.

Q   What was the color of the clothes on that arm, if you remember the sleeve?

A   I am not sure at all about that.

Q   Did you see the color of the jacket or sweater or arm you indicated?

A   At the time of impact?

Q   Yes.

A   No sir, so far as color goes, no.

Q   Now if you did not see the vehicle, you at the present time have no knowledge or idea how fast the other car might have been coming?

A   No sir.

Q   You could not say as to whether it was going fast or slow?

A   Just from the sound of the engine would be the only way.

Q   How soon before the impact would you say that you heard the sound of the engine?

A   Maybe three seconds, or, it was very very fast, right there.

Q   Three seconds would be one, two, three.

A   No, it was closer than that. It all happened right about, the best as I could tell, at the same time.

Q   A snap of the fingers you might say, is that right?

A   Yes.

Q   Prior to that time you heard nothing and you saw nothing? Your answer is "No"?

A   Yes.

MR. McCORMICK: Wait a minute. Now his answer is "Yes, I heard nothing," is that right?

A   Yes. I heard nothing.

MR. BRAZIL: I will reframe the question. We will get it this way:

Q   At that time you neither heard anything or saw anything?

A   No, not pertaining to the car.

Q   That is what I mean.

A   Yes.

Q   You were looking in a generally easterly direction along the traffic on 466?

A   Yes sir.

Q   Did you by any chance apply your brakes?

A   Yes sir, I did.

Q   How did you apply them, with a great force or gradually, if you remember?

A   The best I can recall, great force as soon as I heard it.

Q   In other words the application of brakes came at the time that you heard the motor, rather than the time you saw the car?

A   That is right.

Q   Do you know at this time if you had made any skid marks on the highway.

A   At this time? Yes I do apparently now, that I made them.

Q   Did you check them after the accident?

A   Yes sir.

Q   And were you able to observe any of them at that time?

A   After the accident, yes sir.

Q   Do you know what the distance of the skid marks were?

A   About four or five feet.

Q   Now four or five feet long, you mean?

A   Yes sir.

Q   Was that one or two skid marks?

A   It was all four of them, I believe.

Q   What do you mean by that?

A   All four wheels.

Q   In other words, the back wheels not tracking on the front ones, they made their own individual skid marks?

In this photograph showing Dean's view of the intersection, the location of the skid-marks has been darkened with a pen by Charles Adams.

A   Yes, yes sir.

Q   Did you swerve either way?

A   I tried to swerve to the right, now whether I did or not, that —

Q   At the time however it was so instantaneous that you had no opportunity to make a movement either way?

A   I made a distinct movement of the steering wheel; that part I am sure of.

Q   But not enough reaction so as to get your car out of the path of this oncoming automobile?

A   No sir, I sure did not.

Q   You did not. Do you wear glasses?

A   No sir.

Q   You do not have any restrictions on your driver's license.

A   No.

Q   And you feel that at the time that you started to make the turn you were traveling at about did you say 40 or 45 miles an hour?

A   That would be a rough guess.

Q   May I have some outside limits: Might you have been going as slow as 20 miles an hour?

A   It would be possible, yes.

Q   How about 60 miles an hour?

A   No, I know that I was not.

Q   What would you think would be, in your own honest opinion, the maximum speed that you could have been going at that time?

A   It would be between 40 and 45 in order to make that curve.

Q   Yet you could have been traveling perhaps as low, as you said, as 20 miles?

A   Yes.

Q   However 45 is the top speed you feel you were going?

A   Yes.

Q   Do you know where in that highway it was that the two cars came together?

A   It was on the — that would be the westbound lane, right in the intersection.

Q   The westbound lane of 466, you mean?

A   Yes sir.

Q   And in the general area of the intersection or junction?

A   Yes.

Q   Do you know if any marks were left upon the highway which were caused by either car? That is, gouge marks?

A   There was one set on mine.

Q   Were there any witnesses that you know of, any — rather, any people within that area at the time of the accident?

A   I don't know their names, but there was.

Q   Were any people there?

A   Yes.

Q   How soon after the accident did people arrive at the scene?

A   Right afterwards, there were.

Q   Was it a car coming in what direction, if they were traveling?

A   There was one going east behind me, there was one arrived going west behind Dean that were anywhere —

Q   Close?

A   Close area to that.

Q   Do you know when the Highway Patrol officers arrived on the scene?

A   About two hours later.

Q   Had either of the cars been moved from the time of the accident until they arrived?

A   No sir.

Q   So that whatever investigation they made would have been based on the situation which existed immediately after the accident?

A   Yes sir.

Q   Did the ambulance arrive there?

A   Yes sir.

Q   And who went to the hospital, if you know?

A   Both Dean and the mechanic.

Q   You as I understand it were not injured.

. A   No sir. I was— had minor cuts on me.

Q   So that you were fully conscious at all times of what was going on?

A   Yes sir.

Q   What part of your car came in contact with the car driven by Dean?

A   The left front end and side area of the left.

Q   And was your car badly damaged?

A   Yes sir, it was.

Q   You were not able to drive it away?

A   No sir.

Q   What part of the Dean car came in contact with yours, if you know?

A   The left side and front.

Q   Now you mentioned previously of having seen this arm rise up and — being raised up and covering the face. Would you at this time know as to whether it was the person on the left or on the right side?

A   No sir, until after the accident I had no idea whether there was one or five of them in the car.

Q   Did you later see the people who were in the car?

A   Yes sir.

Q   Had one of them been thrown from the vehicle?

A   Yes sir.

Q   Which one was that?

A   The mechanic.

Q   Do you recall at that time how he was dressed as to color, I am referring to?

A   I believe I sure could not, I know there was two colors involved, but which one had which one I would not want to say.

Q   In other words one person did have on a red colored jacket of some kind?

A   Yes. The other was white.

Q   You do not know which was which?

A   No.

Q   Where was Dean's body located?

A   He was on the right-hand side of the car hanging over the door facing down.

Q   Was this a left or right-hand drive automobile?

A   Left-hand.

Q   Did you see where his feet were at the time, in the car?

A   In the floor board, I believe.

Q   He was dead at that time as I understand it?

Q   That is the way as I understand it.

(Short recess.)

MR. BRAZIL: May I have the last?

(Record read.)

Q Now how far did your car travel if at all from the point of impact to where it came to rest?

A Actually travel, none, but it was turned around in the road sideways.

Q Made a circle around, is that right?

A Yes.

Q Pivoted about the point of impact?

A Yes sir.

Q How far did the Dean car travel if at all from the point of impact to the coming to rest?

A Maybe 60 feet.

Q And in what direction if you know did it go from the point of impact?

A Well it would be in a westerly —

Q Westerly direction?

A Westerly direction, just the way he was headed.

Q Did either car turn over?

A No sir.

Q Didn't Dean's car make several turns?

A No sir.

Q Did you see it as it traveled?

A No, not in flight. It could have turned over.

Q In other words, if you did not see it actually turn over before it came to rest, you were not in a position to see it?

A No sir, that is right.

Q Were you stunned in any way?

A Yes sir, I was.

Q Is your hearing good?

A Yes.

Q And eyesight, was it —

A Yes sir.

Q Were you able to get out of your car right after it came to a stop?

A Yes.

Q What is the color of your car?

A It was black and white.

Q And what is the color of the Dean car?

A Silver gray aluminum color.

Q Does it have any stripes or odd colors?

A No sir. It had numbers on it in black.

Q In black. How big were the numbers?

A Oh I would say maybe a foot or a foot and a half tall.

Q Did you see those before the accident?

A No sir.

Q Were they on the front, back, or side?

A Front and back both. In the photographs they show them on the side too but I did not notice that at the time.

Q   When you heard this motor as you state, was that just a smooth hum of some kind?

A   No sir. It was a scream.

Q   Was there a noise at the impact, loud noise of the two cars coming together, I mean?

A   Yes sir, there was quite a bit of it.

Q   Do you know whether or not there were any application of brakes of the Dean car as shown by the marks on the highway?

A   No sir. There was no marks at all.

MR. BRAZIL: I think that is all we need to question Mr. Turnupseed on.

MR. McCORMICK: All right, sir.

MR. BRAZIL: Thank you very much, sir.

(Discussion.)

MR. BRAZIL: Mr. Turnupseed, I have assumed that your counsel has advised you of the fact that when your deposition is transcribed you are to read it over carefully and to make any changes that you feel should be made, if the statement does not conform to the facts as you believe them to be?

A   O.K.

MR. BRAZIL: And you are to sign the same before a notary public.

MR. McCORMICK: Now the stipulation calls for calls for conditional waiver. If you want him to sign it I will be happy to have him sign it.

MR. BRAZIL: I do want him to sign it. That is only in the event he cannot, but I would like to have him sign it if possible.

Q   I might ask you one question: We have been here now some 30 minutes in this examination, and as you sit there, there is nothing which you have said, in your opinion, that was not exactly as you recall it according to the best of your memory and belief?

A   No sir, there was not.

Q   You have made an honest effort to tell us all the facts as they are in your mind, based upon my questions to you?

A   Yes sir.

MR. BRAZIL: Thank you very much.

Tussaud's Wax Museum

Madame Tussaud's added Jimmy Dean to their waxworks in 1989.

U

UFOs

The president of the Amalgamated Flying Saucer Clubs of America believes that strange lights in the vicinity where Jimmy Dean filmed *Giant* in Texas are due to atmospheric ionization around spacecraft piloted by aliens who have set up bases under nearby mountains. Eerie globes of green light hover over the hills above Cholame where Jimmy died. Hardy visitors who have gone to his gravesite at night see flickering streaks above the surrounding cornfields, and at least one conspiracy death buff believes that Jimmy's death may have been faked by extraterrestrials intent on abducting him to a higher mode of consciousness where he belonged all along.

There may be an explanation for the sightings near the intersection where Dean died: The tragic spot lies almost directly upon an earthquake fault, and geophysicists currently theorize that the grinding of quartz layers produces on a vast scale the same sparking which can be accomplished in the laboratory.

See also curses; ghosts and hauntings.

Unarius Academy of Science

Founded in 1954 by Dr. Ernest L. Norman and his wife Ruth, the Unarius Academy of Science is dedicated to teaching a new science of life for the 21st century. An introduction to their mission states that "humankind is being prepared for a momentous change in consciousness, which will effect all institutions on earth as we come to the end of the sixth cycle of the recessional in the year 2001.... The founders laid down a bridge that is a cosmic link to the Space Brothers. Unarius, an acronym for Universal Articulate Interdimensional Understanding of Science is dedicated to exploring the frontiers of science and expanding our awareness and connection with galactic intelligence."

To this end a transmission was received from James Dean on April 22, 1999, and reprinted on the organization's website under the title "James Dean Speaks":

> Hello Friends, this is Jimmy Dean speaking to you from the Spiritual Side of Life where I have been living and making my abode since the tragic accident, which cut short my former life span as a movie actor. I truly suppose that what I am about to say will result in shocking many of the mul-

tiplied tens of thousands of former teenagers, now grown to adulthood but who still comprise my many fans, however, I am not at all dismayed by that prospect.

Jimmy is communicating to tell prospective Church of Unarius followers about the Afterlife.

As you proceed to read these words you will perceive that the former mixed-up "Rebel Without a Cause," who delighted in nothing better than thumbing his nose at the Establishment, has undergone a dramatic change since arriving here. It will become readily apparent that his main desire above all else is to rectify some of the "confusion wrought" from lodging multiple misconceptions in the plastic minds of gullible and unsuspecting youth via his movies and headstrong attitude.

He digresses to recall the circumstances of his death: "The countryside flashed by us on either side, and it was most exhilarating to feel the wind ruffling and playing havoc with my mop of already unruly hair."

At the instant of the accident, his body was "catapulted out of its physical envelope. This happened in much the same manner as a grapefruit pip or seed pops out of the fruit pulp when someone vigorously squeezes the rind."

Transported to the Healing Wards of Venus, he realized he had transcended time and space. He wants to share his newfound wisdom of the Afterlife with others, and advises, "Just drop a line to the Unarius Academy of Science and you will be well rewarded for your efforts by being put in touch with much vital information which will prove to be invaluable to you in your search for the answers to the real purpose of Life."

unsolved mysteries of James Dean's death

1. WHAT HAPPENED TO THE SPYDER?

Did it disappear in transit to California from an auto show in 1960? Owner George Barris reportedly has a private detective still tracking down leads when they pop up. *See* **car; curses.**

2. DID SANFORD ROTH TAKE PICTURES OF JIMMY DEAD BEHIND THE WHEEL?

That's what he told *Life* magazine in 1956, though his widow adamantly denied it. She said any photos taken were for "insurance purposes," which also sounds rather cold, though, given the circumstances.

3. What Happened to the Blood in His Body?

The mortician said there was not enough blood left to perform a successful blood alcohol test, which would have required only a small amount.

4. What Happened to Rolf's Pan Am Flight Ring?

He said it was a gift that Jimmy had slipped on his finger some two hours before the crash. When he awoke in the hospital, it was missing. He said it was still somewhere out there in the desert.

5. Who Burgled Jimmy's House After His Death?

Jack Simmons is on many folks' short list.

6. Why Did Jimmy Take the Route He Did to His Death?

Many racers, including Johnnie von Neumann (who sold Dean the Porsche), preferred taking Highway 33 from near the foot of the Grapevine. It bypassed Bakersfield and shaved both mileage and time. Smaller and less-traveled, it was preferred by drivers who wanted to speed on the highway. Von Neumann himself was once reportedly ticketed on the highway, and got the ticket dismissed on the basis that his speed was not unsafe because of his driving expertise.

7. Did the Ambulance Attendants Roll Dean's Body?

Bill Hickman, who had been traveling behind Dean at the time of the wreck and who stayed with Dean's body at the mortuary, says they did. It could explain where Rolf's ring went. Locals say it was not an unknown occurrence. But Dean's estate said that some $33 was found on Jimmy's body.

urination

Biographer Donald Spoto writes that during the filming of *Giant*, "Jimmy Dean regularly urinated in public — against a set, in a gutter, in the town square." He gave as a reason the fact that "nothing else was happening."

V

Valentino, Rudolf

When Rudolph Valentino died of a perforated ulcer in 1926 at age thirty-one, thirty thousand people thronged the funeral parlor. Fifty thousand passed his open casket in a single day, many of the women fainting. The public wails of grief had no precedent. A boy and girl in Europe, in unrelated incidents, took to bed beneath carefully arranged photos of their idol and poisoned themselves. Women jumped from buildings. A mother of two drank iodine and shot herself in the head — but survived.

The strongest visual that emerged on the international level was the pictures of Rudy in his coffin surrounded by a squad of Fascisti at attention. Rumor held that they had been sent by Mussolini to garner some of the publicity and sympathy attendant to Rudy's death and to harness some of the power of publicly identifying with him. Mussolini's representatives, however, denied the rumors but said that international Fascisti were allowed to act on their own.

In 1956 it would be written in a fan magazine, "After thirty years of being the world's number one ghoul-magnet, Rudy was suddenly discovering that he has a real tough competitor in the late James Dean."

Vampira *see* **Nurmi, Maila**

vandalism

The ghouls went to the grave with hacksaws. Skulking among the tombstones, they found the object of their quest of desecration. They started sawing beneath the clean jaw line, severing the stem attaching the head to the plinth. Tossing their booty into their vehicle, they sped from the cemetery.

The year was 1957, and even the *Chicago Tribune* took note in a headline that Jimmy's head was missing from the graveyard. Fortunately, the head that was taken was not Jimmy's actual head, but the head that had been cast in bronze by sculptor Kenneth Kendall and installed on a plinth in Park Cemetery.

Who took it? The obvious culprits were rabid Deanfans in search of a unique collectible. For decades, historians assumed that the head wound up as the centerpiece in a private Dean shrine of a private collector. But as the acknowledgment of Dean's bisexuality emerged in biographies in the 1960s and 1970s, so did the stories of the local animosity to the favorite son who had evaded the draft by, as he himself reported, "kissing the doctor."

To the town of Fairmount, Indiana, which in its patriotic fervor had erected near the town center a monument to those who made the ultimate sacrifice in world wars, the presence of a shrine to Dean in the same cemetery where their slain sons rested uncelebrated was an affront and a blight.

Taking matters into their own hands, this theory goes, they removed the offending object d'art and probably destroyed it.

The head was never replaced, though a replica was later erected closer to downtown, where it was presumably safe from the critique of local patriots.

See also **tombstone.**

Van Deuseun, Anna

Psychic who contacted the ghost of James Dean for writer Robert DeKolbe. The posthumous interview resulted in the article "James Dean Speaks from the Grave" which appeared in *True Strange* magazine (September 1956).

See also **ghosts and hauntings.**

velocity report

John Robert White was a certified public accountant with Price, Waterhouse in Los Angeles who was traveling behind Dean's Porsche at the time of the crash. On October 8, 1955, he gave a 19-page deposition in which he described what he saw. The deposition read in part:

> **Mr. White:** Approximately a mile before Highway 466 is joined by Highway 41 we were passed by a foreign sports car which I assumed to be a Porsche. It was of a silver color and bore number 130. At the time we were driving at approximately 65 to 68 miles per hour according to our speedometer. Mrs. White and I both (were) looking at the speedometer immediately after this car passed because we were astonished that it had come up on us in such a burst of speed with only approximately three hundred fifty feet clearance with three oncoming cars proceeding east on Highway 466.
>
> At the time the car passed I would estimate the speed was in excess of 85 miles per hour...
>
> **Q:** ...at the time you saw it (Turnupseed's car) start to make a left turn it was still in its own lane?
>
> **A:** Yes, but it was enough that I was aware that there was gong to be a collision here.
>
> **Q:** And the Dean car was making no effort to slow up?
>
> **A:** No. I knew it was going to be close or a collision. And the next thing I saw, they hit. The Turnupseed car stayed upright. The Dean car spun to the right and rolled over and over. Mrs. White said that she saw an object fly out of the car, which could have been a body or a part of the car.
>
> **Mrs. White:** I immediately covered my eyes. I didn't see them rolling over. He said (Mr. White) "Watch this," and I looked up and saw this thing

hit and something fly out of the car, and I immediately ducked my head and didn't watch anymore."

This account of his deposition is taken from the expert Lee Raskin article "Through James Dean's Rearview Mirror," which appeared in the December 1995 issue of *Excellence*. Raskin cites the deposition as counterpoint to the theory of Failure Analysis Associates that Dean was traveling only 57 mph at the time of collision. (*See* **simulation**.) Eyewitness Don Dooley supports this version of the collision, and Turnupseed himself described looking down into the car at impact, implying it flew up.

Vernon, Jeff

Jeff Vernon is a very talented artist and fan with many Dean portraits and illustrations to his credit. He dates his first encounter with the legend to a visit to the Movieland Wax Museum in 1962 when he was seven. Years later, in high school, he started watching Dean's films and reading biographies. He discovered that in addition to acting, Jimmy was a skilled painter and sketch artist. Perhaps inspired by Dean's example, Vernon has made his career in the arts and is a successful commercial and fine artist. He says, "I was first inspired by his quote, 'Dream as if you'll live forever, Live as if you'll die today.'"

Villa Capri

Dean's favorite restaurant was located on McCadden Place. Owner Patsy D'Amor was also the owner of Jimmy's leased Sherman Oaks house. At the time of his death, Jimmy's tab at the restaurant was $299.95, which was paid by the administrators of Dean's estate.

von Neumann, Johnnie

In an article titled "Far from Eden" (*Car and Driver*, October 1985), Brock Yates wrote:

> Von Neumann and his wife Eleanor had passed through earlier. They had arrived at the moment the Spyder was being hoisted onto the back of a tow truck and they had asked a policeman if Dean had been hurt. The officer replied, "Yeah, he's been hurt real bad. He's dead." They proceeded to Salinas, unaware that their employee Wuetherich had also been in the car.

W

wallet

A wallet authenticated as having belonged to James Dean was auctioned at Sotheby's for $10,500. The leather billfold featured his name in gold.

Warner Bros.

The studio took the position that Jimmy Dean's 1954 contract gave them the right to market Jimmy and get any earnings from his persona. They sued Curtis Management Group of Indianapolis, the licensing agent for Dean's family, and the James Dean Foundation Trust, which was composed of Dean's aunt and two cousins, contending Warners was defrauded of at least $30 million since Curtis started licensing Jimmy. They sought triple the actual damage — a cool $90 million — in addition to marketing rights.

The defendants asserted that Jimmy's Warner Bros. contract expired when the Spyder hit the Ford. They also said that the suit threatened the income of Dean's father, then 86 and suffering from Alzheimer's disease in a nursing home. A lawyer averred, "What they're trying to do is hit the Dean family with a $90 million judgment and take away the only source of income this gentleman has."

wastebasket

The James Dean wastebasket would seem to give the lie to the Dean estate's contention that they licensed Jimmy's image because "there was so much junk out there." It's adorned by his face and sells for $27.95.

waterglobe, musical

This is a limited edition of 7500. It features James Dean in an aqueous solution with a little Porsche Spyder. The globe plays the song "Yesterday." Produced by PCS International, the musical waterglobe retails for around $25.00.

website

The official World Wide Web site of James Dean is the Internet flagship of the merchandising armada that is Curtis Management. It's *all* about merchandising. An uneasy combination of equal parts cornpone and injunction, the home page greets you with an avuncular Marcus Winslow: "Greetings, I'm Jimmy's cousin and I grew up with Jimmy on our farm in Fairmount, Indiana."

It's difficult to believe that anyone has less in common with James Dean than the authors of the site, unless it is the lawyers who proudly display an alphabetized list of their mercantile conquests. "Fushimiueno Kyoshodo, Indiana Department of Commerce, J. Walter Thompson, Levi Strauss, Microsoft, Pepsi, Reader's Digest, Wheel of Fortune...." The list seems endless. Jimmy's name always appears with a little "TM" for Trademark. He's JimmyTM!

The website is translated into Spanish, Italian, French, Japanese, Korean, Chinese, Malay and Indonesian. There is also an extensive list of current promotions and some surprises among the names. William "Buckwheat" Thomas is just a column away from Sir Lawrence Olivier.

"Wet Willie"

This murky nocturnal character was the contact established by writer Ron Smith in his pursuit of a story on the James Dean curse. Smith met Wet Willie in a junkie-filled diner and was directed to a mansion above Mulholland Drive and a Hollywood warlock who had given Jimmy Dean occult instruction in the fifties.

The resultant story, "The Car, the Star — and the Curse that Linked Them," appeared in the *Robb Report* of August 1990.

See also curses.

Whisper

This 1950s scandal magazine jumped on the Dean death bandwagon — or hearse — in a large way with such stories as "The Ghost Driver of Polonio Pass," "Did James Dean Commit Suicide?" and Rolf's "Jimmy Had Good German Steel in His Hands."

White, John Robert *see* velocity report

Who Killed James Dean?

This novel by Warren Beath (Tor, 1996) is the supernatural account of Dean's life and death. The cover copy reads:

> **REBEL WITHOUT A SOUL!**
> September 30, 1955: A rising young star dies tragically on a lonely stretch of California highway. James Dean is dead, but his legend is only beginning....

Forty years later, the cult of James Dean is kept alive by thousands of devoted fans and worshippers. But as the fatal anniversary approaches, and Dean mania grows to a fever pitch, strange events occur. Dean's body disappears from its Indiana grave. A ghostly Porsche cruises the highway at night. And people begin to die.

Who killed James Dean? And why has he returned from the grave?

In this tale, the fatal collision is actually engineered in order to precipitate the formation of the Dean death cult, whose forces will be harnessed for supernatural purposes.

Who Killed Sal Mineo?

"*James Dean Killed Sal Mineo.* It was actor Sal Mineo's love for legendary screen great James Dean that led to his tragic death, says author of a controversial new book...." So begins a story in the August 17, 1982, Boston Globe. But the book in question is actually a novel by Susan Braudy. She claimed that *Who Killed Sal Mineo?* was the result of four years of research.

She apparently interviewed director Nicholas Ray. "I watched Dean seducing Sal on the set every day," he recalled.

In her book, Braudy tells how Mineo got involved with a young man who owed drug dealers a lot of money. After Mineo tried to get the boy off the hook, someone ordered that he should be roughed up to teach him to mind his own business. But he was killed by the thug instead.

Braudy said, "The person he became — the confusion, the inability to cope, the love he held onto for the man who ultimately influenced his life — is all due to James Dean."

See also Mineo, Sal; Williams, Lionel Ray.

Wicks, Chris

Dean fans are notoriously poor, often dipping deeply into their credit cards to acquire holy artifacts and make their various pilgrimages to Dean gatherings. But dashing young Briton Chris Wicks is an exception. The founder of Tomato Inc., a firm producing young men's fashions, he sold his business in the 1980s for fifty million dollars. A longtime Dean aficionado, he also purchased a Porsche replicar from Beck development and drove it to Cholame with his son in emulation of Jimmy's last drive. The amiable Wicks, approached by aspiring film maker Todd Bello, allowed the car to be "dressed" just like Jimmy's with racing stripes and numbers, for footage for a tentative documentary entitled *Who Really Knew Jimmy?*

With a young film crew, footage was shot in the environs of the crash site at roads and intersections that simulated the highway conditions of the 1950s. Unfortunately, the car developed trouble and had to be put up overnight at Blackwell's Corner until a tow truck could be hired from Los Angeles.

Williams, Lionel Ray

Lionel Ray Williams became known as the "Pizza Man" in the abbreviated vernacular of Dean devotees during his trial for the stabbing death of Dean costar Sal Mineo. The Los Angeles Police had been slow to make an arrest, and Williams was slow to come to trial, and the time lags were a Petri dish for the growth of bizarre theories regarding why the inoffensive Mineo should have been killed so savagely during a routine robbery. One of the more interesting stories was that Williams and Mineo were far from strangers, both being habitués of nearby Sunset Strip with its seamy underworld nightlife.

Mineo's obsession with Dean contributed to his professional discrediting when he submitted to tabloid interviews where he discussed his ongoing, and occasionally successful, attempt to reach Jimmy in the afterlife. He confessed a love for the icon, and told how art had imitated life as far as their onscreen homoerotic undercurrents in *Rebel Without a Cause*. The story circulated that Mineo had been obsessively trying to locate any of the items stolen from Dean's Sherman Oaks bungalow after his death, with the object of having something of personal resonance to facilitate the séances of a West Hollywood psychic who was trying to put Sal in touch with Jimmy. Believing the items were located in an abandoned Melrose storefront, Sal became entangled with the small-time thief in a mission to recover them through burglary.

Williams reportedly told his own wife about a series of meetings with Mineo in which he strung him along about the feasibility of the break-in, Mineo fronting him small change for the project in development. Finally convinced he was being scammed, Mineo severed contacts in a blowout that verged on violence. But Williams could not let go of his mark, and repeatedly approached Mineo for handouts. On the night Mineo died, Williams was waiting for him in the parking lot, high on drugs. He approached him again, but this time was in no mood for rejection.

Within moments, Mineo lay bleeding to death on the pavement.

THE MURDER

"Oh God, no! Help! Someone help!" The cries pierced the night of February 13, 1976. Actor Sal Mineo was walking away from his blue Chevelle after parking in the slot at the rear of his West Hollywood apartment off

Sunset Strip when a longhaired man in dark clothes attacked him. A river of blood several yards long was leaving his body when neighbors responded. Stabbed by a "heavy type knife" through the heart, he was gasping for air. He died in five minutes despite mouth-to-mouth resuscitation.

The case would baffle police. Mineo's wallet had not been taken. There was talk of a drug angle, and the inevitable rumors of a trick gone bad. The Strip was infested with male hustlers waiting to be picked up and taken home. Friends tried to raise $10,000 as reward for information on the killer whose trail was growing cold.

It was over a year after the murder that Mrs. Theresa Williams went to authorities and told them that her husband had bragged about killing Mineo. She said her husband, twenty-two-year-old Lionel Ray Williams, had used a $5.28 hunting knife to kill Mineo. Serving time in a Michigan penitentiary, Williams was recalled as a Los Angeles arrestee who had once offered police information on Mineo's murder in a bid for leniency on a robbery bust. Police bought an identical knife and found it was a perfect fit when inserted into Mineo's chest wound, which had been excised and preserved.

His prison bragging about the crime had been dismissed as jail talk, but a tattoo on Williams' body depicted a knife identical to the murder weapon. In January of 1979, three years after the killing, Williams went to trial. He was convicted of Mineo's killing and ten other brutal robberies. The Mineo murder was almost a tacked-on charge. Guilty of second-degree murder, Williams was sentenced to fifty-one years to life.

See also Mineo, Sal.

window wavers

You're driving along, and isn't that James Dean waving to you from the back of that Honda? Could be. Strikin' It Rich Enterprises marketed Starpool Window Waver, a cardboard cutout of Jim for your rear car window! This was the sort of product Curtis Management put the kibosh on as "tasteless."

wine

Sold by VV Wines to collectors for the bottle value rather than the contents, the 1999 Cabernet Sauvignon Edition of James Dean Wine commemorated Dean's screen contributions. The complete issue of "Rebel Red" was limited to 600 cases.

witchcraft *see* **Malecfarum Coven**

Wozniak, David

A Dean aficionado who won the national James Dean lookalike contest in 2001, Wozniak maintains a web site and side business as a Dean impersonator. He has also won at least six Dean lookalike contests in his home state of Michigan. He explains the first time he heard of Dean and his remarkable resemblance to the man:

> When I was thirteen, I was at the mall and a man came up to me and said, "You look like James Dean. Wait until you get older!" I told him I didn't know who James Dean was. He explained a little bit about James Dean and his life. Eight years later, when I turned 21, my mom asked me to watch *Rebel Without a Cause* starring James Dean. I remembered what the man at the mall had said. So, I watched the movie all the way through and then I went to a mirror and looked at myself. I was shocked! I said, "James Dean!" Since then, James Dean has been a huge part of my life.

wreck *see* **accident**

Wuetherich, Rolf

Dean's mechanic, who was riding with Dean and was injured in the collision but survived. Over the years there has been speculation that it was Wuetherich who was driving the Porsche rather than Dean. At the coroner's hearing two witnesses, Tom Frederick and Don Dooley, testified that Dean in his white T-shirt had not been driving the car. The red-shirted Wuetherich had been the driver. One confused juror cried out, "How are we supposed to know who had a white T-shirt on and who had a red one on?"

> DISTRICT ATTORNEY: From seeing the two men after the accident, looking back, could you place the men in the car, on which side of the car they were?
> FREDERICK: I could place one of them.
> DISTRICT ATTORNEY: Which one of them?
> FREDERICK: The one in the red T-shirt.
> DISTRICT ATTORNEY: Which was he?
> FREDERIC : He would be on the left side.... The car was still in motion after the accident, and I could see the man in the red T-shirt on the left side of the car. That is after they hit.
> DISTRICT ATTORNEY: The man in the T-shirt was in the driver's seat?
> FREDERICK: They were both in T-shirts.
> DISTRICT ATTORNEY: Did they both have on red T-shirts?
> FREDERICK: No, Dean had a white one on — or the man that was still in the Porsche.

DISTRICT ATTORNEY: How do you remember that — what makes you remember the one with the red T-shirt being on the left?
FREDERICK: I seen him with his hands up in the air and seen he had a red T-shirt on.
DISTRICT ATTORNEY: When was that?
FREDERICK: Right after they had the accident.

In a surprising twist, the district attorney dismissed the entire matter. In exasperation he told the jurors, "You know as much as we do on it. This court is interested first in who is the deceased person and how he came to his death. It is not really material who had a white T-shirt on...." No ruling was made on who the driver was.

Twenty-eight-year-old Rudoph Karl Wuetherich was born in Heilbronn, Germany, to a locksmith on August 5, 1927. He had been a Luftwaffe pilot late in the war and had entered the Porsche outfit on November 1, 1950. He was the firm's forty-second employee at the factory in Zuffenhausen. As a racing participant, he was reportedly a veteran of Le Mans, Reims, and the Mille Miglia. In 1955 the Zuffenhausen factory sent him for four years to the United States.

When a sedative-addled Rolf was deposed in his hospital bed, it was a comedy of errors. His testimony is garbled because he was testifying via an interpreter and with the additional disadvantage of painkillers and a broken jaw — not to mention missing teeth. He mentioned something about a different speedometer, and "revolutions per minute."

He was quoted as saying the Porsche was traveling at "speeds of 65–60–65 on the open road, not any more," but he was actually referring to revolutions per minute rather than miles per hour. Rolf, as a professional European driver, watched tachometers, rather than speedometers. Used to reading a speedometer in kilometers, he was more comfortable with the tach. In fourth gear at 4,000 rpm, the speed would have been 60 mph. At 6,500 rpm, the Spyder would have been traveling at 98.6 mph.

Rolf had sustained a broken jaw and left femur. His injuries required some eighteen months of convalescence, most of it spent in a wire structure that was made bearable only by the megadoses of painkillers the doctors plied him with. Doctors wanted to remove his leg, but employer Johnnie von Neumann had him taken by ambulance to Glendale, where a German surgeon saved the limb. He received bone grafts, and an eight-inch silver nail was inserted to connect his hip bones.

In the 1960s he was still active as a rally driver for Porsche. In 1965 he placed second in the Monte Carlo Rally with famous Stuttgart race driver Eugen Bohringer. But one day, without warning, he told the team manager, "I'm quitting. I just can't go on."

His German obituary described his last years as tormented. He was addicted to pills and changed jobs ten times. Three marriages broke up. A mini race track which he opened with his fourth wife, a thirty-year-old woman named Doris, was a financial disaster. He wanted to die with her. He took sleeping pills and cut a vein. When she declined to join him, he went for her with a kitchen knife.

His defense lawyers at the ensuing Stuttgart trial said he suffered tremendous guilt because he blamed himself for the star's death because he had given Jimmy the wheel over the strict instructions of Warner Bros. He also blamed himself for the suicides of grief-stricken women who killed themselves after Dean's death.

Dr. Werner Mende, a nerve specialist, said, "Wuetherich has a massive guilt complex. He is a broken man." Another psychiatric expert, Dr. Juergen Bechtal, said, "At the moment of the attack on his wife he was in a state of trance brought on by his deep feelings of guilt." Wuetherich himself told the court, "My conscience won't let me sleep anymore. I shouldn't have let James drive. I knew his studio had forbidden it." He began to sob. "I am a complete failure. Nothing has gone right for me." He felt the only way out was suicide, the court was told.

The court adjudged him "partially irresponsible," after a tearful plea to the judge in which he moaned, "I always see the asphalt in front of me. The road was straight. Jimmy held the wheel. He was relaxed, smiling, happy." He was cleared of the attempted murder charge, but it was recommended he be confined indefinitely to a clinic for psychiatric treatment.

In February of 1968 he terminated his eighteen-year association with the Porsche firm. He left the Cologne area and in March of 1979 came to Hohenlohe to work for Honda dealer Roland Eckert. That didn't last, and soon he was in Neuenstein mounting Turbo engines for Porsche once again.

It was pouring rain at 10:50 P.M. when he left a bar and got into his red Honda Civic on July 20, 1981. He drove down Market Street toward the middle of town on a long curve near the People's Bank. Shortly before Kupferzell, in the Badenwurttemberg District of Hohenlohe, he lost control of his car at a speed of 65 mph. In an extended right hand turn he broke through a chain link fence and hit the wall of a house. The crash pinned him in the car. Emergency workers tried to extract him with the Jaws of Life as a doctor worked furiously over him, but to no avail. Rolf Wuetherich was dead at the age of 53.

Roland Eckert, one of his last employers, said of him in a statement that might serve as his obituary, "He was car crazy."

INJURIES FROM THE DEAN CRASH

Further information on the extent of Rolf's injuries is found in an affidavit filed on August 7, 1958:

> The injuries of plaintiff ... were a badly comminuted fracture of the left trochanteric region of the left femur; that because of the extensive comminuted fracture, it was impossible to do internal fixation and therefore, he had to be treated with traction over an extensive period of time. That plaintiff had a fracture of the mandible on the right side anteriorly and behind a third molar on the left of the mandible posteriorly. The condylar fragment was displaced laterally approximately the width of the mandible. He lost dentures. That because the condition of the plaintiff was not good, the displacement of the fracture in the mandible was left and not reduced. In its early stages, that there was cosmetic changes in the contour of his face and other complications as well as various other injuries.

And later on,

> That it was necessary and plaintiff did enter the Glendale Sanitarium and Hospital on Sunday, April 8th, 1956, and an open reduction was done and pin placed in the left hip. At the time of the operation, it was found that a long spur on the lateral cortex of the femur was apparently dead due to loss of blood supply and that no doubt accounted for the nonunion of the bone. The dead bone was excised, the position sustained by a Neufeld nail plate and bone grafts from the same ileum placed anteriorly and posteriorly as well as laterally. The question of surgical intervention of the jaw or mandible injury was also being considered at that time.

ROLF-JIMMY AFFAIR

Wuetherich was darkly handsome, his rough-hewn good looks enhanced by his panache as a pilot and race car driver. He was the real thing to Jimmy, someone who had lived close to the edge all his life. Was the racing-pit scent of sweat and gas fumes an aphrodisiac for Jimmy Dean? When knowledge of Dean's sexual ambiguity came to the fore in the 1960s, some fans recoiled from the cast it threw on Rolf's bizarrely selective recollections of his days with Jimmy Dean. What was that whole business about the ring Jimmy so affectionately placed on Rolf's finger some two hours before the crash?

The macabre highway death of German expatriate and silent film director F.W. Murnau in the 1920s perhaps gave impetus to the rumors which circulated in the 1960s about Jimmy's death and the cause of the crash. Murnau lost control of his Stutz Bearcat on a winding Santa Barbara highway when his foot tightened in orgasm on the gas pedal as his Filipino house boy performed fellatio on him. Only eleven people came to his funeral.

The rumors went like this: In a playful mood, and ever pushing the envelope, Rolf and Jimmy decided to engage in some sexual experimentation while Jimmy tried to maintain control of the speeding Porsche en route to the races. Rolf's head reportedly spent quite a bit of time under the dash during the death drive — supposedly so he could light Jimmy's endless stream of cigarettes and be shielded from the wind. "Why don't you do me a favor while you're down there?" Jimmy was imagined to have said. The result was a lapse in attention that affected Jimmy's reaction time as they approached the fatal intersection. A cover story was supposedly devised that it was the impact of the crash that tore Jimmy's pants from his legs.

Rolf's subsequent life seems to be one of rampant heterosexuality, though he never had a successful relationship with women. And after he died on another highway in 1981, the news services reported that he had contracted with an American publisher to finally tell the real story of the death of James Dean. Conspiracy theorists weighed in with suggestions he had been silenced to subvert an assault on the memory of Jimmy Dean.

X

X-rated Jimmy Dean

Rumors circulate from Jimmy's hardscrabble New York years that his hand-to-mouth existence included stints as a male hustler who specialized in masochism. He slummed in the waterfront bars of West Village in the train of his wealthy homosexual benefactors, and some claim he appeared in pornographic films. The only foundation seems to be a nude photograph that has been passed around and occasionally reprinted which shows a young man resembling Dean masturbating in a tree.

Dean biographer Val Holley recounts an incident from Martin Russ in which Rogers Brackett showed Russ a wallet photo of Dean naked in a tree, though his genitals were not visible. Holley also wrote, "The rumors of nude photos of Dean in a tree are nonetheless true, according to *Theatre World's* John Willis, who says he has seen them. Earle Forbes, staff photographer to Daniel Blum, Willis's predecessor as *Theatre World* editor, took them, he says. Willis says both Blum and Forbes kept sets of the photos of Dean and many other young men."

Author Donald Spoto claims the photo is actually the retarded and since-deceased cousin of a man named Richard Laselle and was taken in 1957.

Y

Yamada, Naomi

Yamada is a Japanese fan who performs a yearly ritual at Dean's tombstone. She gracefully drapes streamers of cranes over the headstone in the traditional Japanese tribute known as the Thousand Cranes Tribute. Yamada makes the paper cranes by hand throughout the year, her sacrifice an expression of her devotion to the memory of Dean. The finished product looks like tentacles of crepe ribbon festooned with a thousand cranes.

Yokut Indian curse

They were hunter-gatherers, these primitive people who 10,000 years ago inhabited the plains in central California. Even into the twentieth century, their burial mounds were discoverable on both sides of Highway 466 on which Dean rode to his death. The mounds were noted on maps into the 1950s, and then disappeared. Excavated and researched respectfully by sociologists and archeologists, they were eventually victim to cultivation by the superfarms, which cut California up among themselves. The homely memorials were leveled, most of them plundered for the magical artifacts that found their way into museums.

The vicinity where the Indian dead had resided for ten centuries just to the west of Blackwell's Corner has become legendary as one of the more superstition-ridden spots in America. Did the Indian curse for defiling the burial grounds claim a victim in Jimmy Dean? It's definitely an unlucky spot. Having left the familiar urbanization of the Los Angeles area, Dean took a fatal drive down a lonely highway that in local Indian lore is the nexus of an undying curse.

See also curses.

Z

Zavatsky, William

New York educator and writer who authored the article "Epitaph for a Rebel" which appeared in the October 16, 1980, edition of *Rolling Stone*. Zavatsky is cited prominently in David Dalton's *American Icon*.

Bibliography

Adams, Leith, and Keith Burns. *James Dean: Behind the Scene*. New York: Citadel, 2001.

Alexander, Paul. *Boulevard of Broken Dreams: The Life, Times, and Legend of James Dean*. New York: Viking, 1994.

Bast, William. *James Dean*. New York: Buccaneer, 1992.

Beasley, Michael, and John Hawn. "Dean Tales Fact or Fiction? By Now, It's Hard to Tell." *Indianapolis Star*, September 22, 1985.

Beath, Warren Newton. *The Death of James Dean*. New York: Grove, 1988.

Brean, Joe. *Rebels United: The Enduring Reality of James Dean*. New York: Funk & Wagnalls, 1987.

Colman, David. "Rubble Without a Pause." *Excellence*, November 1955.

Cunningham, Terry. *The Timeless James Dean*. London: Stagedoor, 2004.

Dalton, David. *James Dean: The Mutant King*. Chicago: Chicago Review Press, 2001.

_____, and Ron Cayen. *James Dean: American Icon*. New York: St. Martin's, 1986.

Dawber, Martin. *Wish You Were Here, Jimmy Dean*. London: Columbus, 1988.

Decker, Linda. "Rock Hudson Murdered James Dean." *Examiner*, October 31, 1989.

Defechereux, Philippe. *James Dean — The Untold Story of a Passion for Speed*. Los Angeles: Mediavisions, 1996.

Devillers, Marceau. *James Dean on Location*. London: Pan Macmillan, 1989.

Ellis, Royston. *The Rebel*. London: Mayfair, 1961.

Fortune, Dion. *The Mystical Qabalah*. York Beach, Maine: Samuel Weiser, Inc., reprint 1984.

Fuchs, Wolfgang. *James Dean: Footsteps of a Giant*. West Germany: Taco, 1986.

Gilmore, John. *Live Fast — Die Young: My Life with James Dean*. New York: Thunder's Mouth, 1997.

_____. *The Real James Dean*. New York: Pyramid, 1975.

Hall, William. *James Dean*. Gloucestershire, UK: Sutton, 1999.

Herndon, Venable. *James Dean: A Short Life*. Garden City, New York: Doubleday, 1974.

Hoberman, J., and Jonathan Rosenbaum. "The Idolmakers." *American Film*, December 1982.

Holley, Val. *James Dean: The Biography*. New York: St. Martin's, 1997.

Hoskins, Barney. *James Dean: Shooting Star*. London: Virgin, 1990.

Howlett, John. *James Dean: A Biography*. Medford, New Jersey: Plexus, 1997.

Humphreys, Joseph. *Jimmy Dean on Jimmy Dean*. Medford, New Jersey: Plexus, 1994.

Hyams, Joe. *James Dean: Little Boy Lost*. New York: Warner, 1992.

_____. *Mislaid in Hollywood*. New York: P.H. Wyden, 1973.

Jacobs, Timothy. *James Dean*. New York: Smithmark, 1994.

Kreidl, John Francis. *Nicholas Ray*. New York: Twayne, 1977.

Lindahl, John. "My Death Drive with James Dean." *Pix Annual*, Fall 1958.

Martinetti, Ron. *The James Dean Story*. Secaucus, New Jersey: Carol, 1995.

Morrissey, Stephen. *James Dean Is Not Dead*. London: International Music, 1983.

Newton, Michael. *Raising Hell: An Encyclopedia of Devil Worship and Satanic Crime*. New York: Avon, 1993.

O'Dowd, Brian. "Friendship with a Cause." *Hollywood Studio Magazine*, 1986.

Olesky, Walter G. *The Importance of James Dean*. Chicago: Lucent, 2000.

Raskin, Lee. "Little Bastard: The Search for James Dean's Spyder." *Porsche Panorama*, July 1984.

_____. "Through James Dean's Rearview Mirror." *Excellence*, December 1995.

Ravenscroft, Trevor. *The Spear of Destiny*. York Beach, Maine: Samuel Weiser, Inc., reprint 1997.

Riese, Randall. *The Unabridged James Dean: His Life and Legacy from A to Z*. Chicago: Contemporary, 1991.

Roller, Alfred G. "How the Ghouls are Picking at Jimmy Dean." *Fury*, June 1957.

Ross, Walter. *The Immortal*. New York: Simon & Schuster, 1958.

Roth, Beulah. *James Dean*. San Francisco: Pomegranate, 1983.

Roth, Sanford. "Jimmy Dean: The Assignment I'll Never Forget." *Popular Photography*, July 1962.

St. Michael, Mick. *James Dean: In His Own Words*. New York: Music Sales, 1992.

Schaeffer, Sam. "James Dean, the Ghost Driver of Polonio Pass." *Whisper*, December 1957.

Schatt, Roy. *James Dean: A Portrait*. New York: Beaufort, 1985.

Skal, David J. *Hollywood Gothic*. New York: W.W. Norton, 1990.

Smith, Linda D. "Legend: James Dean Lives On in the Collections of His Fans." *Colorado Gazette Telegraph*, September 30, 1983.

Smith, Ron. "The Car, the Star — and the Curse that Linked Them." *The Robb Report*, August 1990.

Spoto, Donald. *Rebel: The Life and Legend of James Dean.* New York: Harper-Collins, 1997.

Stock, Dennis. *James Dean Revisited.* New York: Viking, 1978.

Stout, Larry. "Licensing a Legend." *Hollywood Studio Magazine,* February 1988.

Tanitch, Robert. *Unknown James Dean.* London: B.T. Batsford, 1999.

Tysl, Robert Wayne. *Continuity and Evolution in a Public Symbol: An Investigation into the Creation and Communication of the James Dean Image in Mid-Century America.* Ph.D. dissertation, Michigan State University, 1965.

Volpe, Dante. *The Last James Dean Book.* Richmond, BC: Quill, 1984.

Whitman, Mark. *The Films of James Dean.* San Diego: Greenhaven, 1978.

Winer, Richard, and Nancy Osborn. *Haunted Houses.* New York: Bantam, 1979.

Wuetherich, Rolf. "Death Drive." *Modern Screen,* October 1957.

Yates, Brock. "Far from Eden." *Car and Driver,* October 1985.

Zahn, Debra. "James Dean: Rebel with an Agent." *Los Angeles Times.* September 29, 1985.

Index

251